W9-AEN-619

GERMAN SONGS

The German Library: Volume 53
Volkmar Sander, General Editor

GERMAN SONGS

Popular, Political, Folk, and Religious

Edited by Inke Pinkert-Sältzer

CONTINUUM • NEW YORK

1997

The Continuum Publishing Company
370 Lexington Avenue, New York, NY 10017

The German Library
is published in cooperation with Deutsches Haus,
New York University.
This volume has been supported by Inter Nationes,
and a grant from Robert Bosch Jubiläumsstiftung.

Printed in the United States of America

Library of Congress Cataloging Card Number: 96-85684

Hardcover ISBN: 0-8264-0730-7
Paperback ISBN: 0-8264-0731-5

Acknowledgments will be found on pages 313–14,
which constitute an extension of the copyright page.

Contents

Introduction: Inke Pinkert-Sältzer   xi

Ein feste Burg ist unser Gott / A Mighty Fortress Is Our God
(Luther) 1

POLITICAL SONGS

Songs of the Downtrodden

Es ist ein Schnitter, heißt der Tod / Behold the Reaper
(Traditional) 3
Ich bin ein freier Bauernknecht / I Am a Free Peasant
(Traditional) 5
Wer jetzig Zeiten leben will / We Need a Heart of Courage Now
(Traditional) 7
Wir sind des Geyers schwarzer Haufen / Geyer's Pitch-Dark Gang Are We
(Traditional) 9

Songs in the Time of the French Revolution

Bürgerlied der Mainzer / The Mainz Citizens' Song (Traditional) 11
Freiheit, die ich meine / Come, My Gentle Freedom
(Schenkendorf) 14
Die Gedanken sind frei / Thoughts Are Free (Traditional) 15
O König von Preußen / Oh, King of Prussia (Traditional) 17
Lied freyer Landleute / Song of the Free Country Folk (Lehne) 20

Songs of the German Revolution of 1848

Badisches Wiegenlied / Lullaby of Baden (Pfau) 23
Das Blutgericht / The Blood Court (Traditional) 25
Bürgerlied / The Citizens' Song (Traditional) 26
Der gute Bürger / The Solid Citizen (Freiligrath) 28
Ein neues Lied / A Winters Tale (Heine) 30
Freifrau von Droste-Vischering / Milady Droste-Vischering
(Löwenstein) 31
Das Heckerlied / The Song of Hecker (Schanz) 34
Ich bin ein guter Untertan / A Loyal Subject Am I Then
(Glasbrenner) 36

Lied vom Bürgermeister Tschech / The Mayor Tschech Song
(Traditional) 39
O wag es doch nur einen Tag / Oh, Just Dare, If for Just One Day
(Herwegh) 40
Das Proletariat / The Proletariat (Lüchow) 43
Reveille (Freiligrath) 44
Trotz alledem / Despite It All (Freiligrath) 46
Die beiden Grenadiere / The Two Grenadiers (Heine) 48

Songs of the Workers' Movement

Achtzehnter März / March 18 (Herwegh) 51
Der Arbeitsmann / The Working Man (Dehmel) 53
Die Arbeitsmänner / The Hymn of the Proletariat (Most) 54
Auf, auf, zum Kampf / On to the Battle, to the Battle
(Traditional) 57
Brüder, zur Sonne, zur Freiheit / Go to the Sun, into Freedom (Radin) 58
Bundeslied / Said Wealth to Toil (Herwegh) 59
Einheitsfrontlied / United Front Song (Brecht) 62
Ich bin Soldat, doch bin ich es nicht gerne /
A Soldier Am I, but Don't Like To Be (Traditional) 64
Die Internationale / The Internationale (Pottier) 66
Die junge Garde / The Young Guards (Eildermann) 69
Lied der deutschen Arbeiter / Song of the German Workers (Audorf) 71
Der Revoluzzer / The Amateur Revolutionary (Mühsam) 74
Der rote Wedding / The Reds from Wedding (Weinert) 78
Sozialistenmarsch / The Socialist March (Kegel) 81
Wann wir schreiten Seit an Seit / When We're Marching Side by Side
(Claudius) 83

Anti-Fascist Songs

Ballade von der "Judenhure" Marie Sanders /
Ballad of Marie Sanders, the Jew's Whore (Brecht) 85
Buchenwaldlied / The Buchenwald Song (Böda-Löhner) 86
Komintern-Lied / Comintern (Jahnke / Vallentin) 89
Lied der Internationalen Brigaden / Song of the International Brigades
(Weinert) 92
Mein Vater wird gesucht / They're Looking for My Father (Drach) 95
Die Moorsoldaten / The Peat-Bog Soldiers (Langhoff) 96
Die Moritat von Mackie Messer / The Crimes of Mackie the Knife
(Brecht) 98
Die Thälmann-Kolonne / The Thaelmann Column (Ernst) 100

Songs of East and West Germany

Ach, du mein schauriges Vaterland / Oh, My Gruesome Fatherland
(Wecker) 102
Das Barlach-Lied / The Barlach Song (Biermann) 104
Der Baggerführer Willibald /The Ballad
of Willibald the Power Shovel Operator (Süverkrüp) 105

Contents • vii

Deutscher Sonntag / A German Sunday (Degenhardt) 108
Die hab ich satt! / I'm Sick of It! (Biermann) 114
Ermutigung / Encouragement (Biermann) 116
Erschröckliche Moritat vom Kryptokommunisten / Dreadful
Ballad of the Crypto-Communist (Süverkrüp) 117
Frieden im Land / Peace in the Land (Wecker) 121
Für M. Theodorakis / For M. Theodorakis (Degenhardt) 123
Großes Gebet der alten Kommunistin Oma Meume in Hamburg /
The Communist Grandma Meume's Great Prayer in Hamburg
(Biermann) 125
Das Hölderlin-Lied / The Hoelderlin Song (Biermann) 127
Ja, dieses Deutschland meine ich / This Is the Germany I Mean
(Degenhardt) 129
Kinder / Children (Wegner) 131
Kirschen auf Sahne / Cherries and Cream (Süverkrüp) 133
Lied von der Gedankenfreiheit / Freedom of Thought Song
(Mossmann) 136
Manchmal sagen die Kumpanen / These Days the Guys Might Say
(Degenhardt) 138
Marsch der Minderheit / March of the Minority
(Hüsch) 140
Moritat auf Biermann seine Oma Meume in Hamburg /
Moritat for Biermann's Grandma Meume in Hamburg (Biermann) 142
Ostermarschlied 68/ Easter March Song 1968 (Degenhardt) 144
Sieben Fragen eines Schülers und Sieben freiheitlich-demokratisch-grundor-
dentliche Antworten / Seven Questions from a Schoolboy and Seven Free,
Democratic, Constitutionally Appropriate Answers (Mossmann) 146
Spiel nicht mit den Schmuddelkindern /
Don't Play with Those Filthy Children (Degenhardt) 150
Und als wir ans Ufer kamen / And When We Reached the Lake Shore
(Biermann) 152
Wenn der Senator erzählt / When the Senator Tells His Tales
(Degenhardt) 153

National Anthems of German-Speaking Countries

Nationalhymne der Bundesrepublik Deutschland /
National Anthem of West Germany (Hoffmann von Fallersleben) 158
Nationalhymne der Deutschen Demokratischen Republik /
National Anthem of the GDR (Becher) 160
Nationalhymne der Schweiz / National Anthem of Switzerland
(Widmer) 163
Nationalhymne von Österreich / National Anthem of Austria
(Preradović) 166

SONGS OF THE PEOPLE

Religious Songs

Alle Jahre wieder / Another Year (Hey) 169

Aus tiefer Not schrei ich zu dir / From Depths of Woe I Cry to You
(Luther) 170

Es ist ein Ros entsprungen / Lo, How a Rose Is Growing
(Traditional) 172

Hört, ihr Herrn, und laßt euch sagen / Listen to Me, Gentlemen
(Traditional) 173

Ich steh an deiner Krippe hier / I Stand Beside Thy Cradle Here
(Gerhardt) 175

Ihr Kinderlein, kommet / O Come, Little Children (Schmid) 176

Kommet, ihr Hirten / Come, Ye Men and Women (Riedel) 178

Leise rieselt der Schnee / Softly Flutters the Snow (Ebel) 179

Lobe den Herren / Praise to the Lord (Neander) 180

Maria durch ein'n Dornwald ging / Mary Walks amid the Thorn
(Traditional) 182

Nun danket alle Gott / Now Thank We All Our God (Rinckart) 184

O du fröhliche / Oh, You Joyful (Falk) 185

O Haupt voll Blut und Wunden / Oh, Sacred Head Now Wounded
(Gerhardt) 186

O Tannenbaum / Oh Christmas Tree (Anschütz / Zahneck) 189

Stille Nacht / Silent Night (Mohr) 190

Tochter Zion, freue dich / Daughter of Zion, Come Rejoice (Ranke) 192

Vom Himmel hoch / From Heaven Above to Earth I Come (Luther) 193

Was soll das bedeuten / I Know It's Midnight (Traditional) 195

Songs about the Seasons and the Times of Day

Abend wird es wieder / Eventide's Returning (Hoffmann von Fallersleben) 198

Bunt sind schon die Wälder / All the Leaves Are Turning
(Salis-Seewis) 199

Der Mond ist aufgegangen / Evening Song (Claudius) 201

Es tönen die Lieder / Now Spring Is A-Springing (Traditional) 203

Geh aus, mein Herz, und suche Freud /
Go Out, My Dear, and Find Joy (Gerhardt) 204

Guten Abend, gut' Nacht / Cradle Song (Traditional) 206

Jeden Morgen geht die Sonne auf / Every Morning (Claudius) 208

Jetzt fängt das schöne Frühjahr an / Lovely Spring (Traditional) 209

Kein schöner Land / There Are No Other Lands (Zuccalmaglio) 211

Nun will der Lenz uns grüßen / Spring Sends Us Hearty Greetings
(Reuenthal / Fischer) 212

O, wie wohl ist mir am Abend / Oh, How Lovely Is the Evening
(Traditional) 213

So treiben wir den Winter aus / Let's Drive Out Old Man Winter!
(Traditional) 214

Winter, ade! / Winter, Good-bye! (Hoffmann von Fallersleben) 215
Wem Gott will rechte Gunst erweisen /
Whomever God Decides to Favor (Eichendorff) 216
Wohlauf in Gottes schöne Welt / God's Gorgeous World (Levy) 218
Nun ruhen alle Wälder / Evensong (Gerhardt) 220
Komm, lieber Mai, und mache / Yearning for Spring (Overbeck) 222

Songs of Wanderers

Am Brunnen vor dem Tore / The Linden Tree (Müller) 225
Auf, du junger Wandersmann / Up, Young Traveler, Hi-Ho
(Hensel) 227
Das Wandern ist des Müllers Lust / The Journeyman's Song (Müller) 228
Der Mai ist gekommen / Now May Is Arriving (Geibel) 230
Ein Heller und ein Batzen / A Penny and a Fortune (Schlippenbach) 232
Es, es, es und es / It, It, It, and It (Traditional) 233
Glück auf, Glück auf / Good Luck! Good Luck! (Traditional) 236
Hoch auf dem gelben Wagen / Atop the Yellow Carriage (Baumbach) 237
Im Frühtau zu Berge / Hiking in the Mountain Dew
(Swedish: Thunman; German: Schulten) 239
Im Krug zum grünen Kranze / The Emerald Garland (Müller) 241
Im Märzen der Bauer / Farmwork Song (Hensel) 242
Innsbruck, ich muß dich lassen / Innsbruck, Now I Must Depart
(Traditional) 244
Nun ade, du mein lieb Heimatland / Sweet Homeland, Farewell!
(Disselhoff) 246
Schön ist die Welt / The World Is Beautiful (Traditional) 247
Üb immer Treu und Redlichkeit / Be Always True and Righteous
(Hölty) 248
Was noch frisch und jung an Jahren / Anyone Who's Spry and Youthful
(Traditional) 251

Love Songs

Ännchen von Tharau / Annie of Tharaw (Dach) 253
Du, du, liegst mir im Herzen / You, You Are My True Love
(Traditional) 257
Es dunkelt schon in der Heide / Dark in the Heath (Traditional) 258
Es waren zwei Königskinder / Two Royal Children (Traditional) 260
Heidenröslein / The Wild Rosebud (Goethe) 262
Horch, was kommt von draußen 'rein? / Hark, Who's Coming Inside Here?
(Traditional) 263
In einem kühlen Grunde / The Broken Ring (Eichendorff) 265
Kein Feuer, keine Kohle / Secret Love (Traditional) 267
Kommt ein Vogel geflogen / Little Bird (Bäuerle) 268
Die Loreley / The Lorelei (Heine) 269
Muß i denn / Since I Must . . . (Traditional) 271
Wenn alle Brünnlein fließen / The Flowing Brooks (Kleber) 273
Wenn ich ein Vöglein wär / If I Were But a Bird (Traditional) 274

Children's Songs

Alle Vögel sind schon da / All the Birdies Have Returned
(Hoffmann von Fallersleben) 276

Auf einem Baum ein Kuckuck / A Cuckoo Sitting in a Tree
(Traditional) 277

Der Kuckuck und der Esel / The Cuckoo and the Donkey
(Hoffman von Fallersleben) 279

Ein Jäger aus Kurpfalz / A Hunter from Kurpfalz (Traditional) 280

Ein Männlein steht im Walde / A Little Man Stands in the Woods
(Hoffmann von Fallersleben) 281

Ein Vogel wollte Hochzeit machen / The Bird Wedding (Traditional) 283

Es klappert die Mühle am rauschenden Bach / The Rattling Water Mill
(Anschütz) 287

Fuchs, du hast die Gans gestohlen / Fox, You've Stolen the Goose
(Anschütz) 289

Ich bin der Doktor Eisenbart / I Am Doctor Ironbeard (Traditional) 290

Kuckuck, Kuckuck / Cuckoo, Cuckoo (Hoffmann von Fallersleben) 292

Laterne, Laterne / Lantern, Lantern (Traditional) 293

Notes 294

Index of Composers 315

Index of Poets 316

Index of Titles and First Lines 317

Introduction

This collection of German songs contains two strains of tradition: the political song and the folk song. It is not always clear where one should draw the distinction between the two, since many political songs became folk songs due to their great popularity, and many folk songs have a clear emancipatory, and thus political, dimension.

The popularity that a song gained in either German-speaking or non-German-speaking countries functioned as the criterion for selection,[1] and the reasons for this popularity could be quite various.[2]

Existing historical and present-day collections of songs[3] quickly give a broad overview of the various epochs of German song, making it easier to compile this volume. Producing an adequate version of each text proved to be a more difficult task; numerous political songs, such as those of the German workers' movement, were quickly carried to other countries because of international networking in the movement. In these cases, I have chosen the oldest English translation available.[4]

Because of this wide diffusion of material, great skepticism vis-à-vis folk songs existed in critical circles in the Federal Republic of Germany up into the 1970s. Already during the nineteenth century, at the time of the Franco–Prussian Wars—and particularly during the time of German fascism—representatives of the ruling ideology exploited the folk song to conjure up a nationalism that rigorously rejected everything foreign and "liberal." For that reason, in the postwar era folk songs espoused a conservative or reactionary world view, concealed social grievances, and functioned as stabilizers of the status quo. A change of view did not come about until the 1970s, when the original emancipatory attitude of many German folk songs was rediscovered, due to a new and different awareness of history. While the younger generation in the Federal Republic became increasingly politicized (as expressed in the 1968 student movement and the subsequent civil rights and women's movements), German folk songs and historical–political songs concurrently experienced a revival. People wanted to learn from history and used the progressive tradition of the emancipatory song to do so. The German song henceforth began to be regarded differently by being placed in its historical context, with particular consideration accorded to its genesis, intended effect, reception, and function. This emancipatory tradition was taken up and continued by numerous *Liedermacher*[5] of the Federal Republic and the GDR.

With an acknowledgement of the difficulties of achieving "true socialism" and of the contradiction between political ideals and realities, interest in political songs has declined in the united Germany since 1989, coinciding with a rapid loss of belief in political utopias.

In this context, this volume is an attempt to contribute toward revitalizing the emancipatory tradition of German-language political songs and folk songs, even though the collection remains incomplete[6] and does not correspond to linguistic standards of the time.[7]

The inclusion of the scores offers the opportunity to recognize the songs musically as well. The folk songs are divided according to topic, so that the historical development of a particular topic is clarified.

Since it is primarily historical events,[8] great social grievances,[9] and injustices[10] that have been thematicized in political songs, these texts are arranged according to a historical chronology that, starting with the Peasant Wars,[11] extends to present-day Germany. On the one hand, this chronological presentation shows the historical tradition of political songs;[12] on the other hand, it shows the didactic character of those songs with utmost clarity: in the texts, common notions, ideas, interests, and goals are expressed and transposed into action through group singing. It is no coincidence that the popular movements, political as well as religious, of various epochs have successfully used songs in order to call people to action. Of course, this also always bore the danger that the songs might be misused for ideological and demagogic purposes.

I. P.-S.
Translated by Lance W. Garmer

NOTES

1. Due to copyright restrictions, however, the selection of songs was limited in some cases.
2. See the notes to the individual songs (pp. 294–312). While the topicality of a text was usually the primary concern in German-speaking countries, many songs became popular in non-German-speaking countries primarily because of their very catchy melodies. However, this collection does not

present songs that glorify war, militarism, intolerance, or xenophobia, despite the popularity some of these songs have, for various reasons—a popularity that need not be promoted further.

3. See bibliography.
4. German workers' songs were often presented at trade-union meetings in England just months after they were first performed in Germany.
5. GDR *Liedermacher* (songwriter) Wolf Biermann coined this term, adapting Brecht's expression *Stuckemacher* (playwright).
6. Frequently, only those verses were translated that had contextual relevance to the country in question or had international significance. For example, the English translation of the 1932 song "Komintern" contains only four verses; verses two, three and four are missing in the American version of the song "Die Moorsoldaten."
7. Cf. the English version of "Bundeslied" with the title "Said Wealth to Toil."
8. Wars, revolts, revolutions, assassinations, and so forth.
9. The working conditions of the Silesian weavers in the eighteenth and nineteenth centuries, for example.
10. For example, songs from the time of the Peasant Wars, songs against German fascism, songs of the German student movement.
11. First recorded texts of political songs.
12. This historical tradition is shown in the continued exercise of social criticism as well as in the concrete appropriation of text passages or melodies that, for their part, are to be understood as an indication of the historical context of the grievances criticized.

EIN FESTE BURG IST UNSER GOTT

Text: Martin Luther, 1528
Music: Johann Sebastian Bach

1.
Ein feste Burg ist unser Gott,
Ein gute Wehr und Waffen.
Er hilft uns frei aus aller Not,
Die uns jetzt hat betroffen.
Der alt böse Feind,
Mit Ernst er's jetzt meint.
Groß Macht und viel List
Sein grausam Rüstung ist.
Auf Erd ist nicht seinsgleichen.

2.
Mit unsrer Macht ist nichts getan,
Wir sind gar bald verloren.
Es streit' für uns der rechte Mann,
Den Gott hat selbst erkoren.
Fragst du, wer der ist?
Er heißt Jesus Christ,
Der Herr Zebaoth,
Und ist kein andrer Gott.
Das Feld muß er behalten.

3.

Und wenn die Welt voll Teufel wär
Und wollt uns gar verschlingen,
So fürchten wir uns nicht so sehr,
Es soll uns doch gelingen.
Der Fürst dieser Welt,
Wie saur er sich stellt,
Tut er uns doch nicht.
Das macht, er ist gericht'.
Ein Wörtlein kann ihn fällen.

4.

Das Wort sie sollen lassen stahn
Und Kein' Dank dazu haben.
Er ist bei uns wohl auf dem Plan
Mit seinem Geist und Gaben.
Nehmen sie den Leib,
Gut, Ehr, Kind und Weib,
Laß fahren dahin.
Sie haben's kein Gewinn.
Das Reich muß uns doch bleiben.

A MIGHTY FORTRESS IS OUR GOD

1.

A mighty fortress is our God,
A sword and shield victorious;
He breaks the cruel oppressor's
  rod
And wins salvation glorious.
The old satanic foe
Has sworn to work us woe.
With craft and dreadful
  might
He arms himself to fight.
On earth he has no equal.

2.

No strength of ours can match
  his might.
We would be lost, rejected.
But now a champion comes to
  fight,
Whom God himself elected.
You ask who this may Be?
The Lord of hosts is he,
Christ Jesus, mighty Lord,
God's only Son, adored.
He holds the field victorious.

3.

Though hordes of devils fill the
  land
We tremble not, unmoved we
  stand;
They cannot overpower us.
Let this world's tyrant rage;
In battle we'll engage.
His might is doomed to fail;
God's judgment must prevail!
One little word subdues him.

4.

God's Word forever shall abide,
No thanks to foes, who fear it;
For God himself fights by our side
With weapons of the Spirit.
Were they to take our house,
Goods, honor, child, or spouse,
Though life be wrenched away,
They cannot win the day.
The Kingdom's ours forever!

*Translated in Lutheran
Book of Worship, 1982*

POLITICAL SONGS

Songs of the Downtrodden

ES IST EIN SCHNITTER, HEIßT DER TOD

Text: Traditional, 1638
Music: Traditional, 1638

Es ist ein Schnit-ter, der heißt Tod, hat

G'walt vom gro - ßen Gott. Heut

wetzt er das Mes-ser, es geht schon viel bes-ser, bald

wird er drein-schneiden, wir müs-sens nur lei - den.

Hüt dich, schöns Blü - me - lein!

1.

Es ist ein Schnitter, heißt der Tod,
  Hat G'walt vom großen Gott
Heut wetzt er das Messer,

Es geht schon viel besser,
Bald wird er dreinschneiden,
Wir müssens nur leiden.
Hüt dich, schöns Blümelein!

2.

Was heut noch grün und frisch
    dasteht,
Wird morgen weggemäth;
Die edel Narzissel,
Die englische Schlüssel,
Der schön Hyazinth,
Die türkische Bind.
Hüt dich schöns Blümelein!

3.

Viel hunderttausend ungezählt,
Was nur unter die Sichel fällt:
Rot Rosen, weiß Liljen,
Beid wird er austilgen,

Ihr Kaiserkronen,
Man wird euch nicht schonen.
Hüt dich, schöns Blümelein!

4.

Trutz Tod, komm her, ich
    fürcht' dich nit!
Trutz, komm und tu ein'n
    Schnitt!
Wenn er mich verletzet, so werd'
    ich versetzet:
Ich will es erwarten im
    himmlischen Garten;
Freu dich, schön's Blümelein!

BEHOLD THE REAPER

1.

Behold the reaper called Death,
God-granted power he hath.
He sharpens his long knife
The better to cut life;
Soon our own is taken,
Yet our faith never shaken.
Guard thee well, fairest flow'r!

2.

All that grows and blooms
    today
Will wither, die, and fade away:
The noble narcissus,
The English primrose,
The lovely hyacinth,
The sturdy terebinth.
Guard thee well, fairest flow'r!

3.

Unnumbered thousands Death
    obeyed,

Cut down by the scythe's sharp
    blade:
Red roses, white lillies,
Uprooted are both these,
Proud crown imperials
From death no denials.
Guard thee well, fairest flow'r!

4.

Grim Death, come here, I fear
    thee not!
I humbly accept my lot.
Were I accused harshly,
My fate I accept gladly;
Awaiting my sentence
In God's holy presence.
Rejoice thee now, fairest
    flow'r!

Translated by
Charles Haywood

ICH BIN EIN FREIER BAUERNKNECHT

Text: Traditional, 17th century
Music: Traditional, 17th century

1. Ich bin ein frei - er Bau - ren - knecht,
ob schon mein Stand ist e - ben schlecht,
so deucht ich mich doch wol so gut,
als ei - ner an dem Ho - fe___ tut.
Tral - ti - ra - la, ich will es nicht ach - ten,
ob schon, die Hof - leut auch mich ver-ach - ten.

1.
Ich bin ein freier Bauernknecht,
ob schon mein Stand ist eben
   schlecht,
so deucht ich mich doch wol so
   gut,
als einer an dem Hofe tut.
Traltirala, ich will es nicht
   achten,
ob schon die Hofleut auch mich
   verachten.

2.
Trag ich nicht lange krause Haar
und Pulver drein, das Geld ich
   spar;
den Staub vom Lande weht der
   Wind
des Sommers in mein Haar
   geschwind.
Traltirala, drumb geh ich gestutzet,
obschon mein Haar ist vorn
   geputzet.

3.
Vor Seiden Strümpfe, knapfte
    Schuh,
Bänder, und was gehörig dazu,
zieh ich ein weit Paar Stiefel an,
und doch mit Wahrheit sagen
    kann.
Traltirala, daß vor so viel Jahren
ich sie hab eh denn je getragen.

4.
Ich darf zu Hof schmarutzeln
    nicht,
weil mir dasselbst nichts
    gebricht;
darf nicht Fuchsschwäntzen
    umb das Brod,

arbeite lieber mich zu todt.
Traltirala, ich werd nicht
    belogen,
auch nicht mit Gleißners-
    Worten betrogen.

5.
Was bildet sich der Hofmann
    ein,
Daß er als ich will besser sein?
Da Adam ackert und Eva spann,
wer war damals ein Edelmann?
Traltirala, ich bin noch mein
    eigen,
darf mich vor keinem bücken
    noch neigen.

I AM A FREE PEASANT

1.
A truly free peasant am I,
and though my rank's not
    high,
I see myself as just as good
as someone in a castle would.
Traltiralla, I'm my own man,
needn't bend nor bow 'fore
    anyone.

2.
A beaver hat I don't call mine,
and smokey felt suits me just
    fine.
A green twig put on top of
    that
looks like choice feathers on my
    hat.
Traltiralla, I sure don't mind
if highborn folks laugh at my
    kind.

3.
Don't wear my hair in curls and
    long
and powdered—why spend
    money wrong?
The summer wind blows swift
    and fair
dust from the fields into my
    hair.
Traltiralla, my hair's short, but,
around my face it is well cut.

4.
I don't call a castle my own.
I'm not witty with words and
    tone,
but I live on a farm that's mine,
and always feel just fine.
Traltiralla, and as I go
I learn what a farmer needs to
    know.

5.
I'm usually sound and fit,
my work behind the plough
    helps it.
Those others gorge and gulp so
    that
they're often sick, and they get
    fat.
Traltiralla, I'm in fine whack,
and have what folks at court
    well lack.

6.
His nose up in the air has he,
and thinks he is better than me.
When Adam dug, and Eva span,
well, who was then the
    nobleman?
Traltiralla, I live every day
and easy-go-lucky, carefree and
    gay.

Translated by Sabine Tober

WER JETZIG ZEITEN LEBEN WILL

Text: Traditional, 17th century
Music: Traditional, 17th century

Wer jet - zig Zei - ten le - ben will, muß
es hat der ar - gen Feind so viel, be -

hab'n ein tap - fers Her - ze,
rei - ten ihm groß Schmer - ze. Da

heißt es stehn ganz un - ver - zagt in

sei - ner blan - ken Weh - re, daß sich der Feind nicht

an uns wagt, es geht um Gut und Eh - re.

1.
Wer jetzig Zeiten leben will,
muß hab'n ein tapfers Herze,
es hat der argen Feind so viel,
bereiten ihm groß Schmerze.
Da heißt es stehn ganz unverzagt
in seiner blanken Wehre,
daß sich der Feind nicht an uns
   wagt,
es geht um Gut und Ehre.

2.
Geld nur regiert die ganze Welt,
dazu verhilft Betrügen;
wer sich sonst noch so redlich hält,
muß doch bald unterliegen.
Rechtschaffen hin, rechtschaffen
   her,

das sind nur alte Geigen:
Betrug, Gewalt und List
   vielmehr,
klag du, man wird dir's zeigen.

3.
Doch wie's auch kommt, das
   arge Spiel,
behalt ein tapfers Herze,
und sind der Feind auch noch so
   viel,
verzage nicht im Schmerze.
Steh gottgetreulich, unverzagt
in deiner blanken Wehre:
Wenn sich der Feind auch an
   uns wagt,
es geht um Gut und Ehre!

We Need a Heart of Courage Now

1.
We need a heart of courage now
In this day and age,
For all those many enemies
Cause us hurt and rage.
We've got to bravely stand our
   ground;
Our honor and property
Must be protected at all costs
From any enemy.

2.
The world is ruled by Money
   now,
And Money's sidekick, Fraud.
Most honest men will soon
   succumb,
Despite their fear of God.
O righteous this, o righteous
   that,

Complaining is no use.
For Fraud and Cunning now
   prevail,
Alongside sheer Abuse.

3.
But keep staunch courage in
   your hearts,
Within this ugly game;
There may be many foes right
   now,
But don't despair in pain.
So stand undaunted, trust in God;
Your honor and property
Must be protected at all costs
From any enemy.

*Translated by
Alexandra Chciuk-Celt*

WIR SIND DES GEYERS SCHWARZER HAUFEN

Text: Traditional, 15th century
Music: Traditional, 15th century

1. Wir sind des Gey-ers schwar-zer Hau-fen,
hei - ja - ho, ho! Wir woll'n mit Pfaff und
A - del rau-fen, hei - ja - ho, ho! Spieß vor-an!
Drauf und dran! Setzt aufs Klo-ster-dach den ro-ten Hahn!

1.
Wir sind des Geyers schwarzer
   Haufen, heijaho, ho!
Wir woll'n mit Pfaff und Adel
   raufen, heijaho, ho!
Spieß voran! Drauf und Dran!
Setzt aufs Klosterdach den roten
   Hahn!

2.
Als Adam grub und Eva spann,
   Kyrieleis,
Wo war denn da der Edelmann?
   Kyrieleis.
Spieß voran . . .

3.
Wir wollen's Gott im Himmel
   klagen, Kyrieleis,
Daß wir die Pfaffen nicht dürfen
   totschlagen, Kyrieleis!
Spieß voran . . .

4.
Der Florian Geyer führt uns an,
   heijaho, ho!
Den Bundschuh führt er in der
   Fahn, trotz Acht und
   Bann.
Spieß voran . . .

GEYER'S PITCH-DARK GANG ARE WE

1.
Geyer's pitch-dark gang are we,
    heia hoho,
we'll fight church and nobility,
    heia hoho!
Out the lance!
Let's advance!
On cloister's roof the flames
    shall dance,
on the roof the flames shall
    dance.

2.
When Adam dug, and Eva Span,
    kyrieleis,
well, who was then the
    nobleman? Kyrieleis.
Out the lance, etc.

3.
Our protest to God in his
    heavenly land, kyrieleis,
that we mustn't kill the clerical
    band, kyrieleis!
Out the lance, etc.

4.
Florian Geyer's our head man
in spite of outlawry and ban.
The peasant's clog is in his
    sign,
his armor and helmet in full
    shine.
Out the lance, etc.

Translated by
Sabine Tober

Songs in the Time of the French Revolution

BÜRGERLIED DER MAINZER

Text: Traditional, 1792
Music: Traditional

1.
Auf Brüder! Auf! Die Freiheit
    lacht,
Die Ketten sind entzwei,
Uns hat sie Custine losgemacht,
O Bürger, wir sind frei!
Nun drückt uns kein Despote
    mehr
Und raubt uns unsre Taschen leer,
Der Mainzer ist nun frei!
Der Mainzer ist nun frei!

2.
Auf Brüder! Auf zum Jubelsang,
Und preiset dankend Gott!
Nun hört er auf des Bürgers
    Drang,
Der armen Bauern Not;
Nun ist allein ihr Stand geacht
Und die Despoten sind veracht;
Der Mainzer ist nun frei!
Der Mainzer ist nun frei!

3.
Auf Bürger! schwört den
    Frankeneid!

Den schönsten auf der Erd',
Die Franken haben euch befreit,
Macht euch der Freiheit wert!
Den Tod verlacht der freie
    Mann,
Weil Freiheit nur beglücken
    kann.
Der Mainzer ist nun frei!
Der Mainzer ist nun frei!

4.
O Bürger! welche Seligkeit
Ein freier Mann zu sein!
Dem kein Despote mehr gebeut
Nur das Gesetz allein.
Nun ist es aus, das Adelreich,
Nun sind wir Brüder, alle
    gleich;
Der Mainzer ist nun frei!
Der Mainzer ist nun frei!

5.
O Bürger sprecht: Wie schön es
    läßt,
Wenn ihr, vom Zwang befreit,

Wenn beim Gericht, beim
    Jubelfest
Ihr stets die Ersten seid?
Wenn nicht mehr Stern- und
    Ordensmann
Euch spotten, Euch verhöhnen
    kann;
Denn Mainzer, ihr seid frei!
Denn Mainzer, ihr seid frei!

6.
Ihr Mainzerinnen freuet euch!
Ihr Schönen jubiliert!
Nun seid ihr Edeldamen gleich,
Die stolz euch sonst regiert,
Nun hat bei Ball, bei Spiel und
    Sang

Die Bürgerin den ersten Rang;
Der Mainzer ist nun frei!
Der Mainzer ist nun frei!

7.
Das Eisen, das uns sonst
    gedrückt,
Das unser Recht gekränkt,
O Bürger! Bürger dankt
    entzückt
Ihm, der es so gelenkt!
Das Eisen, aufgestellt vom
    Stolz,
Ha, seht doch Bürger, es
    zerschmolz.
Der Bürger ist nun frei!
Der Bürger ist nun frei!

The Mainz Citizens' Song, 1792

1.
Come, brothers, rejoice in being
    free
now that our chains are gone.
Custine cut them, and fight did
    he!
Citizens, it is done!
No more can despots be
    so bold
and rob us of our hard earned
    gold.
The Mainzer is now free!
The Mainzer is now free!

2.
Let's join in songs of jubilation,
let's praise God in his might
who now sees our tribulation
and the poor peasants' plight.

It's their rank now that's held the
    best,
and all the despots we detest.
The Mainzer is now free!
The Mainzer is now Free!

3.
The Frankens' oath let's take now,
    we
know none as fine on
    earth.
It was the Franks who set you free,
give liberty its worth.
A trifle's death to the free man
rejoicing in freedom as we
    can!
The Mainzer is now free!
The Mainzer is now free.

4.
Oh, citizens, what joy and bliss
in being free at last.
No despot do we have to please,
can just obey the laws.
The feudal system was a shame.
Now we're all brothers, all the
    same.
The Mainzer is now free!
The Mainzer is now free!

5.
Citizens, speak of your feelings
when you, freed of oppression,
at tribunals, at festive dealings
rank first in every session.
And neither noble- nor
    clergyman
can mock, jeer, or insult you
    then.
The Mainzer is now free!
The Mainzer is now free!

6.
And you, our fine Mainz women
    revel,
rejoice, you beauties, for

you are now on an even level
with the ladies who ruled you
    before.
Now at the dance, in song and
    game,
it's the woman citizen who gains
    fame.
The Mainzer is now free!
The Mainzer is now free!

7.
The iron yoke that held us
    down,
insulting our right,
the yoke imposed by
    haughtiness,
is melted by god's might.
Him who thus guided our
    fate
let's give our thanks from morn
    till late.
Free citizens are we!
Free citizens are we!

Translated by
Sabine Tober

FREIHEIT, DIE ICH MEINE

Text: Max von Schenkendorf, 1813
Music: Karl August Groos, 1818

Frei-heit, die ich mei - ne, die mein Herz er -
Komm mit dei-nem Schei - ne, sü - ßes En - gel -

füllt,
bild! Magst du nie dich zei - gen der be -

dräng - ten Welt, füh - rest dei - nen

Rei - gen nur am Ster - nen - -zelt?

1.
Freiheit, die ich meine,
die mein Herz erfüllt,
komm mit deinem Scheine,
süßes Engelsbild!
Magst du nie dich zeigen
der bedrückten Welt?
Führest deinen Reigen
nur am Sternenzelt?

2.
Auch bei grünen Bäumen
in dem lust'gen Wald,
unter Blütenträumen
ist dein Aufenthalt!
Ach, das ist ein Leben,
wenn es weht und klingt,
wenn dein stilles Weben
wonnig uns durchdringt.

3.
Wenn die Blätter rauschen
süßen Freundesgruß,
wenn wir Blicke tauschen,
Liebeswort und Kuß.
Aber immer weiter
nimmt das Herz den Lauf,
auf der Himmelsleiter
steigt die Sehnsucht auf.

4.
Wo sich Gottes Flamme
in ein Herz gesenkt,
das am alten Stamme
treu und liebend hängt;
wo sich Männer finden,
die für Ehr' und Recht
mutig sich verbinden,
weilt ein frei Geschlecht.

COME, MY GENTLE FREEDOM

1.
Come, my gentle freedom,
You who fill my soul,
Show your angel-image
Here unto us all.
Will you never show the
Troubled world your
        face?
Will you only dance with
Stars in outer space?

2.
You can also tarry
'Mid the verdant trees,
In the merry forest
And dream-blossom bees.
When we cry in pain, we
Hope for your sweet kiss:
When your silent flutter
Fills our hearts with
        bliss.

3.
Now the leaves are rustling
Frinedly greetings too,
We're exchanging glances,
Kisses, "I love you."
But our hearts keep rising,
Running ever higher,
And our longing climbs up
Heaven's golden spires.

4.
Where God's golden flame is
Placed within a man,
One who is devoted,
True to his own clan,
Where men have the courage
To organize to fight
For honor and for justice,
There's Freedom and there's Right.

Translated by
Alexandra Chciuk-Celt

DIE GEDANKEN SIND FREI

Text: Traditional, 1230; Ernst Richter, 1780;
A. H. Hoffmann von Fallersleben
Music: Traditional, 1815

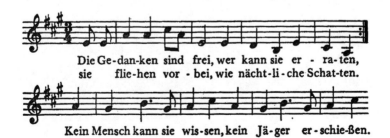

Die Ge-dan-ken sind frei, wer kann sie er - ra-ten,
sie flie-hen vor - bei, wie nächt-li-che Schat-ten.

Kein Mensch kann sie wis-sen, kein Jä-ger er - schie-ßen.

Es blei - bet da - bei: Die Ge - dan - ken sind frei.

1.

Die Gedanken sind frei,
wer kann sie erraten,
sie fliehen vorbei,
wie nächtliche Schatten.
Kein Mensch kann sie wissen,
kein Jäger erschießen.
mit Pulver und Blei,
Die Gedanken sind frei.

2.

Ich denke, was ich will
und was mich beglücket,
doch alles in der Still
und wie es sich schicket.

Mein Wunsch und Begehren
kann niemand verwehren,
es bleibet dabei:
Die Gedanken sind frei!

3.

Und sperrt man mich ein
im finsteren Kerker,
das alles sind rein
vergebliche Werke;
denn meine Gedanken
zerreißen die Schranken
und Mauern entzwei:
Die Gedanken sind frei!

THOUGHTS ARE FREE

1.

Die Gedanken sind frei,
My thoughts freely flower,
Die Gedanken sind frei,
my thoughts give me power,
no scholar can map them,
no hunter can trap them,
no man can deny,
Die Gedanken sind frei.

2.

So I think as I please,
And this gives me pleasure,
My conscience decrees,
This right I must treasure;
My thoughs will not cater

To duke or dictator,
No man can deny—
Die Gedanken sind frei!

3.

And if tyrants take me
And throw me in prison,
My thoughts will burst free,
Like blossoms in season.
Foundations will crumble,
The structure will tumble,
And free men will cry—
Die Gedanken sind frei!

Translated by Arthur Kevess

O KÖNIG VON PREUßEN

Text: Traditional, early 19th century
Music: Traditional

1.
O König von Preußen, du großer
    Potentat,
wie sind wir deines Dienstes
so überdrüssig satt!
Was fangen wir nun an
in diesem Jammertal,
allwo ist nichts zu finden
als lauter Not und Qual?

2.
Und kommt das Frühjahr an,
da ist die große Hitz',
da heißt es exerzieren,
daß ei'm der Buckel schwitzt,
da heißt es exerzieren,
vom Morgen bis Mittag,
und das verfluchte Leben,
das währt den ganzen Tag.

3.

Vom Exerzieren weg
geht's wieder auf die Wacht.
Kein Teufel tut nicht fragen,
ob man gefressen hat.
Kein Branntwein in der
    Flaschen,
kein weißes Brot dabei;
ein schlechtes Tabakrauchen,
das ist der Zeitvertreib.

4.

Und kommt ein' frisch' Parad;
tut man ein falschen Tritt,
so hört man es schon rufen:
Der Kerl muß aus dem Glied!
Patronentaschen runter,
den Säbel abgelegt,
und tapfer drauf geschmissen,
bis er sich nicht mehr regt!

5.

Ihr Herren, nehmt's nicht
    Wunder,
wenn einer desertiert.
Wir werden wie die Hunde
mit Schlägen strapaziert,
und bringen sie uns wieder,

sie henken uns nicht auf.
Das Kriegsrecht wird
    gesprochen:
Der Kerl muß Gassenlauf'!

6.

Und wenn wir Gassen laufen,
dann spielet man uns auf.
Mit Waldhorn und
    Trompeten,
dann geht es tapfer drauf;
dann werden wir gehauen
von manchem Musketier,
der eine hat's Bedauern,
der andre gönnt es mir.

7.

Und werden wir dann alt.
Wo wenden wir uns hin?
Die Gesundheit ist
    verloren,
die Kräfte sind dahin!
Und endlich wird es heißen:
Ein Vogel und kein Nest!
Geh', Alter nimm den
    Bettelsack,
bist auch Soldat gewest!

OH KING OF PRUSSIA

1.

Great king of Prussia, oh,
you mighty potentate,
how utterly and fully
your service we do hate!
What's to become of us
in all this misery
when all that's there for us
is pain and agony?

2.

And once Springtime is here,
we're really getting cooked,
and have to drill and drill
till we're completely soaked.
We must drill every day
from morning until noon,
and in this wretched way
it goes on all afternoon.

3.
Once we are off the drill,
it's guard instead of bed,
and no one ever will
ask us whether we're fed.
No brandy in the crock,
and no white bread to chew,
some poor tobacco smoking
is the best we can do.

4.
If in a new parade
we make a faulty step,
immediately it's said:
Let us pull out that chap!
Your cartridge pockets down,
your sabre off your belt,
and then they let you have it
till nothing can be felt.

5.
You gents, don't be surprised
when some of us desert
because just like the dogs
with beatings we are hurt,
and once they bring us back,
they do not hang us then,

but proclaim martial law:
the man must gauntlet run.

6.
And when we gauntlet run,
they play the music loud,
and with horns and with
    trumpets
we are getting knocked out.
We're struck and we are
    pounded
by many a musketeer,
some treat us with some pity,
some hit us without fear.

7.
And once we're getting on
in years, where can we turn,
once our health is gone,
and our strength forlorn?
Then finally we are
called birds without a nest,
and beggars, nothing more,
with all our soldiers' past.

Translated by Sabine Tober

LIED FREYER LANDLEUTE

Text: Friedrich Lehne, 1792–93
Music: "Le Marseillaise," Claude-Joseph
Rouget de Lisle, 1792.

1.
Wohlan! es geht! es ist
  gegangen!
Uns seegnet Gottes Vater-Blik;
Laßt Sklaven vor Despoten
  bangen!
Die feige Brut verdient kein Glük.
Laß uns der Freyheit würdig
  werden!
Sie ist des Menschen bestes Gut,
Und fliest für sie auch all' sein
  Blut—
Geniest sein Sohn doch Glük auf
  Erden.
Wohlan! die Wahl ist leicht!
Nur Freyheit oder Tod!
Weh' dem! Fluch dem!
Der je es wagt und unsrer
  Freyheit droht!

2.
Wir pflügten willig unsre
  Aekker,
Viel träge Prasser nährten wir;
Doch seht! sie wurden immer
  kekker,
Erniedrigt waren wir zum Thier.
Geblendet von dem schnöden
  Glanze
Den ihnen unser Fleiß verschaft,
War stolz und stark durch unsre
  Kraft
Manch fetter Pfaff, manch geiler
  Schranze.
Wohlan! die Wahl is leicht! . . .

3.
Wann künftig unsre Saaten
  blühen
Dann ärnten wir, nur wir
sie ein;
So werden dann auch unsre
  Mühen
Belohnt durch Gottes Gaben
  sein.
Kein Fürstenknecht darf uns
  mehr kränken,
Nur dem Gesez gehorchen wir,
Und dieses macht uns nicht zum
  Thier
Es siehert uns vor bösen
  Ränken.
Wohlan, die Wahl ist leicht! . . .

4.
Wir selbst, wir machen die
  Gesezze,
Denn wer weiß besser, was un
  nützt?
Dadurch behalten wir die
  Schäzze.
Die dann kein Schwelger mehr
  besizt.
Wir wählen uns gerichte
  Richter,
Die keines Schurken Gold
  besticht
Vertrauen wekket ihr Gesicht
Schrök nie wie jene Amts-
  Gesichter.
Wohlan! die Wähl ist leicht! . . .

5.
Seht diesen Baum all' ihr
    Despoten!
Wir pflanzten unsern Rechten
    ihn;
Und in des Vaterlandes Boden
Soll er noch unsern Enkeln
    blüh'n.
Wir wollen ihr mit Muth
    beschüzzen,
Bis die Gerechtigkeit gesiegt;
In seinem Schatten dann
    vergnügt
Am Abend unsres Lebens sizzen.
Wohlan! die Wahl ist leicht! . . .

6.
O Gott! Beschüzzer alles Guten!

Schenk' unsrer Freyheit deinen
    Schild!
Wir wollen gerne für sie bluten,
Wenn es dein Richter-Wink
    befielt.
Gieb unsren Werken deinen
    Seegen!
Denn der nut gründet unser Glük;
Wir fodern dein Geschenk
    zurük;
Komm' unsrem Muth mit Kraft
    entgegen!
Wohlan! wir schwören dir!
Nur Freyheit oder Tod!
Weh'dem! Fluch dem!
Der je es wagt, und unsrer
    Freyheit droht.

THE SONG OF THE FREE COUNTRY FOLK (1792-93)

1.
Now forward march! We are
    arriving!
And God the Father blesses us!
Slaves quake in fear before a
    tyrant,
A coward-brute deserves no luck.
Let us be worthy of our
    freedom!
It is mankind's most sacred
    good,
For which we may spill all our
    blood—
To bring our children earthly
    boon.
Now march! the choice is clear!
It's liberty or death!
Our curse upon anyone
Who dares to stop us now!

2.
We gladly plowed our fields before.
We fed a lot of parasites—
But they have gotten much too
    cocky
And treat us just like animals.
They're blinded by the tinsel
    glamor
Which is the work of our own
    sweat.
All those fat priests and
    lech'rous toadies
Got pride and power at our
    expense.
Now march! etc.

3.
When crops are in full bloom,
    remember

We planted them, and we alone!
Our efforts shall be compensated
By harvest bountiful from God.
No courtly hack can then insult
us,
The Law will sheild us from
such plots,
And we'll be subject to it only.
This proves that we're not
animals.
Now march! etc.

4.
We'll make the laws all by
ourselves then,
For who knows better what we
need?
We'll keep the riches we created
And not give them to parasites.
Then we'll elect some honest
judges
Who won't be bribed by rascals'
gold;
They'll have these trust-inspiring
faces,
Not fearsome bureaucratic
masks.
Now march! etc.

5.
Look at this tree, oh, all you
tyrants:
We've planted all our rights
within.

We'll see it bloom in this our
homeland
For our grandchildren and
beyond.
And we shall carefully protect it
Till justice is victorious;
And when we reach our golden
years
We'll rest quite happy in its
shade.
Now march!, etc.

6.
O God! Protector of all
goodness!
Give our liberty Thy shield!
We'll gladly spill our blood for
freedom
If Thou, O Judge, decree it so.
Give Thy blessing as the
foundation
Without which all our efforts
are naught!
Give us back Thy present again,
And join Thy power with our
courage.
We swear to Thee, O God:
It's liberty or death!
Our curse upon anyone
Who dares to stop us now!

Translated by
Alexandra Chciuk-Celt

Songs of the German Revolution of 1848

BADISCHES WIEGENLIED

Text: Ludwig Pfau, 1848
Music: Traditional

Refr.: Schlaf, mein Kind, schlaf leis', dort drau-ßen geht der Preuß'! 1. Deinen Va-ter hat er um-ge-bracht, / dei-ne Mut-ter hat er arm ge-macht, und wer nicht schläft in gu-ter Ruh', / dem drückt der Preuß' die Au-gen zu: Schlaf, mein Kind.

1.
Schlaf, mein Kind, schlaf leis',
dort draußen geht der Preuß
Deinen Vater hat er umgebracht,
deine Mutter hat er arm
 gemacht,
und wer nicht schläft in guter
 Ruh',
dem drückt der Preuß die Augen
 zu:
Schlaf, mein Kind, schlaf leis',
dort draußen geht der Preuß.

2.
Schlaf, mein Kind, schlaf leis',
dort draußen geht der Preuß
Der Preuß' hat eine blutige
 Hand,
die streckt er über das badische
 Land
und alle müssen wir stille
 sein,
wie dein Vater unterm Stein.
Schlaf, mein Kind, schlaf leis',
dort draußen geht der Preuß.

3.
Schlaf, mein Kind, schlaf leis',
dort draußen geht der Preuß.
Zu Rastatt auf der Schanze,
da spielt er auf zum Tanze,
da spielt er auf mit Pulver und
    Blei,
so macht er alle Badener frei.
Schlaf, mein Kind, schlaf leis',
dort draußen geht der Preuß.

4.
Schlaf, mein Kindlein, schrei's,
da draußen liegt der Preuß!
Gott aber weiß, wie lang er geht,
bis daß die Freiheit aufersteht,
und wo dein Vater liegt, mein
    Schatz,
da hat noch mancher Preuße Platz,
schrei's, mein Kindlein, schrei's,
da draußen liegt der Preuß'!

LULLABY OF BADEN

1.
Sleep and make no sound,
the Prussians are around.
They came and killed your
    father,
they came and robbed your
    mother,
and unless you're in slumber
    deep
the Prussians will put you to
    sleep.
Sleep and make no sound,
the Prussians are around.

2.
Sleep and make no sound,
the Prussians are around.
The Prussian has a bloody hand,
extends it over Baden land,
and we must all hold our breath
like your father in his death.
Sleep and make no sound,
the Prussians are around.

3.
Sleep and make no sound,
the Prussians are around.

Rastatt bulwark was the site
where he played music, played
    with might.
With gunpowder and lead
    played he,
and set the people of Baden free.
Sleep and make no sound,
the Prussians are around.

4.
Scream and yell, my darling dear:
the Prussian, the Prussian is
    lying out here.
God will know how much time
    to give
until he lets liberty live,
and many a Prussian will yet fit
down with your father in the
    dark pit.
Scream and yell, my darling
    dear:
the Prussian, the Prussian is
    lying out here.

Translated by
Sabine Tober

DAS BLUTGERICHT

Text: Traditional, 1844
Music: Traditional, "Es liegt ein Schloß in Österreich"

1.
Hier im Ort ist das Gericht
Viel schlimmer als die Femen,
Wo man nicht nur das
Urteil spricht,
Das Leben schnell zu nehmen.

2.
Hier wird der Mensch langsam
      gequält,
Hier ist die Folterkammer,
Hier werden Seufzer viel gezählt,
Als Zeugen von dem Jammer.

3.
Die Herren Zwanziger die
      Henker sind,
Die Dierig ihre Schergen.

Davon ein jeder tapferschind't,
Anstatt was zu verbergen.

4.
Ihr Schurken all, ihr Satansbrut,
Ihr höllischen Dämone,
Ihr freßt der Armen Hab und
      Gut,
Und Fluch wird euch zum
      Lohne.

5.
Ihr seid die Quelle aller Not,
Die hier den Armen drücket,
Ihr seid's, die ihm das trockne
      Brot
Noch von dem Munde rücket.

THE BLOOD COURT

1.
A blood court is what we have here
harsher than Vehmic law
with verdicts cruelly more severe
than death plain, swift, and raw.

2.
Relentless torture is our fate,
and we are on the rack.
Hear our sighs from morn to late
while they are on our back.

3.
They Zwanzigers execute all day,
the Dierigs by their side.
They grind us, sweat us, skin
    and flay,
and nothing do they hide.

4.
You villains, oh, you devil's
    brood,
infernal monsters you,
getting fat off the poor man's
    good—
damnation will be your due.

5.
It's you who cause pain, grief,
    despair
for the poor man in this land,
and even snatch with zero
    care
his dry bread from his hand.

*Translated by
Sabine Tober*

BÜRGERLIED

Text: Traditional (Nettler), 1845
Music: "Prinz Eugen, der edle Ritter"

1. Ob wir ro-te, gel-be Kra-gen, Hel-me
o-der Hü-te tra-gen, Stie-fel
tra-gen o-der Schuh', o-der ob wir Rök-ke nä-hen und zu

Schuhen Drähte drehen:Das tut, das tut nichts da- zu.

1.
Ob wir rote, gelbe Kragen,
Helme oder Hüte tragen,
Stiefel tragen oder Schuh',
oder ob wir Röcke nähen
und zu Schuhen Drähte
drehen:
Das tut, das tut nichts dazu.

2.
Ob wir können präsidieren,
oder müssen Akten schmieren
ohne Rast und ohne Ruh;
ob wir just Collegia lesen,
oder aber binden Besen,
das tut, das tut nichts dazu.

3.
Ob wir stolz zu Rosse
reiten,
oder ob zu Fuß wir schreiten,
immer unserm Ziele zu;
ob uns Kreuze vorne schmücken,
oder Kreuze hinten drücken,
das tut, das tut nichts dazu.

4.
Aber ob wir Neues bauen,
oder Altes nur verdauen,
wie das Gras verdaut die Kuh;
ob wir in der Welt was schaffen,
oder nur die Welt begaffen,
das tut, das tut was dazu.

5.
Ob wir rüstig und geschäftig,
wo es gilt zu wirken kräftig,
immer tapfer greifen zu;
oder ob wir schläfrig denken:
"Gott wird's schon im Schlafe
schenken",
das tut, das tut was dazu.

6.
Drum, ihr Bürger, drum, ihr
Brüder,
alle eines Bundes Glieder:
Was auch jeder von uns tu!
Alle, die dies Lied gesungen,
so die Alten, wie die Jungen,
tun wir, tun wir was dazu!

THE CITIZENS SONG

1.
Wear your collars red or yellow
wear your hats hard, wear them
mellow
wear a boot or wear a shoe;
go and sew skirts for a living,
or with wires keep shoes from
giving—

all the same is what you do.

2.
You may lead, control, preside,
or
be a mere desk clerk and writer
with long working hours too;

be professor and truth finder
or just work as a broom
    binder—
all the same is what you do.

3.
Move along on horseback
    proudly,
walk meekly, or parade loudly
toward our goal that's pulling
    you;
wear your crosses on your gown,
or let your crosses weigh you
    down—
all the same is what you do.

4.
But whether we dig up what's
    novel
or just keep gazing at the
    shovel,
eat like cattle and say moo;
whether we just sit and wonder

or else actively go yonder—
not the same is what we do.

5.
Whether we are quick to act,
give assistance, swift, direct,
and get going as it's due;
or whether we think
    sleepily
"God is sure to act for me"—
not the same is what we do.

6.
Citizens, my brothers, we're
part of one alliance here,
no matter what moves me or
    you;
all of us who just have
    sung,
be we old or be we young—
critical is what we do.

Translated by
Sabine Tober

DER GUTE BÜRGER

Text: Ferdinand Freiligrath, early 19th century
Music: Jürgen Rohland, 1969

1.
So hab ich's doch nach all den
    Jahren
zu diesem Posten noch gebracht.
Und leider allzuoft erfahren,
wer hier im Land das Wetter
    macht.
Du sollst, verdammte Freiheit,
    mir
die Ruhe fürder nicht gefährden.
Lisett, noch ein Gläschen Bier!
Ich will ein guter Bürger
    werden.

2.
Diogenes in seiner Tonne—
vortrefflich!—wie beneid ich ihn.
Es war noch keine Juni-Sonne,
die jenen Glücklichen beschien.
Was Monarchie, was Republik?
Wie sich die Leute toll gebärden!
Zum Teufel mit der Politik,
ich will ein guter Bürger werden.

3.
Gewiß, man tobt sich einmal
    aus.

Es wär ja um die Jugend schade.
Doch führt man erst ein eigen
    Haus,
dann werden Fünfe plötzlich
    grade.
In welcher Mühle man uns
    mahlt,
das macht mir nimmermehr
    Beschwerden.
Der ist mein Herr, der mich
    bezahlt.
Ich will ein guter Bürger werden.

4.
Jedwedem Umtrieb bleib ich fern.
Der Henker mag das Volk
    beglücken.
Der Orden ist ein eigner Stern,
wer einen hat, der soll sich
    bücken.
Bück dich, mein Herz! Bald
    fahren wir
zur Residenz mit eigenen
    Pferden.
Lisett, noch ein Gläschen Bier.
Ich will ein guter Bürger werden.

THE SOLID CITIZEN

1.
So after all these years I've
    managed
To get this job; to my dismay,
I found out just a bit too often
Who makes the rules we must
    obey.
Damned Freedom, just leave me
    alone,
Stop making trouble. Once again,
Bring me a glass of beer, Lisette!
I am a Solid Citizen.

2.
Diogenes didn't give a damn
About republics, monarchies,
Or all those other things that
    make
Folks fierce so they disturb the
    peace.
He lived inside a barrel—oh,
That's so sublime!—I envy
    him!
To hell with politics, I say—
I am a Solid Citizen.

3.
It's quite all right to sow wild oats,
Or else one's youth would be a
    waste.
But once a master in one's house,
One learns how to avoid disgrace.
I now do anything for money,
No matter what the regimen;
I don't complain about my boss:
I am a Solid Citizen.

4.
Let common people flirt with
    danger!
I'll only watch it from afar.
I've my position to consider,
I have to follow my own star.
So bow to higher-ups, my hearts!
We'll soon be driving our own
    train
Of horses, visiting the Count.
For I'm a Solid Citizen.

Translated by
Alexandra Chciuk-Celt

Ein neues Lied

Text: Heinrich Heine, 1844
Music: Dieter Süverkrüp, 1969

1.
Ein neues Lied, ein besseres
    Lied,
O Freunde, will ich euch
    dichten!
Wir wollen hier auf Erden schon
Das Himmelreich errichten.

2.
Wir wollen auf Erden glücklich
    sein
Und wollen nicht mehr
    darben;
Verschlemmen soll nicht der
    faule Bauch,
Was fleißige Hände erwarben.

3.
Es wächst hienieden Brot genug
Für alle Menschenkinder,
Auch Rosen und Myrten,
    Schönheit und Lust,
Und Zuckererbsen nicht minder.

4.
Ja, Zuckererbsen für jedermann
    Sobald die Schoten platzen!

Den Himmel überlassen wir
Den Engeln und den
    Spatzen.

5.
Und wachsen uns Flügel nach
    dem Tod,
So wollen wir euch besuchen
Dort oben, und wir, wir essen
    mit euch
Die seligsten Torten und
    Kuchen.

6.
Ein neues Lied, ein besseres
    Lied,
Es klingt wie Flöten und
    Geigen!
Das Miserere ist vorbei,
Die Sterbeglocken schweigen.

7.
Die Jungfer Europa ist
    verlobt
Mit dem schönen Geniusse
Der Freiheit, sie liegen einander
    im Arm,
Sie schwelgen im ersten Kusse.

A Winter's Tale

1.
A different song, a better song,
I'd write: one baked with leaven!
Oh let us here on our good earth
set up the kingdom of heaven.

2.
Oh, let us here on earth be glad,
we're tired of want and pain.
The lazy belly shall not consume
what toiling fingers gain.

3.
There's bread enough grows out
    of earth
for all the children of mankind,
and roses and myrtle, beauty
    and joy,
and green peas and things of
    that kind.

4.
Yes, green peas aplenty for every
    man,
as soon as the crop of them
    mellows!
The heavens we shall gladly leave
to the angels and the
    sparrows.

5.
And if wings shall grow on us
    after death,

why then we shall betake
ourselves to heaven and eat with
    you
the blessedest coffee cake,

6.
A different song, a better song,
it sounds like the viol and flute!
The miserere is over and done,
the funeral bell is mute.

7.
The virgin, Europe, is engaged
to the beautiful young spirit
of freedom, and they lie
    embraced.
Their first kiss—you can hear it.

Translated by
Herman Salinger

FREIFRAU VON DROSTE-VISCHERING

Text: Rudolf Löwenstein, 1844
Music: Traditional

1. Frei- frau von Dro- ste - Vi- sche- ring,
   zum heil'- gen Rock nach Trier hin- ging,

Vi- va- Vi-sche-ring, sie kroch auf al- len
Tri- Tra- Trier hin-ging; sie tat sich sehr ge-

vie- ren, sie wollt' gern' oh- ne Krük- ken
nie- ren, durch die- ses Le- ben rük- ken.

Ach, herr-je, o je-mi-ne, je-mi-ne, ja, ach, herrje, o

je-mi-ne, o je-mi-ne! Jo-seph und Ma-ri-a!

1.
Freifrau von Droste-Vischering,
Vi-Va-Vischering,
zum heil' gen Rock nach Trier
    hinging,
Tri-Tra-Trier hinging;
sie kroch auf allen vieren,
sie tat sich sehr genieren,
sie wollt' gern' ohne Krücken
durch dieses Leben rücken.
Ach, herrje, o jemine, jemine, ja,
ach, herrje, o jemine,
    o jemine!
Joseph und Maria!

2.
Sie schrie, als sie zum Rocke
    kam, Ri-Ra-Rocke kam,
Ich bin an Händ' und Füßen
    lahm, Fi-Fa-Füßen lahm,
Du Rock bist ganz unnäthig,
Drum bist du auch so gnädig;
Hilf mir mit deinem Lichte,
Ich bin des Bischoffs Nichte.
Ach, herrje . . .

3.
Drauf gab der Rock in seinem
    Schrein,
Si-sa-seinem Schrein,
Auf einmal einen hellen Schein,
Hi-ha-hellen Schein,
Gleich fährt's ihr in die Glieder,
Sie kriegt das Laufen wieder;
Getrost zog sie von hinnen,
Die Krücken ließ sie drinnen.
Ach, herrje . . .

4.
Freifrau von Droste-Vischering,
Vi-Va-Vischering,
Noch selb'gen Tags zum
    Kuhschwof ging,
Ki-Ka-Kuhschwof ging.
Dies Wunder göttlich
    grausend,
Geschah im Jahre Tausend
Achthundertvierundvierzig
Und wer's nicht glaubt, der irrt
    sich.
Ach, herrje . . .

MILADY DROSTE-VISCHERING

1.
Milady Droste-Vischering, Vi-
   Va-Vischering,
Went to Trier to the Holy Robe,
   Hi-Ha-Holy Robe;
She crawled around on hands
   and knees,
As embarrassed as she
   could be;
She wanted to get through life
Without having to use
   crutches.
Oh, Lordy, Lordy mine, oh,
   Lordy, Lordy mine.
Oh, Lordy, Lordy mine, St.
   Joseph and St. Mary!

2.
She cried when she the Robe did
   see, Ri-Ra-Robe did see,
I'm lame in both my hands and
   feet, hi-ha-hands and feet;
Oh, Robe, you are quite
   seamless,
So please be generous with me,
Oh, holy light, please help poor
   me,
For I'm the bishop's niece, you
   see.
Oh, Lordy . . .

3.
The Robe within its sacred
   shrine, si-sa-sacred shrine,
At once gave off the brightest
   shine, bri-bra-brightest
   shine;
It then shot right through all her
   limbs,
She found that she could walk
   again,
She walked off feeling satisfied.
Her crutches, there they lay
   inside.
Oh, Lordy . . .

4.
Milady Droste-Vischering, Vi-
   Va-Vischering,
That same day went to a dairy
   ball, di-da-dairy ball;
This wonder awesome and
   divine
Took place in the year one
   thousand
Eight hundred four and forty
And those who doubt it are
   wrong.

*Translation by
Richard J. Rundell*

DAS HECKERLIED

Text: Ludwig Schanz, 1848
Music: Traditional

1.

Es klingt ein Name stolz und
    prächtig
Im ganzen deutschen Vaterland;
Und jedes Herz erzittert mächtig,
Wenn dieser Name wird
    genannt.
Ihr kennt ihn wohl, den edlen
    Mann:
"Es lebe Hecker, stoßet an!"

2.

Wir wurden lang' genug
    beraten,
Hinweg mit jedem feigen Rat!
Wir wollen Männer, wollen
    Taten,
Und Hecker ist der Mann der Tat,

Der kühn für Freiheit fechten
    kann:
"Es lebe Hecker! Stoßet an!"

3.

Wollen nichts vom Frieden
    hören,
Bis durchgekämpft der letzte
    Krieg,
Wir lassen nie mehr uns
    betören,
Die Losung bleibt: Tod oder
    Sieg!
Und wer mit Mut uns geht
    voran:
"Es lebe Hecker! Stoßet
    an!"

4.

Die Scharen jener feigen
    Lumpen
Verachten wir für alle Zeit;
Die ihn geehrt bei vollen
    Humpen
Und ihn verließen in dem
    Streit,
Des Volkes Acht wirft sie in
    Bann:
"Es lebe Hecker! Stoßet an!"

5.

Die Freiheit ist noch nicht
    verloren;
Bald in des Ruhmes
    Flammenschein
Zieht er beim Fest geschmückter
    Tore
Im Vaterlande wied'rum ein.
Und allerwärts ertönt es
    dann:
"Es lebe Hecker! Stoßet an!"

THE SONG OF HECKER

1.

One name resounds through all
    of Germany,
A name that's mighty, straight,
    and proud,
And everyone feels his heart
    flutter
When that name is pronounced
    out loud.
You know him well throughout
    this land:
"Three cheers for Hecker, he's
    our man!"

2.

We've had too much
    deliberation,
Throw out the cowardly advice!
We need real men now, we need
    action,
And our man Hecker's brave
    and wise.
He'll fight for freedom in this
    land:
"Three cheers for Hecker, he's
    our man!"

3.

We will not listen to that peace
    talk
Until the final war is won.
We won't be duped into surrender,
It's "Victory or death," my son.
Who leads us bravely through
    the land?
"Three cheers for Hecker; he's
    our man!"

4.

We'll always have contempt for
    rabble
Who cheered and clapped while
    it was fun;
Those ragged cowards then
    absconded
As soon as fighting had begun.
Just hear the people in this land:
"Three cheers for Hecker, he's
    our man!"

5.

Our freedom is not yet a lost
    cause;

Soon he shall march by torch-
    light flames
Through gestive decorated portals,
Recov'ring Fatherland and fame!
You'll hear it echo through the
    land:

"Three cheers for Hecker, he's
    our man!"

Translated by
Alexandra Chciuk-Celt

ICH BIN EIN GUTER UNTERTAN

Text: Adolf Glasbrenner, 1848
Music: Traditional

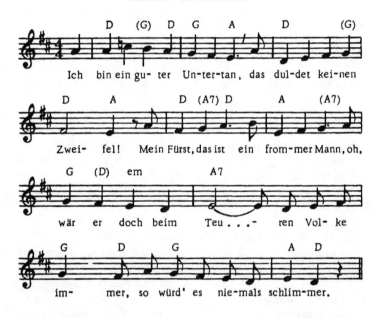

1.
Ich bin ein guter Untertan,
das duldet keinen Zweifel!
Mein Fürst, das ist ein frommer
    Mann,
oh, wär er doch beim
    Teu . . . ren Volke immer,
so würd' es niemals
    schlimmer.

2.
Wir haben ihn wohl oft
    betrübt,
doch nimmermehr
    belogen.
Er sagte, daß er uns geliebt,
doch hat er uns betro . . . offen
    oft mit Taten,
die er uns nicht geraten.

3.
Die Staatsbeamten taten
  recht,
sie wahrten seine Rechte,
und der war ihm der liebste
  Knecht,
der sich recht viel erfre . . .
  eulich zu uns neigte
und Mitleid uns bezeugte.

4.
Den Schwur, den er geleistet
  hat,
Erfüllung alles dessen,
was seine Pflicht an Gottes
  Statt—,
den hat er ganz verge . . . ebens
  halten wollen,
es hat nicht glücken sollen.

5.
Die Polizei, die dazu da,
das wilde Volk zu zügeln,
die möchte ich nur einmal, ja,
so recht von Herzen prü. . . fen
  und sie fragen,
wer über sie könnt' klagen.

6.
Ihr Ritter des Philistertums
und ihr gelehrten Raben
am Friedenshof des Altertums,
o laßt euch doch begr . . . eiflich
  machen,
wie sehr wir euch stets achten.

7.
Ihr Mönche, vornehm, schwarz
  und weiß!
Das Volksglück, das verpuffte,
wird euer steten Mühen Preis,
denn ihr seid große Schul. . .
  gerechte Lehrer
und eifrige Bekehrer.

8.
Ihr Stolzen, ihr im deutschen
  Land
vom Rheine bis nach Polen,
ihr seid mir durch und durch
  bekannt;
euch soll der Kuckuck ho. . . hes
  Alter melden,
euch weisen Friedenshelden!

A LOYAL SUBJECT AM I THEN

1.
A loyal subject am I then,
There is no doubt, I tell,
My sovereign is a pious man,
I wish he were in hel. . .pful
  closeness to us all
to keep things well under
  control.

2.
We must have made him often
  sad,

but we're no lying mob.
He speaks of love he for us had,
but he would come and rob. . .ustly
  surprise us with some acts
that are quite far from our pacts.

3.
His civil servants did well here,
they watched his rights, were
  aimful.
And those of them to him are dear

that are the utmost shame. . .
  faced about what they do,
and show us some empathy too.

4.
A solemn oath one time took he,
to give it all he'd got
in acting as God's deputy,
but now he has forgo. . . ne
  what is his self-interest.
And if things failed; he gave his
  best.

5.
The police force which always
  should
control the wild folks' heat,
if I just once, that would be
  good,
could give them a nice b. . .it of
  study to find out
what the complaints are all
  about.

6.
Philistines in your ivory cage,
you many a learned rave,

on the rest ground of ancient
  age
go find yourselves a grave. . . ly
  given verification
that we cherish you with
  dedication.

7.
You clerics, noble, black and
  white!
public welfare forgotten,
that is your work's result all
  right
for you are really rot. . und and
  eloquent teachers
and most capable preachers.

8.
You haughty folks in Germany
'tween Rhine and Poland
  clamped,
so intimately known to me,
oh, may you all be dam. . . age
  free, old that is,
you very wise heroes of peace.

Translated by Sabine Tober

❦

LIED VOM BÜRGERMEISTER TSCHECH

Text: Traditional, 1844
Music: Traditional

1.
Wer war wohl je so frech
wie der Bürgermeister Tschech?
Denn er schoß ein ganz klein
    wenig
Vorbei an unserm guten König.
Ihm ging's durch'n Mantel,
Ihr ging's durch'n Hut, Hut,
    Hut, Hut,

Ihm ging's durch'n Mantel und
    ihr
ging's durch'n Hut, Hut, Hut,
    Hut, Hut, Hut.

2.
Duncker hat es gleich
    erraten,

Daß er wollte attentaten,
Als er kam so grau bemäntelt
Über'n Schloßpark hergewentelt
Ihr ging's durch'n Mantel . . .

3.
Und er schoß in blinder Wut
Unsrer Kön'gin durch den
    Hut,
Der verfluchte Attentäter,
Königsmörder, Hochverräter.

Ihr ging's durch'n Mantel . . .

4.
Wir kamen so bei einem
Haar
Um unser edles Königspaar.
Hieraus nun jedermann
    ersicht:
Traut keinem Bürgermeister
    nicht.
Ihr ging's durch'n Mantel . . .

THE MAYOR TSCHECH SONG

1.
Who could have been as cheeky
as Mayor Tschech! His bullet
just missed our good royal
couple, whizzing through the
king's cape and the queen's hat.

2.
Duncker (Berlin's notorious
police commissioner) guessed
right away that a plot was
underfoot when Tschech,
swathed in a gray coat, saun-
tered into the royal park.

3.
And he shot our queen through
the hat, that accursed assassin-
plotter, regicide, and traitor.

4.
So we missed losing our royal
couple by just a hair's breadth!
The obvious moral to the story:
mayors are not to be trusted.

Translated by
Alexandra Chciuk-Celt

O, WAG ES DOCH NUR EINEN TAG

Text: Georg Herwegh, 1845
Music: Traditional

1. Frisch auf, mein Volk, mit Trommel-schlag   im

Zor - nes - wet - ter - schein! O wag es doch nur ei - nen

Tag, nur ei - nen, frei zu sein! Und ob der Sieg vor

Ster - nen-licht dem Fein - de schon ge - hört, nur

ei - nen Tag! Es rech - net nicht ein

Herz, das sich em - pört! Nur ei - nen Tag! Es

rech - net nicht ein Herz, das sich em - pört!

1.
Frisch auf, mein Volk, mit
    Trommelschlag
Im Zorneswetterschein!
O wag es doch nur einen Tag,
Nur einen, frei zu sein!
Und ob der Sieg vor Sternenlicht
Dem Feinde schon gehört,
Nur einen Tag! Es rechnet
    nicht
Ein Herz, das sich empört!

2.
O wart' in deiner tiefen Not
Auf keinen Ehebund;
Wer liebt, der gehet in den Tod

Für eine Schäferstund';
Und wer die Ketten knirschend
    trug,
Dem ist das Sterben Lust
Für einen freien Atemzug
Aus unterdrückter Brust.

3.
O tilg' nur einen Augenblick
Aus deiner Sklaverei,
Und zeig dem grollenden
    Geschick,
Daß sie nicht ewig sei;
Erwach aus deinem bösen
    Traum:

Reif ist, die du gesucht,
Und schüttle nicht zu spät vom
    Baum,
Wenn sie gefault, die Frucht.

4.
Wach auf! Wach auf! Die
    Morgenluft
Schlägt mahnend an dein Ohr

Aus deiner tausendjähr'gen
    Gruft
Empor, mein Volk, empor!
Laß kommen, was da kommen
    mag:
Blitz auf, ein Wetterschein!
Und wag's und wär's nur einen
    Tag,
Ein freies Volk zu sein!

OH, JUST DARE, IF FOR ONE DAY

1.
Come on, my people, beat the
    drums,
let your fury like firebolts be,
and were it for one day, just
    once
go and dare to be free.
And if your foe later that night
already'll have you downed,
if for one day, dare, hearts that
    fight,
they surely do not count.

2.
Oh, don't wait for the nuptial
    tie
in your inmost distress.
A true lover will gladly die
for a short time of bliss.
And those are apt to embrace
    death
who angrily bore their chains,
and rather die for a free breath
into their chest in pain.

3.
Erase a moment, do not wait,
off your time in slavery,
and prove it to a gloomy fate
that eternal it won't be.
Wake up now from your
    nightmare, see,
ripe's what you wish you had.
Don't shake too late it off the
    tree:
the fruit might well go bad.

4.
Wake up, wake up, open your ears
to the morning air's advice—
out of your grave of a thousand
    years
rise up, my people, rise!
The future can bring what it may,
let there a lightning be,
and dare to, if just for one day,
be a free people, free.

Translated by Sabine Tober

DAS PROLETARIAT

Text: J. Chr. Lüchow, 1848
Music: Traditional

1.
Es quillt und keimt von unten
    auf,
Wie frisch gesäte Saat;
Es wächst wohl aus der Erd'
    heraus:
Das Proletariat!

2.
Es ist erwacht der vierte
    Stand,
Der nützlichste im Staat;
Denn wer ernährt das ganze
    Land?
Das Proletariat!

3.
Es schindet sich nur für den Sarg,

O Schande, Volksverrat!
Es zehrt von seinem Lebensmark
Das Proletariat!

4.
Die ihr in weichen Kissen ruht,
Im Überfluß und Staat,
Denkt, wenn ihr satt und
    wohlgemut,
Ans Proletariat!

5.
Was nützt noch hohler Phrasen
    Schwall,
Frisch auf zur ernsten Tat!
Es regt und reckt sich überall
Das Proletariat!

THE PROLETARIAT

1.

It sprouts and swells from down
    below
like freshly planted seed,
from within the earth it seems to
    grow:
the proletariat.

2.

The fourth estate's alive now,
    and
the most useful for that,
for who is it that feeds the
    land?
The proletariat!

3.

They toil and work just for the
    grave,
shame and betrayal that,

off their very essence they live
    and slave,
the proletariat!

4.

You, lounging there on a soft
    bed
who live in pomp and glut,
think, when you're full and
    when you're glad,
of the proletariat.

5.

What use is empty phrases' sound,
let's start the pressing deed!
It stirs and stretches all around,
the proletariat!

Translated by Sabine Tober

REVEILLE

Text: Ferdinand Freiligrath, 1844
Music: "Le Marseillaise" Claude-Joseph
Rouget de Lisle, 1792

1.

Frisch auf zur Weise von
    Marseille,
frisch auf ein Lied mit hellen
    Ton!
Singt es hinaus als die Reveille
der neuen Revolution!
der neuen Revolution!
Der neuen, die mit Schwert und
    Lanze
die letzte Fessel bald zerbricht
der alten , halben singt es nicht!

Uns gilt die neue nur, die ganze!
Die neue Rebellion!
Die ganze Rebellion!
Marsch! Marsch!
Marsch! Marsch!
Marsch!—Wär's zum Tod!
Und unsre Fahn' ist rot!

2.

Der Sommer reift des Frühlings
    Boten,

drum folgt der Juni auf den
März.
O Juni, komm und bring uns
Taten!
Nach frischen Taten lechzt das
Herz!
Nach frischen Taten lechzt das
Herz!
Laß deine Wolken schwarz sich
ballen,
bring uns Gewitter, Schlag auf
Schlag!
Laß in die ungesühnte Schmach
der Rache Donnerkeile fallen!
Die neue Rebellion . . .

3.
An unsre Brust, an unsre Lippen
der Menschheit Farbe, heil'ges Rot!
Wild schlägt das Herz uns an die
Rippen—
Fort in den Kampf! Sieg oder Tod!
Fort in den Kampf! Sieg oder
Tod!
Hurra, sie sucht des Feindes
Degen!
Hurra, die ew'ge Fahne wallt!
Selbst aus der Wunden breitem
Spalt
springt sie verachtend ihm
entgegen!
Die neue Rebellion . . .

REVEILLE

1.
Let's sing a Marseillaise of our
own,
One that rings as clear as a bell,
Let's sing it as the reveille
Of the new revolution!
The new one whose swords and
lances
Will soon break the very last
chain.
Let's sing for the new, all-out
revolution,
Not for some half-measure old one.
The new rebellion!
All-out rebellion!
E'en unto death!
Our flag is red, you see!

2.
The summer ripens spring-sown
crops,

That is why June comes after
March.
Oh, come and bring effective
action,
O month of June, our hearts are
starved!
Bring on the black and gathering
clouds,
Bring on the lightning and the
thunder!
Revenge's lightning-bolt must strike
Into our unavenged shame.
The new rebellion, etc.

3.
O color red, man's holy color,
We press you to our lips and
breast.
And our hearts beat wild in our
ribcage.

Into battle! Death or
  victory!
Hurrah, the enemy's dagger is
  parried!
Hurrah, the flag flutters
  eternally!

The color red sneers at the
  enemy
From slits no bigger than a
  wound.
The new rebellion, etc.

Translator unknown

TROTZ ALLEDEM

Text: Ferdinand Freiligrath, 1848
Music: "Lady Mackintash's Reel"

1. Das war 'ne hei - ße Mär - zen - zeit, trotz
Re - gen, Schnee und al - le - dem! Nun
a - ber, da es Blü - ten schneit, nun
ist es kalt, trotz al - le - dem, trotz
al - le - dem und al - le - dem, trotz
Wien, Ber - lin und al - le - dem, ein
schnö - der, schar - fer Win - ter - wind durch -
frö - stelt uns trotz al - le - dem!

1.

Das war' ne heiße Märzenzeit
Trotz Regen, Schnee und
    alledem!
Nun aber, da es Blüten schneit,
Nun ist es kalt, trotz alledem!
Trotz alledem und alledem—
Trotz Wien, Berlin und alledem,
Ein schnöder, scharfer
    Winterwind
Durchfröstelt uns trotz alledem!

2.

Die Waffen, die der Sieg uns
    gab,
Der Sieg des Rechts trotz
    alledem,
Die nimmt man sacht uns
    wieder ab,
Samt Kraut und Lot und
    alledem!
Trotz alledem und alledem—
Trotz Parlament und alledem—
Wir werden unsre Büchsen los,
Soldatenwild trotz alledem!

3.

Doch sind wir frisch und
    wohlgemut
Und zagen nicht trotz alledem!
In tiefer Brust des Zornes Glut,
Die hält uns warm, trotz
    alledem!

Trotz alledem und alledem,
Es gilt uns gleich trotz alledem!
Wir schütteln uns, ein garst'ger
    Wind,
Doch weiter nichts, trotz
    alledem!

4.

So füllt denn nur der Mörser
    Schlund
Mit Eisen, Blei und alledem:
Wir halten uns auf unserm
    Grund,
Wir wanken nicht trotz alledem,
Trotz alledem und alledem,
Und macht ihr's gar, trotz
    alledem,
Wie zu Neapel dieser Schuft;
Das hilft erst recht, trotz
    alledem!

5.

Nur was zerfällt, vertretet ihr!
Seid Kasten nur, trotz
    alledem!
Wir sind das Volk, die
    Menschheit wir!
Sind ewig drum, trotz alledem,
Trotz alledem und alledem!
So kommt denn an, trotz
    alledem!
Ihr hemmt uns, doch ihr zwingt
    uns nicht—
Unser die Welt, trotz alledem!

DESPITE IT ALL

1.

The month of March was very hot
despite the rain and snow and all,
but now that trees have
    blossoms got,

it's bitter cold despite it all.
Despite this, despite that,
though Vienna and Berlin we
    had,

a frosty bitter winterwind
gives us the shudders after all.

2.
The weapons gained by
    victory,
triumph of justice after all,
they subtly take from you
    and me,
gunpowder, lead, and the likes
    of all.
Despite this, despite that,
despite the Parliament we had
we're loosing our rifles yet,
are soldier prey despite it all.

3.
This little chap here is called
    "Sir,"
just note his bearing, pride,
    and all,

and he who makes those big
    crowds stir
remains a wretch despite it all.
Despite this, despite that,
in spite of ribbon, star, and hat,
a man of independent thought
looks on and smiles despite it
    all.

4.
If Parliament makes foolish
    pacts,
dogmatical despite it all,
and if the devil then reacts
with hoof and horn and fireball,
despite this, despite that,
we finally will have it that
people all over will reach out
for brother handshakes after all.

*Translated by
Sabine Tober*

DIE BEIDEN GRENADIERE

Text: Heinrich Heine, 1850
Music: Robert Schumann (op. 49, no. 1)

1.
Nach Frankreich zogen zwei
    Grenadier,
Die waren in Rußland gefangen.
Und als sie kamen ins deutsche
    Quartier,
Sie ließen die Köpfe hangen.

2.
Da hörten sie beide die traurige
    Mär:
Daß Frankreich verloren
    gegangen,

Besiegt und geschlagen das
    tapfere Heer
Und der Kaiser, der Kaiser
    gefangen!

3.
Da weinten zusammen die
    Grenadier
Wohl ob der kläglichen Kunde.
Der eine sprach: Wie weh wird
    mir,
Wie brennt meine alte Wunde!

4.

Der andere sprach: Das Lied ist
    aus,
Auch ich möcht mit dir
    sterben,
Doch hab ich Weib und Kind zu
    Haus,
Die ohne mich verderben.

5.

Was schert mich Weib, was
    schert mich Kind,
Ich trage weit bessres
    Verlangen;
Laß sie betteln gehn, wenn sie
    hungrig sind,—
Mein Kaiser, mein Kaiser
    gefangen!

6.

Gewähr mir, Bruder, eine Bitt:
Wenn ich jetzt sterben werde,
So nimm meine Leiche nach
    Frankreich mit,
Begrab mich in Frankreichs Erde.

7.

Das Ehrenkreuz am roten
    Band
Sollst du aufs Herz mir legen;
Die Flinte gib mir in die Hand,
Und gürt mir um den Degen.

8.

So will ich liegen und horchen
    still,
Wie eine Schildwach, im Grabe,
Bis einst ich höre
    Kanonengebrüll
Und wiehern der Rosse
    Getrabe.

9.

Dann reitet mein Kaiser wohl
    über mein Grab,
Viel Schwerter klirren und
    blitzen;
Dann steig ich gewaffnet hervor
    aus dem Grab—
Den Kaiser, den Kaiser zu
    schützen!

THE TWO GRENADIERS

1.

To France were returning two
    grenadiers
who had been captured in
    Russia;
and when they came to the
    German land
they hung their heads.

2.

For there they heard the sad
    news
that France was lost,
the great army defeated and
    destroyed
and the Emperor a prisoner.

3.

The grenadiers wept
    together
over the miserable tidings.
One spoke: "Woe is me!
How my old wound burns!"

4.
The other said: "It is all over.
I too would like to die with you,
but I have a wife and child at
    home
who without me would perish.

5.
"What do I care for wife and
    child?
I have more important concerns.
Let them go begging if they are
    hungry—
my Emperor is a prisoner!

6.
"Brother, grant me one request
if I must die now;
take my body to France with
    you,
bury me in French earth.

7.
"My cross of honor, with the
    red ribbon,

you must lay on my heart;
put my rifle in my hand
and fasten my sword-belt
    around me.

8.
"So will I lie still and listen,
like a sentry in the grave,
until I hear the noise of cannon
and the hooves of whinnying
    horses.

9.
"Then should my Emperor ride
    over my grave,
with many swords clanking and
    clashing;
then I will arise, fully armed,
    from my grave,
to defend my Emperor!"

Translated by
Philip Lieson Miller

Songs of the Workers' Movement

ACHTZEHNTER MÄRZ

Text: Georg Herwegh, 1873
Music: Josef Scheu

1. Acht - zehn - hun - dert vier - zig und acht, als im Len - ze das Eis ge - kracht, Ta - ge des Fe - bruar, Ta - ge des Mär - zen, wa - ren es nicht Pro - le - ta - rier - her - zen, die voll Hoff - nung zu - erst er - wacht acht - zehn - hun - dert vier - zig und acht? Acht - zehn - hun - dert vier - zig und acht?

1.

Achtzehnhundertvierzig und
    acht,
Als im Lenze das Eis
    gekracht,
Tage des Februar, Tage des
    Märzen,
Waren es nicht
    Proletarierherzen,
Die voller Hoffnung zuerst
    erwacht,
Achtzehnhundertvierzig und
    acht?

2.

Achtzehnhundertvierzig und
    acht,
Als du dich lange genug
    bedacht,
Mutter Germania, glücklich
    verpreußte,
Waren es nicht Proletarierfäuste,
Die sich ans Werk der Befreiung
    gemacht,
Achtzehnhundertvierzig und
    acht?

3.

Achtzehnhundertvierzig und
    acht,
Als du geruht von der
    nächtlichen Schlacht,
Waren es nicht
    Proletarierleichen,
Die du, Berlin, vor den
    zitternden, bleichen
Barhaupt grüßenden Cäsar
    gebracht,
Achtzehnhundervierzig und
    acht?

4.

Achtzehnhundertsiebzig und
    drei,
Reich der Reichen, da stehst du,
    juchhei!
Aber wir Armen, verkauft und
    verraten,
Denken der Proletariertaten—
Noch sind nicht alle Märze
    vorbei,
Achtzehnhundertsiebzig und
    drei!

MARCH 18

1.

Eighteen hundred and forty-eight,
Winter ice began cracking late.
Days of February, days of
    March—
Didn't then proletarian hearts
First awake to a hopeful fate,
Eighteen hundred and forty-eight?

2.

Eighteen forty-eight Germany,
Mother-Prussianed so happily,
Evidently one fact you missed:

Didn't those proletarian fists
Liberation-work undertake
In eighteen hundred and forty-
    eight?

3.

Eighteen forty-eight: when,
    Berlin,
ou'd rested after night-battle din,
Weren't those proletarian dead
You'd rested after night-battle din,
Weren't those proletarian dead

You showed to Caesar's
uncovered head
As he trembled and paled and
waved,
Eighteen hundred and forty-eight?

4.
Eighteen hundred and seventy-
three:
Commonwealth of the wealthy,
whee!

But we paupers, betrayed, sold
out,
Will support proletarian
clout!
This is not the last spring we'll
see,
Eighteen hundred and seventy-
three!

Translated by
Alexandra Chciuk-Celt

DER ARBEITSMANN

Text: Richard Dehmel, 1890
Music: Richard Strauss (op. 35, no. 3), 1897–98;
Hans Pfitzner (op. 30, no. 4), 1922

1.
Wir haben ein Bett, wir haben
ein Kind,
mein Weib!
Wir haben auch Arbeit, und gar
zu zweit,
und haben die Sonne und Regen
und Wind,
und uns fehlt nur eine
Kleinigkeit,
um so frei zu sein, wie die Vögel
sind:
Nur Zeit.

2.
Wenn wir sonntags durch die
Felder gehn,
mein Kind,
und über den Ähren weit und
breit

das blaue Schwalbenvolk blitzen
sehn,
oh dann fehlt uns nicht das
bißchen Kleid,
um so schön zu sein, wie die
Vögel sind:
Nur Zeit.

3.
Nur Zeit! wir wittern
Gewitterwind,
wir Volk.
Nur eine kleine Ewigkeit;
uns fehlt ja nichts, mein Weib,
mein Kind,
als all das, was durch uns
gedeiht,
um so kühn zu sein, wie die
Vögel sind:
Nur Zeit.

The Working Man

1.
We've got a bed, we've got a
 child,
my wife,
we both have work which is a
 bliss,
and sun and rain and wind so
 mild,
and just a small thing is amiss
to feel free like birds in the wild:
just time.

2.
When Sundays through the
 fields we strive,
my child,
and glimpse above the cornfields
 wide
the blue swallows' flight so
 brightly alive,

oh, there is nothing we're
 lacking, and nothing to hide
to feel beautiful like birds in the
 wild:
just time.

3.
Just time. We see the
 stormclouds piled,
my people,
just a little time to be alive,
for nothing is missing, my wife,
 my child,
but that one thing that lets us
 thrive
and be bold like birds in the
 wild:
just time.

Translated by Sabine Tober

Die Arbeitsmänner

Text: Johannes Most, 1869
Music: "Zu Mantua in Baden"

1. Wer schafft das Gold zu-ta-ge? Wer häm-mert Erz und Stein? Wer we-bet Tuch und Sei-de? Wer bau-et Korn und Wein? Wer

gibt den Rei - chen all ihr Brot und lebt da-bei in bitt - rer

Not? __ Das sind die Ar - beits - män - ner, das

Pro-le - ta - ri - at! __ Das sind die Ar - beits -

män - ner, das Pro - le - ta - ri - at! __

1.
Wer schafft das Gold zutage?
Wer hämmert Erz und Stein?
Wer webet Tuch und Seide?
Wer bauet Korn und Wein?
Wer gibt den Reichen all ihr Brot
und lebt dabei in bittrer Not?
Das sind die Arbeitsmänner,
das Proletariat!

2.
Wer plagt vom frühen Morgen
sich bis zur späten Nacht?
Wer schafft für andre Schätze,
Bequemlichkeit und Pracht?
Wer treibt allein das Weltrad
und hat dafür kein Recht im
    Staat?
Das sind die Arbeitsmänner,
das Proletariat!

3.
Wer war von je geknechtet

von der Tyrannenbrut?
Wer mußte für sie kämpfen
und opfern oft sein Blut?
O Volk, erkenn, daß du es bist,
das immerfort betrogen ist!
Wacht auf, ihr Arbeitsmänner!
Auf, Proletariat!

4.
Rafft eure Kraft zusammen
und schwört zur Fahne rot!
Kämpft mutig für die Freiheit!
Erkämpft euch bessres Brot!
Beschleunigt der Despoten Fall!
Schafft Frieden dann dem
    Weltenall!
Zum Kampf, ihr Arbeitsmänner!
Auf, Proletariat!

5.
Ihr habt die Macht in Händen,
wenn ihr nur einig seid.

Drum haltet fest zusammen,
dann seid ihr bald befreit.
Drängt Sturmschritt vorwärts in
   den Streit,

wenn auch der Feind
   Kartätschen speit!
Dann siegt, ihr Arbeitsmänner,
das Proletariat!

THE HYMN OF THE PROLETARIAT

1.

Who hammers brass and stone?
Who raiseth from the mine?
Who weaveth cloth and silk?
Who tilleth wheat and vine?
Who worketh for the rich to
   feed,
Yet lives himself in sorest
   need?—
It is the men who toil, the
   Proletariat.

2.

Who strives from earliest morn?
Who toils till latest night?
Who brings to OTHERS wealth,
Ease, luxury, and might?
Who turns alone the world's
   great wheel,
Yet has no right in common
   weal!—
It is the men who toil, the
   Proletariat.

3.

Who is from aye a slave
To all the tyrant brood?
Who oft for them must fight?
Oft sacrifice his blood?—
O fool! hast thou not yet
   perceived,

'Tis THOU that ever art deceived!
Awake, ye men who labor! Up,
   Proletariat!

4.

Together join your powers!
And swear to banner red!
For Freedom boldly fight!
So win ye better bread!
Then quicken ye the despot's
   fall,
Bring peace unto the nations all,
To battle, ye who labor! Up,
   Proletariat!

5.

In YOUR hands lie the means;
Work but with UNITY,
Hold ye but firm together
Then ye will soon be FREE,
With quick-march forward to
   the fight,
Though scorn the foe in grape-
   shot might!
Then win, ye men who labor!
   Win, Proletariat!

Translator unknown

AUF, AUF, ZUM KAMPF

Text: Traditional, 1907, 1919
Music: "Auf, auf, zum Kampf"

1.
Auf, auf, zum Kampf, zum Kampf!
Zum Kampf sind wir geboren.
Auf, auf, zum Kampf, zum
    Kampf sind wir bereit!
Dem Karl Liebknecht haben
    wir's geschworen,
Der Rosa Luxemburg reichen
    wir die Hand.

2.
Wir fürchten nicht, ja nicht
Den Donner der Kanonen!
Wir fürchten nicht, ja nicht die
    grüne Polizei.

Den Karl Liebknecht haben wir
    verloren,
Die Rosa Luxemburg fiel durch
    Mörderhand.

3.
Es steht ein Mann, ein Mann
So fest wie eine Eiche.
Er hat gewiß, gewiß schon
    manchen Sturm erlebt.
Vielleicht ist er schon morgen
    eine Leiche,
Wie es so vielen unsrer Brüder
    geht.

On to the Battle, the Battle

1.

On to the battle, the battle!
For the battle we are born.
On to the battle, the battle!
To the battle we are torn.
We promised it to Karl
    Liebknecht,
and take Rosa Luxemburg's
    hand.

2.

We're not afraid as all
of the cannons' thunderclaps.
Nor are we afraid at all

of the green police chaps.
Our Karl Liebknecht we have lost,
and Rosa Luxemburg was slain.

3.

Here stands a man, a man
as sturdy as an oak.
He has quite certainly
weathered many a storm.
He might be dead tomorrow
like so many Red Guards before.

Translated by Sabine Tober

Brüder, zur Sonne, zur Freiheit

Text: Leonid P. Radin (Russian), 1897;
Hermann Scherchen (German), 1917
Music: Hermann Scherchen

Brü - der, zur Son - ne, zur Frei - heit,   Brü - der, zum

Lich - te em - por ___ !   Hell aus dem dunk - len Ver -

gang - nen   leuch - tet die Zu - kunft her - vor.

1.

Brüder, zur Sonne, zur Freiheit,
Brüder, zum Lichte empor!
Hell aus dem dunklen
    Vergangnen
Leuchtet die Zukunft hervor.

2.

Seht, wie der Zug von Millionen
endlos aus Nächtigem quillt,
bis euer Sehnsucht Verlangen
Himmel und Nacht
    überschwillt!

3.

Brüder, in eins nun die Hände,
Brüder, das Sterben verlacht!

Ewig, der Sklav'rei ein Ende,
heilig die letzte Schlacht!

GO TO THE SUN, INTO FREEDOM

1.

Go to the sun, into freedom,
Brethren, go into the light.
Out of the past's murky
    darkness,
The future is shining so bright.
Out of the past's murky
    darkness,
The future is shining so bright.

2.

See how the millions are teeming
Endlessly out of the mire,
Till both the night and the
    darkness
Overflow with your desire.

Till both the night and the
    darkness
Overflow with your desire.

3.

Let us join hands now, my
    brethren,
Death cannot give us a scare.
Let this last battle be sacred:
Slavery will perish fore'er.
Let this last battle be sacred:
Slavery will perish fore'er.

Translated by
Alexandra Chciuk-Celt

BUNDESLIED

Text: Georg Herwegh, 1863
Music: Peter Heinz; Hans von Bülow

1. "Bet' und ar-beit!" ruft die Welt. Be-te kurz, denn Zeit ist Geld! An die Tü-re pocht die Not, be-te kurz, denn Zeit ist Brot!

1.
"Bet' und arbeit!" ruft die Welt,
Bete kurz, denn Zeit ist Geld.
An die Türe pocht die Not—
Bete kurz, denn Zeit ist Brot.

2.
Und du ackerst, und du säst,
Und du nietest, und du nähst,
Und du hämmerst, und du
    spinnst—
Sag, o Volk, was du gewinnst!

3.
Wirkst am Webstuhl Tag und
    Nacht,
Schürfst im Erz- und
    Kohlenschacht,
Füllst des Überflusses Horn,
Füllst es hoch mit Wein und
    Korn—

4.
Doch wo ist *dein* Mahl bereit?
Doch wo ist *dein* Feierkleid?
Doch wo ist *dein* warmer Herd?
Doch wo ist *dein* scharfes
    Schwert?

5.
Alles ist dein Werk! o sprich,
Alles, aber nichts für dich!
Und von allem nur allein,
Die du schmiedst, die Kette,
    dein?

6.
Mann der Arbeit, aufgewacht!
Und erkenne deine Macht!
Alle Räder stehen still,
Wenn dein starker Arm es
    will.

7.
Deiner Dränger Schar
    erblaßt,
Wenn du, müde deiner Last,
In die Ecke lehnst den Pflug,
Wenn du rufst: Es ist genug!

8.
Brecht das Doppeljoch
    entzwei!
Brecht die Not der Sklaverei!
Brecht die Sklaverei der Not!
Brot ist Freiheit, Freiheit
    Brot!

SAID WEALTH TO TOIL

1.
Said Wealth to Toil, Pray thou,
    but labor too;
And—time is money—let thy
    prayers be few.
Pale Hunger always hovers o'er
    thy head;
Then let thy prayers be short,
    for time is bread.

2.
Ye sow and reap, and plough
    the furrowed field,
Your heavy hammers evermore
    ye wield;
Unwearied still ye weave and
    stitch and spin;
Then say, O people, what
    reward ye win.

3.

At loom and shuttle day and
    night ye sit,
Dig coal and metal deep in
    darksome pit,
Fill high rich plenty's
    overflowing horn
With earth's best gifts of wine
    and oil and corn.

4.

But where is then your rich
    reward, and where
Your gala garment and your
    festal fare?
Where the home comforts of
    your bed and board,
And where the shining of your
    sharpened sword?

5.

All these are fashioned by your
    arm alone;
And have ye naught that ye may
    call your own?

Of all ye forge does naught
    indeed remain—
Naught but the links and rivets
    of your chain?

6.

Ye sons of labor, up! Awake!
    Arise!
Learn all the virtue in your
    strength that lies.
The world's great wheels and
    works refuse to go
Unless your stalwart arms the
    force bestow.

7.

Pale grow your proud
    oppressors in their fear,
If ye, o'erweary of your evil
    cheer,
Refuse for once to plod behind
the plough,
And cry "Enough! We'll toil no
    longer now!"

8.

O break at last your double
    yoke in twain,
And burst asunder slavery's iron
    chain!
Cast off the servitude of want
    and need;
For bread is Freedom—Freedom
    bread indeed.

Translated by J. L. Joynes

EINHEITSFRONTLIED

Text: Bertolt Brecht, 1934
Music: Hanns Eisler

Und weil der Mensch ein Mensch ist, drum braucht er was zum Es-sen, bit-te sehr. Es macht ihn ein Ge-schwätz nicht satt, das schafft kein Es-sen her. Drum links, zwei, drei! Drum links, zwei, drei! Wo dein Platz, Ge-nos-se, ist! Reih' dich ein in die Ar-bei-ter- Ein-heits-front, weil du auch ein Ar-bei-ter bist!

© Deutscher Verlag für Musik, Leipzig

1.

Und weil der Mensch ein
    Mensch ist,
Drum braucht er was zum
    Essen, bitte sehr.
Es macht ihn ein Geschwätz
    nicht satt,
Das schafft kein Essen her.

Drum links, zwei, drei!
Drum links, zwei, drei!
Wo dein Platz, Genosse, ist!
Reih' dich ein in die
    Arbeitereinheitsfront,
Weil du auch ein Arbeiter
    bist!

2.
Und weil der Mensch ein
    Mensch ist,
Drum braucht er auch noch
    Kleider und Schuh'.
Es macht ihn ein Geschwätz
    nicht warm
Und auch kein Trommeln dazu.
Drum links . . .
3.
Und weil der Mensch ein
    Mensch ist,
Drum hat er Stiefel im Gesicht
    nicht gern,

Er will unter sich keinen Sklaven
    sehn
Und über sich keinen Herrn.
Drum links . . .

4.
Und weil der Prolet ein Prolet ist,
Drum wird ihn kein anderer
    befrei'n,
Es kann die Befreiung der
    Arbeiter nur
Das Werk der Arbeiter sein!
Drum links . . .

UNITED FRONT SONG

1.
And because a man is human,
He'll want to eat, and thanks a
    lot,
But talk can't take the place of
    meat
Or fill an empty pot.
So left, two, three!
So left, two, three!
Comrade, there's a place for
    you.
Take your stand in the workers'
    united front
For you are a worker too.

2.
And because a man is human,
He'll need to wear some clothes
    and some shoes.

But talk can't keep him really
    warm
Nor can the drumming do.
So left, two, three!

So left, two, three!
Comrade, there's a place for
    you.
Take your stand in the workers'
    united front
For you are a worker too.

3.
And because a man is human,
He won't care for a kick in the
    face.
He doesn't want slaves under him
Or above him a ruling class.
So left, two, three!
So left, two, three!
Comrade, there's a place for you.
Take you stand in the workers'
    united front
For you are a worker too.

4.
And because a worker's a
    worker,

No one else will bring him
   liberty.
It's nobody's work but the
   workers' own
To set the worker free.
So left, two, three!
So left, two, three!

Comrade, there's a place for you.
Take your stand in the workers'
   united front
For you are a worker too.

*Tranlated by
Desmond J. Vesey*

ICH BIN SOLDAT, DOCH BIN ICH ES NICHT GERNE

Text: Traditional, 1870–71

Music: Traditional

1. Ich bin Sol-dat, doch bin ich es nicht ger- ne, als ich es
   Man riß mich fort, hin-ein in die Ka- ser- ne, ge-fan-gen

ward', hat man mich nicht ge- fragt.
ward' ich wie ein Wild ge-
                                        Ja, von der
                                        jagt.   denk' ich dar-

Hei- mat und des Liebchens Her- zen mußt ich hin-
an, fühl' ich der Weh-mut Schmer-zen, fühl' in der

weg   und von der Freun-de Kreis;
Brust   des Zor- nes Glut so   heiß.

1.
Ich bin Soldat, doch bin ich es
   nicht gerne,
als ich es ward', hat man mich
   nicht gefragt.
Man riß mich fort, hinein in die
   Kaserne,

gefangen ward' ich wie ein Wild
   gejagt.
Ja, von der Heimat und des
   Liebchens Herzen
mußt ich hinweg und von der
   Freunde Kreis;

denk' ich daran, fühl' ich der
    Wehmut Schmerzen,
fühl in der Brust des Zornes
    Glut so heiß.

2.
Ich bin Soldat, doch nur mit
    Widerstreben;
Ich lieb' ihn nicht, den blauen
    Königsrock,
Ich lieb' es nicht, das blut'ge
    Waffenleben,
Mich zu verteid'gen wär' genug
    ein Stock.
O sagt mir an, wozu braucht ihr
    Soldaten?
Ein jedes Volk liebt Ruh' und
    Frieden nur,
Allein aus Herrschsucht und
    dem Volk zum Schaden,
Laßt ihr zertreten, ach, die
    gold'ne Flur!

3.
Ich bin Soldat, muß Tag und
    Nacht marschieren,
Statt an der Arbeit, muß ich
    Posten steh'n,
Statt in der Freiheit, muß ich
    salutieren,

und muß den Hochmut frecher
    Buben seh'n.
Und geht's ins Feld, so muß ich
    Brüder morden,
Von denen keiner mir zuleid
    was tat,
Dafür als Krüppel trag' ich
    Band und Orden,
Und hungernd ruf ich dann:
    «Ich war Soldat!»

4.
Ihr Brüder all', ob Deutsche, ob
    Franzosen,
Ob Ungarn, Dänen, ob vom
    Niederland,
Ob grün, ob rot, ob blau, ob
    weiß die Hosen,
Gebt euch statt Blei zum Gruß
    die Bruderhand!
Auf, laßt zur Heimat uns
    zurückmarschieren,
Von den Tyrannen unser Volk
    befrei'n;
Denn nur Tyrannen müssen
    Kriege führen,
Soldat der Freiheit will ich gerne
    sein!

A Soldier Am I but Don't Like to Be

1.
A soldier am I, but don't like to
    be,
When I was made one, they
    didn't ask me.
They took me away and brought
    me here,
hunting me like they would
    some deer.

My home and my sweetheart I
    had to forgo
and the group of friends I
    cherish so.
My heart is heavy, painfully
    sad,
and with the fire of anger
    mad.

2.

A soldier am I, it's not my choice,
'gainst the king's blue garb I
    raise my voice.
The blood-work of weapons is
    not mine,
for my defense a stick would do
    fine.
Tell me what you need soldiers
    for
when all the people love peace
    and hate war.
The thirst for power harms us all,
lets golden fields get crushed and
    fall.

3.

A soldier am I, must march
    night and day,
instead of working, on guard I
    stay.
I can't be free, have to salute,
and pay to arrogance my
    tribute.
Once we're in battle, they force
    me to slay

brothers who never before
    crossed my way.
A cripple with medals, I shall
    shout;
I'm an ex-soldier, my belly
    growls loud.

4.

My brothers, Germans,
    Frenchmen, Danes,
men from Hungary and the
    Netherlands,
be red or green or blue your
    pants,
don't greet with lead, greet with
    your hands.
Let's march back home, and let
    us see
that our people can be free.
Just tyrants benefit from
    war.
A soldier for freedom I'll be
    evermore.

Translated by Sabine Tober

DIE INTERNATIONALE

Text: Eugène Pottier (French original), 1871;
Emil Luckhardt (German)
Music: Pierre Degeyter, 1888

1. Wacht auf, Ver-damm-te die-ser Er-de, die

stets man noch zum Hun-gern zwingt! Das Recht, wie

Glut im Kra-ter-her-de, nun mit Macht zum Durch-bruch dringt! Rei-nen Tisch macht mit den Be-drängern, Heer der Skla-ven, wa-che auf! Ein Nichts zu sein, tragt es nicht län-ger! Al-les zu wer-den, strömt zu Hauf! Völ-ker, hört die Sig-na-le! Auf zum letz-ten Ge-fecht! Die In-ter-na-tio-na-le er-kämpft das Men-schen-recht! Völ-ker hört die Sig-na-le! Auf zum letz-ten Ge-fecht! Die In-ter-na-tio-na-le er-kämpft das Men-schen-recht!

1.

Wacht auf, Verdammte dieser Erde,
die stets man noch zum Hungern
   zwingt!
Das Recht wie Glut im
   Kraterherde
nun mit Macht zum Durchbruch
   dringt.
Reinen Tisch macht mit den
   Bedrängern!

Heer der Sklaven, wache auf!
Ein Nichts zu sein, tragt es nicht
   länger,
alles zu werden, strömt
   zuhauf!
Völker, hört die Signale!
Auf, zum letzten Gefecht!
Die Internationale
erkämpft das Menschenrecht!

2.
Es rettet uns kein höh'res
  Wesen,
kein Gott, kein Kaiser, noch
  Tribun.
Uns aus dem Elend zu erlösen,
können wir nur selber tun!
Leeres Wort: des Armen Rechte!
Leeres Wort: des Reichen
  Pflicht!
Unmündig nennt man uns und
  Knechte,
duldet die Schmach nun länger
  nicht!
Völker, hört . . .

3.
In Stadt und Land, ihr
  Arbeitsleute,
wir sind die stärkste der Partei'n
Die Müßiggänger schiebt
  beiseite!
Diese Welt muß unser sein;
unser Blut sei nicht mehr der
  Raben
und der mäch'gen Geier Fraß!
Erst wenn wir sie vertrieben
  haben,
dann scheint die Sonn' ohn'
  Unterlaß!
Völker, hört . . .

THE INTERNATIONALE

1.
Arise! ye starvelings from your
  slumbers,
Arise ye criminals of want,
For reason in revolt now
  thunders,
And at last ends the age of cant.
Now away with all
  superstitions,
Servile masses, arise! arise!
We'll change forthwith the old
  conditions,
And spurn the dust to win the
  prize.
Then comrades, come rally,
The last fight let us face,
L'Internationale
Unites the human race.

2.
No saviors from on high deliver,
No trust have we in price or peer;

Our own right hand the chains
  must shiver,
Chains of hatred, of greed and
  fear,
Ere the thieves will disgorge
  their booty,
And to all give a happier lot,
Each at his forge must do his
  duty
And strike the iron when it's
  hot.
Then comrades, etc.

3.
We, peasants, artisans, and
  others,
Enroll'd among the sons of toil,
Let's claim the earth henceforth
  for brothers,
Drive the indolent from
  the soil.

On our flesh long has fed the raven,
We've too long been the vulture's prey;
But now farewell this spirit craven,

The dawn brings in a brighter day.
Then comrades, etc.

Translated by
E. Pottier

DIE JUNGE GARDE

Text: Heinrich Eildermann, 1907
Music: Andreas Hofer, "Zu Mantua in Baden"

1. Dem Mor - gen - rot ent - ge - gen, ihr
Kampf - ge - nos - sen all! Bald siegt ihr al - ler -
we - gen, bald weicht der Fein - de Wall! Mit
Macht her - an und hal - tet Schritt! Ar -
bei - ter - ju - gend? Will sie mit? Wir
sind die jun - ge Gar - de des Pro - le - ta - ri -
ats! Wir sind die jun - ge
Gar - de des Pro - le - ta - ri - ats!

1.
Dem Morgenrot entgegen,
ihr Kampfgenossen all!
Bald siegt ihr allerwegen,
bald weicht der Feinde Wall!
Mit Macht heran und haltet
    Schritt!
Arbeiterjugend? Will sie mit?
Wir sind die junge Garde
des Proletariats!

2.
Wir haben selbst erfahren
der Arbeit Frongewalt
in düstren Kinderjahren
und wurden früh schon alt.
Sie hat an unserm Fuß geklirrt,
die Kette, die nur schwerer
    wird.
Wir sind die junge Garde
des Proletariats!

3.
Die Arbeit kann uns lehren
und lehrte uns die Kraft,
den Reichtum zu vermehren,
der unsre Armut schafft.
Nun wird die Kraft, von uns
    erkannt,
die starke Waffe unsrer Hand!
Wir sind die junge Garde
des Proletariats.

4.
Wir reichen euch die Hände,
Genossen all, zum Bund!
Des Kampfes sei kein Ende,
eh' nicht im weiten Rund
der Arbeit freies Volk gesiegt
und jeder Feind am Boden
    liegt.
Vorwärts, du junge Garde
des Proletariats!

THE YOUNG GUARDS

1.
We're marching toward the
    morning,
We're struggling comrades all.
Our aims are set on victory,
Our enemies must fall.
With ordered step, red flag
    unfurled,
We'll make a better world.
We are the youthful guardsmen
of the Proletariat.

2.
We knew the chains of labor
In earliest childhood years;
We've toiled in dusty factories,

We've shed our blood and
    tears,
We're going forth with all our
    might,
We've toiled and we have
    learned to fight.
We are the, etc.

3.
The days we've spent in labor
Have given us the pow'r
To overthrow oppressors and
Bring on the workers' hour,
We are a strong, determined
    band,

Each with a weapon to his
    hand.
We are the, etc.

4.
Young comrades, come and join
    us,

Our struggle will endure
Till every enemy is down
And victory is sure.
In struggle and valiant fight
We're marching to the workers'
    right.
We are the, etc.

LIED DER DEUTSCHEN ARBEITER

Text: Jacob Audorf, 1864
Music: "Le Marseillaise," Claude-Joseph
Rouget de Lisle, 1792

1. Wohl-an, wer Recht und Wahr-heit ach - tet, zu uns-rer

Fah - ne steh' zu-hauf! Wenn auch die Lüg' uns noch um -

nach-tet, bald steigt der Morgen hell herauf, bald steigt der

Mor - gen hell her - auf! Ein schwerer Kampf ist's, den wir__

wa - gen, zahl - los ist uns-rer Fein-de Schar! Doch

ob wie Flammen die Ge-fahr mög' ü - ber uns zusammen

schla-gen, nicht zäh - len wir den Feind, nicht

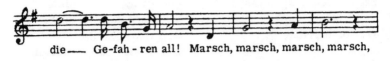

die— Ge-fah-ren all! Marsch, marsch, marsch, marsch,

und sei's zum Tod, denn uns-re Fahn' ist rot!

1.

Wohlan, wer Recht und
    Wahrheit achtet,
Zu unsrer Fahne steht zu Hauf!
Wenn auch die Lüg' uns noch
    umnachtet,
Bald steigt der Morgen hell herauf!
Ein schwerer Kampf ist's, den
    wir wagen,
Zahllos ist unsrer Feinde Schar,
Doch ob wie Flammen die
    Gefahr
Mög' über uns zusammen-
    schlagen,
Nicht zählen wir den Feind,
Nicht die Gefahren all':
Der kühnen Bahn nur folgen wir,
Die uns geführt *Lassalle*!

2.

Der Feind, den wir am tiefsten
    hassen,
Der uns umlagert schwarz und
    dicht,
Das ist der Unverstand der
    Massen,
Den nur des Geistes Schwert
    durchbricht.
Ist erst dies Bollwerk
    überstiegen,
Wer will uns dann noch
    widerstehn?

Dann werden bald auf allen
    Höh'n
Der wahren Freiheit Banner
    fliegen!
Nicht zählen . . .

3.

«Das freie Wahlrecht ist das
    Zeichen,
In dem wir siegen»; nun,
    wohlan!
Nicht predigen wir Haß den
    Reichen,
Nur gleiches Recht für
    Jedermann,
Die Lieb' soll uns
    zusammenketten,
Wir strecken aus die
    Bruderhand,
Aus geist'ger Schmach das
    Vaterland,
Das Volk vom Elend zu erretten!
Nicht zählen . . .

4.

Von uns wird einst die Nachwelt
    zeugen;
Schon blickt auf uns die
    Gegenwart.
Frisch auf, beginnen wir den
    Reigen!

Ist auch der Boden rauh und hart.
Schließt die Phalanx in dichten
  Reihen!
Je höher uns umrauscht die Fluth,
Je mehr mit der Begeist'rung
  Gluth
Dem heil'gen Kampfe uns zu
  weihen!
Nicht zählen . . .

5.
Auf denn, Gesinnungs-
  kameraden,

Bekräftigt heut' aufs Neu' den
  Bund,
Daß nicht die grünen
  Hoffnungssaaten
Gehn vor dem Erntefest zu
  Grund.
Ist auch der Säemann
  gefallen,
In guten Boden fiel die Saat:
Uns aber bleibt die kühne Tat,
Heil'ges Vermächtniß sei sie
  Allen!
Nicht zählen . . .

SONG OF THE GERMAN WORKERS

1.
Ye who love justice and love
  peace
behind our banner unite,
the darkness of lies is around us,
but soon the morn will be
  bright.
It's a hard battle that we dare
and countless are our foes.
If high the flame of danger
  goes,
seems to devour us there:
We do not count our foes,
don't mind the dangers all
as we pursue the daring course
shown to us by Lasalle.

2.
One enemy most hated stands
gloomy and dense is it;
it's the masses' profound
  ignorance
which the mind's sword shall
  beat.

And once this bulwark stands
  no more,
who then will dare to fight?
Then we shall see in lofty flight
the banners of freedom and lore.
We do not, etc.

3.
Free elections! That's the sign
with which we'll win. Come on!
We don't teach hatred of the
  rich
but justice for everyone.
Love be the link between us.
Here is our brother-hand
to save from shame our
  fatherland,
from misery its people.
We do not, etc.

4.
Posterity will tell of us
the present world's aware of us.

Let's go and start the dance!
The ground we're on is hard and
 rough.
Let's form a phalanx and be
 tough.
The higher the floods may rise
 and roar,
the better we'll fight this holy
 war,
Aflame with the fire of passion!
We do not, etc.

5.

All you who think within our
 scope,
let's reconfirm we're together,
so that the fresh green sprouts of
 hope
won't die in the harsh weather.
Even if the sowman had to fall,
on fertile ground fell his seed:
Let us accomplish the bold deed
that's legacy to all!
We do not, etc.

DER REVOLUZZER

Text: Erich Mühsam, ca. 1920
Music: Bela Reinitz

1. War ein - mal ein Re - vo - luz - zer, im Zi -
vil - stand Lam - pen - put - zer, ging im Re - vo - luz - zer -
schritt mit den Re - vo - luz - zern mit. Und er
schrie: "Ich re - vo - lüz - ze!" Und die Re - vo - luz - zer -
müt - ze schob er auf das lin - ke Ohr, kam sich
höchst ge - fähr - lich vor. Doch die Re - vo - luz - zer

schrit-ten mit-ten in der Stra-ßen Mit-ten, wo er

son-sten un-ver-drutzt al-le Gas-la-ter-nen

putzt, putzt. Sie vom Bo-den zu ent-

fer-nen, rupf-te man die Gas-la-ter-nen aus dem

Stra-ßen-pfla-ster aus, zwecks des Bar-ri-ka-den-

-bau's, aus dem Stra-ßen-pfla-ster aus, zwecks des

Bar-ri-ka-den-bau's. A-ber

un-ser Re-vo-luz-zer schrie: "Ich bin der Lampen-

put-zer die-ses gu-ten Leuch-te-lichts. Bit-te,

bit-te, tut ihm nichts! Wenn wir ihm das Licht aus-

dre-hen, kann kein Bür-ger nichts mehr se-hen.

Laßt die Lam-pen stehn, ich bitt! Denn sonst

spiel ich nicht mehr mit, nicht mehr mit, nicht mehr

mit, denn sonst spiel ich nicht mehr mit!" Doch die

Re - vo - luz - zer lach-ten, und die Gas - la - ter - nen

krach-ten, und der Lam-pen-put-zer schlich fort und

wein - te bit - ter, - bit - - ter - - --

lich. Dann ist er zu Haus ge - blie-ben und hat

dort ein Buch ge - schrie-ben: nämlich, wie man re - vo -

luzzt, näm -lich, wie man re - vo - luzzt, näm - lich

wie man re - vo - luzzt und da - bei, und da -

bei, und da - bei doch Lam - pen putzt.

1.
War einmal ein Revoluzzer,
Im Zivilstand Lampenputzer;
Ging im Revoluzzerschritt
Mit den Revoluzzern mit.

2.
Und er schrie: «Ich revolüzze!»
Und die Revoluzzermütze
Schob er auf das linke Ohr,
Kam sich höchst gefährlich vor.

3.
Doch die Revoluzzer schritten
Mitten in der Straßen Mitten,
Wo er sonsten unverdrutzt
Alle Gaslaternen putzt.

4.
Sie vom Boden zu entfernen,
Rupfte man die Gaslaternen
Aus dem Straßenpflaster aus.
Zwecks des Barrikadenbaus.

5.
Aber unser Revoluzzer
schrie: «Ich bin der Lampenputzer

Dieses guten Leuchtelichts.
Bitte, bitte, tut ihm nichts!

6.
Wenn wir ihm das Licht
    ausdrehen.
Kann kein Bürger nichts mehr
    sehen.
Laßt die Lampen stehn, ich
    bitt!—
Denn sonst spiel ich nicht mehr
    mit!»

7.
Doch die Revoluzzer lachten,
Und die Gaslaternen krachten,
Und der Lampenputzer schlich
Fort und weinte bitterlich.

8.
Dann ist er zu Haus gelieben
Und hat dort ein Buch
    geschrieben:
Nämlich, wie man revoluzzt
Und dabei doch Lampen
    putzt.

THE AMATEUR REVOLUTIONARY

1.
Once there was an amateur
    revolutionary,
A lamplighter in civilian life.
He walked with a revolutionary
    step
Along with other revolutionaries.

2.
And he yelled, "I'm revoluting!"

As he tipped his revolutionary cap
Over his left ear in rakish fashion
And considered himself quite
    dangerous.

3.
But the revolutionaries marched
Right into the middle of the
    street

Where he usually made his
    rounds
Lighting all the gas street lamps.

4.
To get them out of the way,
They tore the street lamps
Right out of the pavement
To build their barricades.

5.
But our amateur revolutionary
Yelled, "Hey, I'm the one who
    lights
These good people's street
    lamps,
So please don't damage them!

6.
If we turn off their street lights,
No citizen will be able to see
    anything;

Leave the street lamps standing,
    please—
Or else I won't play along any
    more!"

7.
But the revolutionaries
    laughed
As the street lamps crashed,
And our lamplighter crept
Away home and cried
    bitterly.

8.
Then he stayed at home
And there he wrote a book
All about how to revolute
And still light the street lamps.

*Translated by
Richard J. Rundell*

DER ROTE WEDDING

Text: Erich Weinert, 1929
Music: Hanns Eisler

1. Links, links, links, links! Die Trommeln werden ge-rührt. Links, links, links, links! Der ro-te Wedding mar-schiert. Hier wird nicht ge-meckert, hier gibt es Dampf! Denn bet-teln nicht mehr um Ge-rechtigkeit! Wir

uns-re Pa-ro-le ist Klas-sen-kampf nach
stehn zum entscheiden-den An-griff be-reit, zur Ver-

blu-ti-ger Me-lo-die! Wir
trei-bung der Bour-ge-oi-sie!

Ro-ter Wedding grüßt euch Genossen, haltet die Fäu-ste be-

reit! Hal-tet die ro-ten Rei-hen ge-schlos-sen,

denn un-ser Tag ist nicht weit! Drohend stehen die Fä-

schi-sten drü-ben am Ho-ri-zont! Prole-ta-rier,

ihr müßt rü-sten! Rot Front! Rot Front!

1.

Links, links, links, links!	zur Vertreibung der
Die Trommeln werden gerührt!	Bourgeoisie!
Links, links, links, links;	Roter Wedding grüßt euch,
der Rote Wedding marschiert!	Genossen!
Hier wird nicht gemeckert, hier	Haltet die Fäuste bereit!
gibt es Dampf!	Haltet die roten Reihen
Denn unsre Parole ist	geschlossen,
Klassenkampf	denn unser Tag ist nicht weit!
nach blutiger Melodie!	Drohend stehen die Faschisten
Wir betteln nicht mehr um	drüben am Horizont!
Gerechtigkeit!	Proletarier, ihr müßt
Wir stehn zum entscheidenden	rüsten!
Angriff bereit,	Rot Front! Rot Front!

2.
Links, links, links, links;
trotz Faschisten und Polizei!
Links, links, links, links!
Wir gedenken des Ersten
    Mai!
Der herrschenden Klasse
    blut'ges Gesicht,
der Rote Wedding vergißt es
    nicht,
und die Schande der SPD!
Sie wolln uns das Fell über die
    Ohren ziehn!
Doch wir verteidigen das rote
    Berlin,
die Vorhut der Roten
    Armee!
Roter Wedding . . .

3.
Links, links, links, links!
Die Fahne weht uns voran!
Links, links, links, links!
Der Rote Wedding tritt an!
Wenn unser Gesang durch die
    Straßen braust,
dann zittert der Feind vor der
    Arbeiterfaust!
Denn die Arbeiterklasse
    erwacht!
Wir stürzen die Säulen des
    Ausbeuterstaats
und gründen die Herrschaft des
    Proletariats.
Kameraden, erkämpft euch die
    Macht!
Roter Wedding . . .

THE REDS FROM WEDDING

1.
Left, left, left, left,
bang the drums,
here come the Reds from
    Wedding!
No bellyaching, nothing but
    action,
for our slogan is "bloody class
    struggle."
No more begging for justice:
we are ready to attack
and chase out the bourgeoisie!
Greetings, comrades,
from the Reds of Wedding,
keep your fists at the ready
and your ranks closed,
for our day is coming soon!
The menacing Fascists are
gathering at the horizon;

proletarians, we must unite
into a Red Front!

2.
Left, left, left, left,
in spite of Fascists and
    police!
Remember May 1st!
Remember the bloodied
face of the ruling class
and the disgrace of the Socialist
    party!
The Reds from wedding won't
    forget,
nor will we let them
pull the wool over our eyes.
Let's defend Red Berlin,
forefront of the Red Army!

3.
Left, left, left, left,
follow the rippling flag,
here come the Reds from
  Wedding.
When our song thunders
  through the streets,
the enemy cowers before the
  workers' fist,

for the working class is awakening!
We will tear down the pillars of
  the exploiter state
and establish new proletarian
  rule.
Fight for your power, comrades!

Translated by
Alexandra Chciuk-Celt

SOZIALISTENMARSCH

Text: Max Kegel, 1891
Music: Carl Gramm

1. Auf So - zia - li - sten, schließt die Rei - hen! Die
Trom - mel ruft, die Ban - ner wehn. Es gilt die
Ar - beit zu be - frei - en, es gilt der
Frei - heit Auf - er - stehn! Der Er - de Glück, der
Son - ne Pracht, des Gei - stes Licht, des Wis - sens
Macht, dem gan - zen Vol - ke sei's ge - ge - ben!
Das ist das Ziel, das wir er - stre - ben!

Das ist der Ar - beit heil' - ger Krieg!

Das ist der Ar - beit heil' - ger Krieg!

Mit uns das Volk! Mit uns der Sieg! Mit

uns das Volk! Mit uns der Sieg!

1.
Auf, Sozialisten, schließt die
    Reihen!
Die Trommel ruft, die Banner
    wehn.
Es gilt, die Arbeit zu befreien,
es gilt der Freiheit Auferstehn!
Der Erde Glück, der Sonne Pracht,
des Geistes Licht, des Wissens
    Macht,
dem ganzen Volke sei's gegeben!
Das ist das Ziel, das wir erstreben!
Das ist der Arbeit heil'ger Krieg!
Das ist der Arbeit heil'ger Krieg!
Mit uns das Volk! Mit uns der
    Sieg!
Mit uns das Volk! Mit uns der Sieg!

2.
Ihr ungezählten Millionen
in Schacht und Feld, in Stadt
    und Land,
die ihr um kargen Lohn müßt
    fronen,
und schaffen treu mit fleiß'ger
    Hand;
Noch seufzt ihr in des Elends
    Bann!
Vernehmt den Weckruf! Schließt
    euch an!
Aus Qual und Leid euch zu
    erheben,
das ist das Ziel, das wir
    erstreben!
Das ist der Arbeit . . .

THE SOCIALIST MARCH

1.
The flag unfurls, the bugles call
    us,
Up, Socialists, in close array!
Shake off the shackles that
    enthrall us,

Let labor burst her bonds today!
The joy of earth and sun and
    sky,
The dawn of light and liberty,
To all the people now, forever!

This be the goal of our endeavor,
Let this be labor's battle cry!
Ours, ours is right and victory!

2.

Ye countless million brother-
    toilers
In mine and mill, by field and
    wave,
Who give your lives for your
    despoilers,

And for a scanty pittance slave.
Why cringe so long in joyless
    plight?
The cry resounds, "Unite!
    unite!"
Put off your fetters now,
    forever!
This be the foal, etc.

*Translated by
H. D. Harben*

WANN WIR SCHREITEN SEIT' AN SEIT'

Text: Hermann Claudius, 1915
Music: Michael Englert, 1916

1. Wann wir schrei-ten Seit an Seit und die al - ten Lie - der
sin - gen und die Wäl - der wi - der - klin - gen, füh - len
wir, es muß ge - lin - gen: Mit uns zieht die
neu - e Zeit, mit uns zieht die neu - e Zeit!

1.
Wann wir schreiten Seit an Seit
und die alten Lieder singen
und die Wälder widerklingen,
fühlen wir, es muß gelingen:
Mit uns zieht die neue Zeit!

2.
Einer Woche Hammerschlag,
einer Woche Häuserquadern
zittern noch in unsern Adern;
aber keiner wagt zu hadern!
Herrlich lacht der Sonnentag!

3.
Birkengrün und Saatengrün:
Wie mit bittender Gebärde
hält die alte Mutter Erde,
daß der Mensch ihr eigen werde,
ihm die vollen Hände hin.

4.
Mann und Weib und Weib und
    Mann
sind nicht Wasser mehr und
    Feuer.

Um die Leiber legt ein neuer
Frieden sich, wir blicken freier,
Mann und Weib, uns fürderan,
Mann und Weib, uns fürderan.

5.
Wann wir schreiten Seit an Seit
und die alten Lieder singen
und die Wälder widerklingen,
fühlen wir, es muß gelingen:
Mit uns zieht die neue Zeit!

WHEN WE'RE MARCHING SIDE BY SIDE

1.
When we're marching side by
    side,
Singing all the olden songs,
And the woods reverberate,
We feel that we must succeed:
This new era dawns with us,
This new era dawns with us.

2.
One whole week of hammering,
One whole week of quarrying,
Still are thund'ring in our veins,
yet nobody dares to quarrel
On this glorious sunny day,
On this glorious sunny day.

3.
Green the trees and green the
    crops:
Stretching out her hands of
    plenty
In a supplicating gesture,
Ancient Mother Earth is hoping

To make man her own again,
To make man her own again.

4.
Man and woman, man and wife
Are no longer fire and water.
Bodies now are clothed anew
In the peace of liberty.
Man and woman, lead us
    forward!
Man and woman, lead us
    forward!

5.
When we're marching side by
    side,
Singing all the olden songs,
And the woods reverberate,
We feel that we must succeed,
This new era dawns with us,
This new era dawns with us.

*Translated by
Alexandra Chciuk-Celt*

Anti-Fascist Songs

Ballade von der "Judenhure" Marie Sanders

Text: Bertolt Brecht, 1935
Music: Hanns Eisler

1.
In Nürnberg machten sie ein
    Gesetz
Darüber weinte manches Weib,
    das
Mit dem falschen Mann im Bett
    lag.
«Das Fleisch schlägt auf in den
    Vorstädten.
Die Trommeln schlagen mit
    Macht.
Gott im Himmel, wenn sie etwas
    vorhätten,
Wäre es heute nacht.»

2.
Marie Sanders, dein Geliebter
Hat zu schwarzes Haar.
Besser, du bist heute zu ihm
    nicht mehr
Wie du zu ihm gestern warst.
«Das Fleisch . . . »

3.
Mutter, gib mir den Schlüssel
Es ist alles halb so schlimm.
Der Mond sieht aus wie immer.
«Das Fleisch . . . »

4.
Eines Morgens, früh um neun
    Uhr
Fuhr sie durch die Stadt
Im Hemd, um den Hals ein
    Schild, das Haar geschoren.
Die Gasse johlte. Sie
Blickte kalt.
«Das Fleisch schlägt auf in den
    Vorstädten.
Der Streicher sprich heute
    nacht.
Großer Gott, wenn wir ein Ohr
    hätten,
Wüßten wir, was man mit uns
    macht.»

Ballad of Marie Sanders, the Jew's Whore

1.
In Nuremberg they made a law
At which many a woman wept
    who'd
Lain in bed with the wrong man.
"The price is rising for butcher's
    meat.

"The drumming's now at its
    height.
God alive, if they are coming
    down our street
It'll be tonight."

2.
Marie Sanders, your lover's
Hair is too black.
Take our advice, and don't you
    be to him
What you were yesterday.
"The price . . .", etc.

3.
Mother, give me the latchkey
It can't be so bad
The moon's the same as ever.
"The price . . .", etc.

4.
One morning, close on nine
She was driven through the
    town
In her slip, 'round her neck a
    sign, her hair all
    shaven.
The street was yelling. She
Coldly stared.
"The price is rising for butcher's
    meat.
And Streicher's speaking
    tonight.
God alive, if we'd an ear to hear
    his speech
We would start to make sense of
    our plight."

*Translated by
Desmond J. Vesey*

BUCHENWALDLIED

Text: Fritz Böda-Löhner, 1938
Music: Hermann Leopoldi

Wenn der Tag er - wacht, eh' die Son-ne lacht, die Ko-
lon - nen ziehn zu des Ta - ges Mühn hin - ein in den
grau - en - den Mor - gen. Und der Wald ist schwarz und der
Him - mel rot, und wir tra - gen im Brot - sack ein

Stück-chen Brot und im Her-zen, im Her-zen die Sor-

gen. O Bu - chen-wald, ich kann dich nicht ver-

ges - sen, weil du mein Schick - sal bist. Wer

dich ver-ließ, der kann es erst er-mes-sen, wie

wun - der - voll die Frei - heit ist! O

Bu - chen-wald, wir jam - mern nicht und kla-gen, und

was auch uns-re Zu - kunft sei___ wir wol - len

trotz-dem "ja" zum Le - ben sa - gen, denn ein-mal

1.
kommt der Tag, dann sind wir frei! Wir wol - len

2.
kommt der Tag, dann sind wir frei!

1.

Wenn der Tag erwacht, eh' die
  Sonne lacht,
Die Kolonnen ziehn zu des
  Tages Mühn
Hinein in den grauenden
  Morgen.
Und der Wald ist schwarz und
  der Himmel rot,
Und wir tragen im Brotsack ein
  Stückchen Brot
Und im Herzen, im Herzen die
  Sorgen.
O Buchenwald, ich kann dich
  nicht vergessen,
Weil du mein Schicksal
  bist.
Wer dich verließ, der kann es
  erst ermessen,
Wie wundervoll die Freiheit
  ist!
O Buchenwald, wir jammern
  nicht und klagen,
Und was auch unsere Zukunft
  sei—
Wir wollen trotzdem "ja" zum
  Leben sagen,
Denn einmal kommt der Tag—
Dann sind wir frei!

2.

Unser Blut ist heiß und das
  Mädel fern,
Und der Wind singt leis, und ich
  hab sie so gern,
Wenn treu, wenn treu sie mir
  bliebe!
Die Steine sind hart, aber fest
  unser Schritt,
Und wir tragen die Picken und
  Spaten mit
Und im Herzen, im Herzen die
  Liebe!
O Buchenwald . . .

3.

Die Nacht ist so kurz und der
  Tag so lang,
Doch ein Lied erklingt, das die
  Heimat sang,
Wir lassen den Mut uns nicht
  rauben!
Halte Schritt, Kamerad, und
  verlier nicht den Mut,
Denn wir tragen den Willen zum
  Leben im Blut
Und im Herze, im Herzen den
  Glauben!
O Buchenwald . . .

THE BUCHENWALD SONG

1.

Ere the sun's come up at the
  break of day
Tired columns trudge through
  the morning gray
Resuming their prison-camp labor.
When the woods are black and
  the sky is red

And our knapsacks hold but a
  bit of bread,
Each heart is as heavy as its
  neighbor's.
O Buchenwald, I simply can't
  forget you,
None can appeciate

How precious freedom is until
    they've left you,
You seem to be my fate.
O Buchenwald, we don't
    complain or grumble
About you, come what may—
We want to keep saying "yes"
    to life here,
For there will come the day
When we'll be free!

2.
My girl's far away and I miss
    her so,
And my blood is hot and the
    wind hums low,
I hope she'll be faithful to me!
Steady is our step though the
    rocks are rough,
And we carry shovels and picks
    enough,

And hearts full of loving have
    we!
O Buchenwald . . .

3.
Though the night's too short
    and the day's too long,
We still hear the notes of our
    back-home song,
They can't take our courage
    away!
Buddy, keep in step and don't
    lose your nerve,
For our hearts still hold our
    desire to live,
We must keep our faith up each
    day!
O Buchenwald . . .

Translated by
Alexandra Chciuk-Celt

KOMINTERN-LIED

Text: Franz Jahnke / Maxim Vallentin, 1929
Music: Hanns Eisler, 1929

Ver - laßt die Ma - schi - nen, her -
aus, ihr Pro - le - ten! Mar-schie - ren, mar-
schie - ren, zum Sturm an - ge - tre - ten! Die

Fah - nen ent-rollt, die Ge - weh - re ge -

fällt, im Sturm-schritt marsch, marsch! Wir er -

o - bern die Welt! Wir er - o - bern die Welt!

1.
Verlaßt die Maschinen, heraus,
 ihr Proleten!
Marschieren, marschieren, zum
 Sturm angetreten!
Die Fahnen entrollt, die
 Gewehre gefällt,
im Sturmschritt marsch, marsch!
Wir erobern die Welt! Wir
 erobern die Welt!

2.
Wir standen im «Vorwärts»,
 zum Tode entschlossen,
und hatten die letzten Patronen
 verschossen.
Sie warfen Granaten und Minen
 hinein,
wir mußten erliegen, wir
 standen allein,
wir standen allein.

3.
Wir haben die Besten zu Grabe
 getragen,
zerfetzt und zerschossen und
 blutig geschlagen,

von Mördern umstellt und ins
 Zuchthaus gesteckt,
uns hat nicht das Wüten, der
 Weißen geschreckt!
der Weißen geschreckt!

4.
Die letzten Kämpfer heran, ihr
 Genossen!
Die Fäuste geballt und die
 Reihen geschlossen!
Marschieren, marschieren zum
 neuen Gefecht,
wir stehen als Sturmtrupp für
 kommendes Recht!
Für kommendes Recht!

5.
In Rußland, da siegten die
 Arbeiterheere,
sie stellten zusammen die heißen
 Gewehre.
Von London, Paris, Budapest
 und Berlin,
Genossen, heraus, zum Kongreß,
 zu Lenin!
Zum Kongreß, zu Lenin!

6.
Beratung, Beschluß, hört den
    Ruf: Zu den Waffen!
Wir haben's gewagt, und wir
    werden es schaffen!
Herbei, ihr Soldaten der
    Revolution,
zum Sturm! Die Parole heißt:
    Sowjetunion!
heißt: Sowjetunion!

7.
Von Pflug und Maschinen,
    heraus, ihr Proleten!
Marschieren, marschieren, zum
    Sturm angetreten!
Die Fahnen entrollt, die
    Gewehre gefällt,
im Sturmschritt marsch, marsch!
    Wir erobern die Welt!
Wir erobern die Welt!

COMINTERN

1.
Rise up, fields and
    workshops,
come out, workers, farmers!
To battle march onward,
march on, world stormers!
Eyes sharp on your guns,
red banners unfurl'd.
Advance proletarians
to conquer the world!
Advance proletarians
to conquer the world!

2.
Oh you who are missing,
Oh comrades in dungeons,
You're with us, you're
    with us
his day of our vengeance!
No fascists can daunt us,
No terror can halt—
All lanes will take flame
With the fire of revolt,
All lands . . .

3.
The Comintern calls you,
Raise high Soviet banner
In steeled ranks to battle!
Raise Sickle and Hammer!
Our answer: Red Legions
we arise in our might;
Our answer: Red storm troops
We lunge to the fight.
Our answer: Red storm troops . . .

4.
From Russia victorious
The Workers' October
Comes storming reaction's
Regime the world over.
We've coming with Lenin
For Bolshevik work
From London, Havana,
Berlin and New York.
From London . . .

Translated by Victor Jerome
                (1932)

LIED DER INTERNATIONALEN BRIGADEN

Text: Erich Weinert, 1936–37
Music: Rafael Espinosa / Carlos Palacio

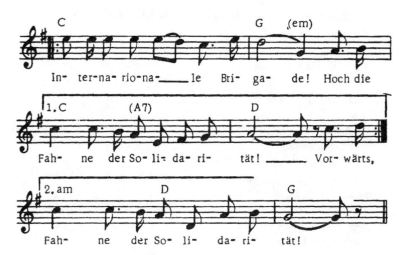

In- ter-na- rio-na-___ le Bri- ga- de! Hoch die

Fah- ne der So- li= da- ri- tät! ___ Vor- wärts,

Fah- ne der So- li- da- ri- tät!

1.

Wir, im fernen Vaterland geboren,
nahmen nichts als Haß im
  Herzen mit.
Doch wir haben die Heimat
  nicht verloren:
Uns're Heimat ist heute vor
  Madrid,
uns're Heimat ist heute vor
  Madrid!
Spaniens Brüder steh'n auf der
  Barrikade,
uns're Brüder sind Bauern und
  Prolet.
Vorwärts, Internationale
  Brigade!
Hoch die Fahne der Solidarität!
Vorwärts, Fahne der Solidarität!

2.

Spaniens Freiheit heißt jetzt
  uns're Ehre,
unser Herz ist international.
Jagt zum Teufel die
  Fremdenlegionäre,

jagt ins Meer den
  Banditengeneral!
Träumte schon in Madrid sich
  zur Parade,
doch wir waren schon da, er
  kam zu spät!
Vorwärts, Internationale
  Brigade . . .

3.

Mit Gewehren, Bomben und
  Granaten
wird das Ungeziefer
  ausgebrannt.
Frei das Land von Banditen und
  Piraten,
Brüder Spaniens, denn euch
  gehört das Land!
Dem Faschistengesindel keine
  Gnade,
keine Gnade dem Hund, der uns
  verrät!
Vorwärts, Internationale
  Brigade . . .

SONG OF THE INTERNATIONAL BRIGADES

1.

Far away is the land that we
    come from,
hatred in our hearts we've quite
    a bit,
yet we didn't lose our lover for
    our homeland,
for our homeland is now before
    Madrid
with our Spanish brothers on
    the barricades,
the peasants and the proletariat.
Let's advance, International
    Brigades!
Raise the flag of solidarity!
Advance, flag of solidarity!

2.

To Spain's freedom we pay now
    homage, so
our heart is all international.
Let those foreign legionaires all
    to hell go,
in the sea drown the treacherous
    general!
Saw himself in Madrid and at
    the parades,
yet too late, for in Madrid there
    were we!

Let's advance, International
    Brigades . . .

3.

With bombs, and with guns, and
    with grenades

the vermin shall forever be
    banned.
And a Spain free of bandits and
    of pirates,
Spanish brothers, that truly is
    your land.
It's the fascist mob here that we
    hate,
for the traiotrs no
    generosity!
Let's advance, International
    Brigades . . .
Saw himself in Madrid and at
    the parades,
yet too late, for in Madrid there
    were we!
Let's advance, International
    Brigades . . .

*Translated by
Sabine Tober*

☙❦

MEIN VATER WIRD GESUCHT

Text: Hans Drach, 1936
Music: Gerda Kohlmey, 1936

1.
Mein Vater wird gesucht,
Er kommt nicht mehr nach Haus.
Sie hetzen ihn mit Hunden,
Vielleicht ist er gefunden
Und kommt nicht mehr nach
  Haus.

2.
Die Mutter aber weint,
Wir lasen im Bericht:
Der Vater sei gefangen,
Und hätt' sich aufgehangen,
Das glaub' ich aber nicht.

3.
Er hat uns doch gesagt
So etwas tät er nicht.
Es sagten die Genossen,
SA hätt' ihn erschossen,
Ganz ohne ein Gericht.

4.
Heut' weiß ich ganz genau,
Warum sie das getan.
Wir werden doch vollenden,
Was er nicht konnt'
  beenden
Und Vater geht voran!

THEY'RE LOOKING FOR MY FATHER

1.
They're looking for my father;
he won't come home again.
They hung him with the hound,
and maybe he was found,
and won't come home again.

2.
But our mother cries.
In the report it said
that Father had been got,
put 'round his neck a knot.
I do not believe that.

[3.
The SA often came,
asked for his whereabouts;
we wouldn't tell and didn't know,
and they beat us ever so.
We didnt' cry out loud.]

4.
Because he always said,
he hated such denial.
And our comrades say,

he was shot by the SA,
was shot without a trial.

5.
Today I understand
why they did what they did.
We shall yet follow through
what father couldn't do,
and father, he shall lead.

Translated by Sabine Tober

DIE MOORSOLDATEN

Text: Wolfgang Langhoff, 1935
Music: Rudi Goguel; Hanns Eisler, 1935

1.
Wohin auch das Auge blicket,
Moor und Heide nur ringsum.
Vogelsang uns nicht erquicket,
Eichen stehen kahl und krumm.
Wir sind die Moorsoldaten
und ziehen mit dem Spaten
ins Moor.

[2.]
Hier in dieser öden Heide
ist das Lager aufgebaut,
wo wir ferne jeder Freude
hinter Stacheldrahtverhau.
Wir sind die Moorsoldaten . . .

[3.]
Morgens ziehen die Kolonnen
in das Moor zur Arbeit hin.
Graben bei dem Brand der
    Sonnen,
doch zur Heimat steht ihr Sinn.
Wir sind die Moorsoldaten . . .

[4.]
Heimwärts, heimwärts jeder
    sehnet
nach den Eltern, Weib und Kind.
Manche Brust ein Seufzer dehnet,
weil wir hier gefangen sind.
Wir sind die Moorsoldaten . . .

5.
Auf und nieder gehn die Posten,
keiner, keiner, kann hindurch.
Flucht wird nur das Leben kosten,
vierfach ist umzäunt die Burg.
Wir sind die Moorsoldaten . . .

6.
Doch für uns gib es kein Klagen,
ewig kann's nicht Winter sein.
Einmal werden froh wir sagen:
Heimat, du bist wieder mein.
Dann ziehn die Moorsoldaten
nicht mehr mit dem Spaten
ins Moor!

THE PEAT-BOG SOLDIERS

1.
Far and wide as the eye can
    wander,
Heath and bog are ev'rywhere.
Not a bird sings out to cheer us,
Oaks are standing gaunt and
    bare.
We are the peat-bog soldiers;
We're marching with our spades
To the bog.
(*Repeat last 3 lines*)

[2–4]
* * *

5.
Up and down, the guards are
    pacing.
No one, no one can go through.
Flight would mean a sure death
    facing.
Guns and barb'd wire greet our
    view.
We are the peat-bog soldiers,
    etc.

6.
But, for us there is no
    complaining.

Winter will in time be past;
One day we shall cry, rejoicing,
"Homeland, dear, you're mine
at last!"
Then will the peat-bog
soldiers

March no more with their
spades
To the bog. (Repeat last 3 lines)

Translated by Norman
Luboff and Win Strache

DIE MORITAT VON MACKIE MESSER

Text: Bertolt Brecht, 1928 (1946)

Music: Kurt Weill

1.
Und der Haifisch, der hat Zähne
Und die trägt er im Gesicht
Und Macheath, der hat ein
Messer
Doch das Messer sieht man
nicht.

2.
Ach, es sind des Haifischs
Flossen
Rot, wenn dieser Blut vergießt!
Mackie Messer trägt 'nen
Handschuh
Drauf man keine Untat liest.

3.
An der Themse grünem Wasser
Fallen plötzlich Leute um!
Es ist weder Pest noch Cholera
Doch es heißt: Macheath geht um.

4.
An 'nem schönen blauen Sonntag
Liegt ein toter Mann am Strand
Und ein Mensch geht um die
Ecke
Den man Mackie Messer nennt.

5.
Und Schmul Meier bleibt
verschwunden
Und so mancher reiche Mann
Und sein Geld hat Mackie
Messer
Dem man nichts beweisen kann.

6.
Jenny Towler ward gefunden
Mit 'nem Messer in der Brust
Und am Kai geht Mackie Messer
Der von allem nichts gewußt.

7.
Wo ist Alfons Glite, der
Fuhrherr?
Kommt das je ans Sonnenlicht?
Wer es immer wissen könnte—
Mackie Meseer weiß es nicht.

8.
Und das große Feuer in Soho
Sieben Kinder und ein Greis—
In der Menge Mackie Messer,
den
Man nicht fragt und der nichts
weiß.

9.

Und die minderjährige
   Witwe
Deren Namen jeder weiß

Wachte auf und war
   geschändet—
Mackie, welches war dein Preis?

THE CRIMES OF MACKIE THE KNIFE

1.

For the shark, he has his teeth
   and
You can see them in his face,
And MacHeath, he has his knife
   but
Hides it in a different place.

2.

For the shark has fins of crimson
When his victim's blood is shed,
But MacHeath, he keeps his
   gloves on
And you cannot see the red.

3.

Down along by Thames' green
   waters
Suddenly there's someone falls
Not from plague and not from
   cholera,
It's MacHeath has
paid his calls . . .

* * *

5.

And Sam Meyer still is missing
Many a rich man's been
   removed
And MacHeath, he has their
   money

But there's nothing can be
   proved.

6.

When they found her, Jenny
   Towler,
With the knife stuck in her
   breast,
Mackie walks along the
   quayside,
Knows no more than all the rest.

7.

Where is Alfonse Glite, the
   coachman?
Will that ever see the day?
Some there are, perhaps, who
   know it—
Mackie really couldn't say.

8.

Burnt alive were seven
   children
and an old man, in Soho—
Midst the crowd is standing
   Mackie, who
Isn't asked and
doesn't know . . .

Translated by
Christopher Isherwood

DIE THÄLMANN-KOLONNE

Text: Karl Ernst, 1936
Music: Paul Dessau / Peter Daniel, 1936

1. Spa-niens Him- mel brei-tet sei-ne Ster- ne ü-ber
uns'- re Schüt-zen-grä- ben aus, und der
Mor- gen grüßt schon aus der Fer- ne, bald geht
es zu neu- em Kampf hin- aus! (Refrain): Die
Hei- mat ist weit, doch wir sind be- reit: Wir
kämp-fen und sie- gen für dich, Frei- heit!

1.
Spaniens Himmel breitet seine Sterne
Über unsre Schützengräben aus.
Und der Morgen grüßt schon aus der Ferne,
Bald geht es zum neuen Kampf hinaus.
Die Heimat ist weit,
Doch wir sind bereit.

Wir kämpfen und siegen für
dich: Freiheit!

2.

Dem Faschisten werden wir
nicht weichen,
Schickt er auch die Kugeln
hageldicht.
Mit uns stehn Kameraden
ohnegleichen,
Und ein Rückwärts gibt es für
uns nicht.
Die Heimat . . .

3.

Rührt die Trommel! Fällt die
Bajonette!
Vorwärts, marsch! Der Sieg ist
unser Lohn!
Mit der Freiheitsfahne brecht die
Kette!
Auf zum Kampf, das Thälmann-
Bataillon.
Der Heimat ist weit,
Doch wir sind bereit.
Wir kämpfen und siegen für
dich: Freiheit!

THE THAELMANN COLUMN

1.

Spanish heavens spread their
brilliant starlight
High above our trenches in the
plain;
From the distance morning
comes to greet us,
Calling us to battle once
again.
Far off is our land,
Yet ready we stand.
We're fighting and winning for
you: Freedom!

2.

We'll not yield a foot to
Franco's fascists,
Even though the bullets fall like
sleet.

With us stand those peerless
men, our comrades,
And for us there can be no
retreat.
Far off is . . .

3.

Beat the drums! Ready!
Bayonets, charge!
Forward, march! Victory our
reward!
With our scarlet banner! Smash
their column!
Thaelmann Battalion! Ready,
forward, march!
Far off is . . .

Translator unkown

Songs of East and West Germany

ACH, DU MEIN SCHAURIGES VATERLAND

Text: Konstantin Wecker, 1982
Music: Konstantin Wecker

1.
Ach, du mein schauriges
    Vaterland,
du Land der Richter und Lenker!
Gestern noch hast du Europa
    verbrannt,
und jetzt spielst du schon wieder
    den Henker.

2.
Ach, du mein schauriges
    Vaterland
mit deinen geschmeidigen
    Mannen.
Wir sind wieder mal vor uns
    davongerannt,
aber ewig grünen die Tannen.

3.
Über dreißig Jahre Gelegenheit,
alte Wunden auszuheilen,
war doch eigentlich genügend Zeit.
Oder wollen wir uns gar nicht
    beeilen?

4.
Wir suchen uns ja immer noch
in den Gesten und Blicken der
    andern,

und sollten doch endlich das
    eigene Ich
mit all seinen Schwächen
    durchwandern.

5.
Soll das auch noch die Schuld
    unserer Väter sein?
Hier gehts nur noch um unser
    Versagen.
Wir haben blind und ganz allein
unsere Freiheit begraben.

6.
Und jetzt würgt uns eine
    Demokratie,
deren Recht so verdächtig
    gerecht ist,
deren Ordnung hysterisch wie
    noch nie
alles prügelt, was offen und echt
    ist.

7.
Ach, du mein schauriges
    Vaterland,
du Land der Richter und
    Lenker!

Gestern noch hast du Europa
    verbrannt,
und jetzt spielst du schon wieder
    den Henker.

8.
Ach, du mein schauriges
    Vaterland,
mit deinen geschmeidigen
    Mannen.
Wir sind wieder mal vor uns
    davongerannt,
aber ewig grünen die Tannen.

9.
Wir sind nicht unbedingt weiser
    geworden
seit jenen Schrecklichkeiten.
Die Ja-Sager sind etwas leiser
    geworden,
die Schwurgerichsräte sind
    greiser geworden.
Man erwartet kältere Zeiten.

10.
Gestern noch hast du Europa
    verbrannt,
und jetzt spielst du schon wieder
    den Henker.

OH, MY GRUESOME FATHERLAND

1.
Oh, my gruesome fatherland,
You land of judges and hustlers.
Yesterday you were burning up
    Europe
And now you're again playing
    hangman.

2.
Oh, my gruesome fatherland
with your compliant gentlemen.
We escaped ourselves yet once
    again,
but the fir trees are evergreen.

3.
More than thirty years of
    chances
for the old wounds to heal up

—that was actually enough time
or aren't we in that much of a
    hurry?

4.
We're still trying to find ourselves
in the gestures and glances of
    others,
but ought to get to know our
    true selves
with all of our weaknesses.

5.
Is that, too, our father's fault?
Here it's merely a matter of our
    own failure.
Blindly and all by ourselves, we
have buried our own freedom.

6.
And now a democracy's choking us
with a justice that's so
    suspiciously just,
with a more hysterical order
    than ever,
beating everything that's open
    and true.

7.
Oh, my gruesome fatherland,
You land of judges and
    hustlers.
Yesterday you were burning up
    Europe
And now you're again playing
    hangman.

8.
Oh, my gruesome fatherland,
with your compliant
    gentlemen.
We escaped ourselves yet once
    again,
but the fir trees are evergreen.

9.
We haven't necessarily grown
    any wiser
since those terrible events.
The yea-sayers have grown a bit
    softer,
the court judges are a little more
    ancient.
People are expecting colder times.

10.
Yesterday you were burning up
    Europe
And now you're again playing
    hangman.

Translated by Richard J. Rundell

DAS BARLACH-LIED

Text: Wolf Biermann, 1965
Music: Wolf Biermann, 1965

1.
Ach Mutter mach die Fenster zu
Ich glaub es kommt ein Regen
Da drüben seht die
    Wolkenwand
Die will sich auf uns legen.
Was soll aus uns noch werden
Uns droht so große Not
Vom Himmel auf die Erden
Fallen sich die Engel tot.

2.
Ach Mutter mach die Türe zu

Da kommen tausend Ratten
Die hungrigen sind vorneweg
Dahinter sind die satten.
Was soll aus . . .

3.
Ach Mutter mach die Augen zu
Der Regen und die Ratten
Jetzt dringt es durch die Ritzen
    ein
Die wir vergessen hatten.
Was soll aus . . .

☙❧

THE BARLACH SONG

1.

O Mother close the windows
  tight;
Big rains are coming now.
A wall of clouds is looming
  there
And wants to squash us down.
What's going to happen to us?
I feel a danger-dread.
The angels won't stop falling
Down to the earth stone-dead.

2.

O Mother close the door real
  tight;

I see a thousand rats.
The hungry ones are right up front,
The full ones are in back.
What's going to happen , etc.

3.

O Mother close your eyes now;
The rain, the thousand rats,
They're coming right inside the
  house
Through long-forgotten cracks.
What's going to happen , etc.

*Translated by
Alexandra Chciuk-Celt*

DER BAGGERFÜHRER WILLIBALD

Text: Dieter Süverkrüp, 1973
Music: Dieter Süverkrüp, 1973

Es ist am Mor-gen kalt. Da kommt der Wil - li -

-bald. Er klettert in den Bag-ger undbaggert auf dem

Ak -ker ein großes tiefes Loch. Was noch?

Letzte Strophe

Wie Wil-li-bald das sagt, so wird es auch ge -

macht. Die Bau-ar-bei-ter le-gen los und bau-en Häuser
schön und groß, wo je-der gut drin wohnen kann weil jeder sie be-
-zah-len kann. Der Bag-gerführer Wil-libald baut ei-ne neu-e
Schwimmanstalt. Da spritzen sich die Leu-te naß. Das
macht so-gar dem Bag - ger Spaß.

1.
Es ist am Morgen kalt.
Da kommt der Willibald.
Er klettert in den Bagger
und baggert auf dem Acker
ein großes tiefes Loch.
Was noch?

2.
Naja, so fängt das an.
Dann kommen alle Mann.
Sie bauen erst den Keller.
Dann baun sie immer schneller.
Was kommt dabei heraus?
Ein Haus!

3.
Und in das Haus hinein
ziehn feine Leute ein.
Die Miete ist sehr teuer.
Kost' siebenhundert Eier.

Wer kriegt die Miete bloß?
Der Boß!

4.
Der Boß kommt groß heraus.
Dem Boß gehört das Haus.
Dem Boß gehört der Bagger,
der Kran und auch der Acker.
Und alles, was da ist.
So'n Mist!

5.
Der Boß steht meistens rum
und redet laut und dumm.
Sein Haus, das soll sich
lohnen.
Wer Geld hat, kann drin
wohnen.
Wer arm ist, darf nicht rein!
Gemein!

6.
Der Willibald kriegt Wut.
Er sagt: "Das ist nicht gut!"
Er steigt auf eine Leiter:
"Hört her, ihr Bauarbeiter,
der Boß ist, wie ihr seht,
zu blöd!

7.
Sein Haus, das bauen wir!
Was kriegen wir dafür?
Der Boß zahlt uns den Lohn aus.
Die Miete für sein Wohnhaus,
die ist in unsrem Lohn
nicht drin!

8.
Das hat doch keinen Zweck!
Der Boß geht besser weg!
Dann baun wir für uns selber

ein schönes Haus mit Keller.
Da ziehen wir alle ein.
Au, fein!"

9.
Wie Willibald das sagt,
so wird es auch gemacht.
Die Bauarbeiter legen los
und bauen Häuser, schön und
    groß,
wo jeder gut drin wohnen
    kann,
weil jeder sie bezahlen kann.
Der Baggerführer Willibald
baut eine neue Schwimmanstalt.
Da spritzen sich die Leute
    naß.
Das macht sogar dem Bagger
    Spaß.

THE BALLAD OF WILLIBALD
THE POWER-SHOVEL OPERATOR

1.
A really chilly dawn.
Now Willibald climbs on
The power excavator
And shovels through the acre,
And digs a great big hole.
Behold!

2.
And that's how things get
    started.
More men come from afar, and
A basement they start making.
What is this undertaking
They're working on, dear Klaus?
The boss!

3.
Who moves into that house?
Some classy people, Klaus.
The rent is quite expensive,
It's sixty dozen hen's eggs.
Who gets that rent, dear
    Klaus?
The boss!

4.
The boss comes strutting out,
The owner of the house.
He owns the excavator,
The crane too, and the acre,
The whole and sundry lot.
What rot!

5.

He usually stands around,
Huffs like a stupid clown.
High rent? He will live off it,
His house must turn a profit.
The poor can't come inside.
How snide!

6.

So Willi says to Klaus:
"This blockhead is a louse!"
He climbs onto a ladder:
"I'm getting ever madder.
Men, this guy is a hood,
No good!

7.

Who built that house of his?
What do we get for this?
The boss pays us our wages,
But his apartment rent is
None of our business.
What's this?!

8.

What bloody use is he?

He'd better leave, so we
Can work on our own buildings
With cellars in our dwellings,
And move in with our crates!
How great!"

9.

And when his speech is done,
That very work's begun!
Construction workers soon have
    built
Big lovely homes upon the silt
Where anyone can live, for each
Will find these homes within his
    reach.
The power-shoveller Willi then
Consructs a swimming-pool,
    and when
The folks are splashing happily,
You'd say the shovel shares their
    glee.

Translated by
Alexandra Chciuk-Celt

DEUTSCHER SONNTAG

Text: Franz Josef Degenhardt, 1965
Music: Franz Josef Degenhardt

Sonn-tags in der klei-nen Stadt, sonn-tags in der klei-nen
Stadt. Wenn die Spin-ne Lan-ge-wei-le Fä-den spinnt und

oh-ne Ei-le___ gif-tig-grau die Wand hoch-kriecht, wenn's

blank und frisch ge-ba-det riecht_____, dann bringt mich

kei-ner auf die Stras-se, und aus Angst und Är-ger

las-se ich mein ro-tes Bart-haar stehn und laß den

Tag vor-ü-ber gehn. Hock am Fen-ster, le-se

mei-ne Zei-tung, dek-ke Bein mit Bei-ne,

seh, hör und rie-che ne-ben-bei das gan-ze

Sonn-tags-ei-ner-lei. Pam pa-dam, pam, pam,

pa-dam, pam, pam, pa-dam, jam, pam, pam, pam, pam.

Intro/Refrain:
Sonntags in der kleinen Stadt,
sonntags in der kleinen Stadt.

1.
Wenn die Spinne Langeweile
Fäden spinnt und ohne Eile
giftiggrau die Wand
      hochkriecht,
wenn's blank und frisch gebadet
      riecht,
dann bringt mich keiner auf die
      Straße,
und aus Angst und Ärger lasse
ich mein rotes Barthaar stehn
und laß den Tag vorüber gehn.
Hock am Fenster, lese meine
Zeitung decke Bein mit Beine,
seh, hör und rieche nebenbei
das ganze Sonntagseinerlei.
Pam padam, pam, pam, padam,
pam, pam, padam, jam, pam,
      pam, pam, pam.

2.
Da treten sie zum Kirchgang an,
Familienleittiere voran.
Hütchen, Schühchen, Täschchen
      passend,
ihre Männer unterfassend,
die sie heimlich vorwärts
      schieben,
weil sie gern zu Hause blieben.
Und dann kommen sie zurück,
mit dem gleichen bösen Blick,
Hütchen, Schühchen, Täschchen
      passend,
ihre Männer unterfassend,
die sie heimlich heimwärts ziehn,
daß sie nicht in Kneipen fliehn.
Pam padam, pam, pam . . .

3.
Wenn die Bratendüfte wehen,
Jungfraun den Kaplan
      umstehen,
der so nette Witzchen macht,
und wenn der dann so harmlos
      lacht,
wenn auf allen Fensterbänken
Pudding dampft, und aus den
      Schenken
schallt das Lied vom
      Wiesengrund,
und daß am Bach ein Birklein
      stund.
Alle Glocken läuten mit,
die ganze Stadt kriegt Appetit.
Das ist dann genau die Zeit,
dann frier ich vor
      Gemütlichkeit.
Pam padam, pam, pam . . .

4.
Da hockt die ganze Stadt und
      mampft,
daß Bratenschweiß aus Fenstern
      dampft.
Durch die fette Stille dringen
Gaumenschnalzen,
      Schüsselklingen,
Messer, die auf Knochen stoßen,
und das Blubbern dicker Soßen.
Hat nicht irgendwas geschrien?
Jetzt nicht aus dem Fenster sehn,
wo auf Hausvorgärtenmauern
ausgefranste Krähen lauern.
Was nur da geschrien hat?
Ich werde so entsetzlich satt.
Pam padam, pam, pam . . .

5.
Wenn Zigarettenwolken
      schweben,

aufgeblähte Nüstern beben,
aus Musiktruhn Donauwellen
plätschern, über Mägen quellen,
dann hat die Luft sich angestaut,
die ganze Stadt hockt und
    verdaut.
Woher kam der laute Knall?
Brach ein Flugzeug durch den
    Schall?
Oder ob mitmal die Stadt
ihr Bäuerchen gelassen hat?
Die Luft riecht süß und säuerlich,
ich glaube, ich erbreche mich.
Pam padam, pam, pam . . .

6.
Dann geht's zu den
    Schlachtfeldstätten,
um im Geiste mitzutreten,
mitzuschießen, mitzustechen,
sich für wochentags zu rächen
um im Chor Worte zu röhren,
die beim Gottesdienst nur
    stören.
Schinkenspeckgesichter lachen
treuherzig, weil Knochen
    krachen
werden. Ich verstopf die Ohren
meiner Kinder. Traumverloren
hocken auf den Stadtparkbänken
Greise, die an Sedan denken.
Pam padam, pam, pam . . .

7.
Und dann die Spaziergangstunde
durch die Stadt, zweimal die
    Runde.

Hüte ziehen, spärlich nicken,
wenn ein Chef kommt, tiefer
    bücken.
Achtung, daß die Sahneballen
dann nicht in den Rinnstein
    rollen.
Kinder baumeln, ziehen Hände.
Man hat ihnen bunte, fremde
Fliegen, Beine ausgefetzt,
sorgsam an den Hals gesetzt,
daß sie die Kinder beißen solln,
wenn sie zum Bahndamm fliehen
    woll'n.
Pam padam, pam, pam . . .

8.
Wenn zur Ruh die Glocken
    läuten,
Kneipen nur ihr Licht
    vergeuden,
dann wird's in Couchecken
    beschaulich,
das ist dann die Zeit, da
    trau ich
mich hinaus, um nachzusehen,
ob die Sterne richtig stehen.
Abendstille überall, bloß
manchmal Lachen wie ein
    Windstoß
über ein Mattscheiben-
    späßchen.
Jeder schlürft noch rasch ein
    Gläschen
und stöhnt über seinen Bauch
und unsern kranken Nachbarn
    auch.
Pam padam, pam, pam . . .

☙❧

A GERMAN SUNDAY

Intro/Refrain:
Small-town Sundays,
Small-town Sundays.

1.
When the spider poison-grey
Spins her threads and climbs
    away
Up the wall, I'm mad and
    scared,
I won't groom my beard or hair.
When things smell so clean and
    new,
I get the German Sunday blues;
I won't go out on the street;
I read my paper, rest my feet
High up on the window-sill,
Smell the boring Sunday swill;
I just watch the day flow by
From the corner of my eye.
Pam padam, pam, pam, padam,
Pam, pam, padam, jam, pam,
    pam, pam, pam.

2.
This herd's off to church, I
    grunt;
See the lead-mare up in front
In her matching hat-bag-shoes,
Linking arms with Hubby, who's
Cranky, for he'd rather stay
Home; he must be nudged today.
Grimly they come trudging back
In their matching bag-shoes-hat,
Linking arms with Hubby, who
Would prefer to duck into
Taverns, where he'd rather stay,
So he must be nudged today.
Pam padam, pam, pam . . .

3.
When the roasts waft fragantly
And the girls attentively
Listen to the curate's jests,
Harmless jokes he laughs at
    best,
When the window-sills are
    gleaming
And the fresh-baked pies are
    steaming,
And the church-bells all start
    ringing
And the taverns all start singing
Birches-meadows-oh-so-pretty,
Appetite befalls the city.
I then feel so cozy, I
Shiver, freeze, and almost cry.
Pam padam, pam, pam . . .

4.
Busily the city's lunching,
Greasy silence coats the
    munching,
Aromatic steam escapes,
Smacking gums and clanging
    plates,
Clinking keys and cutlery,
Gravy bubbling merrily.
Didn't I just hear a shriek?
No, and don't you take a peek—
It's just mangy crows, that's all,
Lurking on the garden wall.
I'm so full—what was that din?
Wonder what that could've
    been . . .
Pam padam, pam, pam . . .

5.
Cigarette-clouds fill the air

Billows smoke and nostrils flare,
Radio's playing Danube ditties.
Now's the time when all the
    city
Sits and lets its belly rest;
Music helps it to digest.
What was that noise? Some
    more champagne?
Was that a supersonic plane?
Maybe somebody's really hurt—
Or did the city just go burp?
The air smells sickly sweet and
    sour,
I think I'm going to vomit now.
Pam padam, pam, pam . . .

6.
And now, off to historic sites—
We help the heroes shoot and
    fight.
Pretend to be artillery,
Revenge for weekday drudgery.
A chorus now is bellowing
Words that no church-choir ever
    sings.
Guiless bacon-faces beam,
Expecting broken bones and
    screams.
I hold my children's ears shut
    tight.
On benches in the sunshine
    bright,
Some old men sunk in reverie
Think back on wartime
    victories.
Pam padam, pam, pam . . .

7.
It's time to go out for a walk
To town and back, tip hats,
    don't talk,

Just nod hello, except you
    bow
If that's your boss you see right
    now.
Make sure you don't lose your
    dessert!
Kids hang and tug at Mommy's
    skirt.
They've got these unfamiliar ties
Around their necks like awful
    flies
Which are supposed to bite
    them if
They feel like chasing to the cliff
Or running off or having fun—
Such things simply never done!
Pam padam, pam, pam . . .

8.
When the church-bells peal
    good-night
And taverns waste their neon
    light,
Then peace descends upon the
    crowd
And I can dare venture out
Onto the street, and check to
    see:
The stars are where they ought
    to be?
Evening quiet blankets all,
All except a laughter-squall
When they like some boob-tube
    joke.
Sipping one more for the road,
Everybody sighs, "My belly,"
Then complains about Aunt
    Nellie.
Pam padam, pam, pam . . .

Translated by
Alexandra Chciuk-Celt

DIE HAB ICH SATT!

Text: Wolf Biermann, 1969
Music: Wolf Biermann, 1969

1.

Die kalten Frauen, die mich
    streicheln
Die falschen Freunde, dir mir
    schmeicheln
Die scharf sind auf die scharfen
    Sachen
Und selber in die Hosen machen
In dieser durchgerissnen Stadt
—die hab ich satt!

2.

Und sagt mir mal: Wozu ist gut
Die ganze Bürokratenbrut?
Sie wälzt mit Eifer und Geschick
Dem Volke über das Genick
Der Weltgeschichte großes Rad
—die hab ich satt!

3.

Was haben wir denn an denen
    verlorn:
An diesen deutschen Professorn
Die wirklich manches besser
    wüßten
Wenn sie nicht täglich fressen
    müßten
Beamte! Feige! Fett und platt!
—die hab ich satt!

4.

Die Lehrer, die Rekruten-
    schinder
Sie brechen schon das Kreuz der
    Kinder

Sie pressen unter allen Fahnen
Die idealen Untertanen:
Gehorsam—fleißig—geistig matt
—die hab ich satt!

5.

Die Dichter mit der feuchten
    Hand
Dichten zugrund das Vaterland
Das Ungereimte reimen sie
Die Wahrheitssucher leimen sie
Dies Pack ist käuflich und
    aalglatt
—die hab ich satt!

6.

Der legendäre Kleine Mann
Der immer litt und nie gewann
Der sich gewöhnt an jeden Dreck
Kriegt er nur seinen
    Schweinespeck
Und träumt im Bett vom Attentat
—den hab ich satt!

7.

Und überhaupt ist ja zum
    schrein
Der ganze deutsche Skatverein
Dies dreigeteilte deutsche Land
und was ich da an Glück auch
    fand
Das steht auf einem andern
    Blatt
—dich hab ich satt!

I'M SICK OF IT!

1.
Cold bitches who keep kissing
    me
And two-faced friends who
    flatter me—
So hot on all the hot safe bets,
You shit yourselves at the
    slightest threat:
In this city torn in two,
    I'm sick of you!

2.
And tell me now what is the good
Of that whole bureaucratic
    brood
Who roll so keenly with such
    skill
World history's relentless wheel
Right across our people's back?
    I'm sick of that!

3.
What would we stand to lose in
    those
Our famous German professors,
Who really might know a thing
    or two
It they weren't so full of
    patriotic stew?
Officials! Cowards! Fat and trite!
    I'm sick of it!

4.
The teachers, those parade-
    ground hacks
Who bend and break our
    children's backs
And with their standards
    fluttering

Produce the ideal underling
Obedient, willing—dead in the
    head:
    I'm sick of them!

5.
You poets with your clammy
    hands
Who rhyme to death the fatherland
Make two and two add up to
    five
While those after truth you bury
    alive—
You're all for sale and slippery
    too!
    I'm sick of you.

6.
You legendary little man,
Who always lost and never won,
Who learns to take all kinds of
    shit—
For your daily bread you'll
    swallow it
Then dream in bed of bloody
    coups—
    I'm sick of you.

7.
But worst of all—it makes you
    scream
Our German national poker game
It's not two nations here but
    three
And as for the happiness I see
That's written on another sheet.
    I'm sick of it.

Translated by Steve Gooch

ERMUTIGUNG

Text: Wolf Biermann, 1968
Music: Wolf Biermann

Du, laß dich nicht verhär-ten   in dieser har-ten Zeit.

Die all - zu hart sind, bre-chen, die all-zu spitz sind, stechen

und bre-chen ab so - gleich,   und bre-chen ab so - gleich.

1.
Du, laß dich nicht verhärten
in dieser harten Zeit.
Die allzu hart sind, brechen,
die allzu spitz sind, stechen
und brechen ab sogleich,
und brechen ab sogleich.

2.
Du, laß dich nicht verbittern
in dieser bittren Zeit.
Die Herrschenden erzittern
—sitzt du erst hinter Gittern—
doch nicht vor deinem Leid,
doch nicht vor deinem Leid.

3.
Du, laß dich nicht erschrecken
in dieser Schreckenzeit.
Das wolln sie doch bezwecken,
daß wir die Waffen strecken

schon vor dem großen Streit,
schon vor dem großen Streit.

4.
Du, laß dich nicht verbrauchen,
gebrauche deine Zeit.
Du kannst nicht untertauchen.
Du brauchst uns, und wir
        brauchen
grad deine Heiterkeit,
grad deine Heiterkeit.

5.
Wir wolln es nicht verschweigen
in dieser Schweigezeit:
Das Grün bricht aus den
        Zweigen.
Wir wolln das allen zeigen,
dann wissen sie Bescheid,
dann wissen sie Bescheid.

ENCOURAGEMENT

Dedicated to Peter Huchel

1.
Don't let yourself be hardened
In these hard times of ours.
The hard ones break so easy,
The sharp ones sting so easy,
And then are dead in hours.

2.
Don't let yourself be bitter
In bitter times like ours.
While in a cell you're sitting,
The rulers will be fretting
Though not for you, of course.

3.
Don't let yourself be frightened
Though these are frightening
    times.
That's all they want, the bastards,

That long before the fight starts
We offer up our arms.

4.
Don't let yourself be misused,
Make full use of your hours.
You can't just disappear now.
You need us and we need somehow
That cheerfulness of yours.

5.
We'll make no secret of it
Our times may be obscure:
But soon each branch will flower,
There'll be no need to cower,
And then they'll know for sure.

Translated by Steve Gooch

ERSCHRÖCKLICHE MORITAT VOM KRYPTOKOMMUNISTEN

Text : Dieter Süverkrüp, 1966
Music : Dieter Süverkrüp

hä - re-nem Bet - te auf steht. Er

wäscht sich nur un-gern und blickt in den Spie-gel mit

sei - nem Mon-go-len - ge - sicht, er

putzt sich die Zäh-ne mit Branntwein und trinkt ei - nen

Wod-ka, mehr früh-stückt er nicht.

Dann zieht der Kom - mun -

ist die Un - ter - wan-der-stie-fel an und dann

geht er an sein il - le - ga - les

Un - ter - tag-werk ran. Hu - hu, hu-

hu! Hu - hu, hu - hu!

1.

Wenn die Sonne bezeichnenderweise im Osten und rot
hinter Wolken aufgeht, ja, das
  ist dann die Zeit,
da er flach wie ein Tiger aus
  härenem Bette aufsteht.
Er wäscht sich nur ungern und
  blickt in den Spiegel
mit seinem Mongolengesicht,
er putzt sich die Zähne mit
  Branntwein
und trinkt einen Wodka, mehr
  früstückt er nicht.
Dann zieht der Kommunist die
  Unterwanderstiefel an
und dann geht er an sein
  illegales Untertagwerk ran.
Hu-hu, hu-hu! Hu-hu,
  hu-hu!

2.

Und dann fletscht er die Zähne,
  die Hand hält er vor, denn
das darf ja kein Mensch niemals
  sehn.
Um neun Uhr zehn frißt er das
  erste Kind, blauäugig,
blond, aus dem Kindergarten.
Um elf brennt die Kirche, es
  drängen sich hilfsbereit
Feuerwehr, Bürger und Christ.
Derweil diskutiert er mit
  Schwester Theres, bis die
auch für den Weltfrieden ist.
Der Kommunist ist so geschickt,
  dagegen kann man nicht!
Und zu Mittag schreibt er gar
  noch ein politisches
  Gedicht.
Huhuuuu . . .

3.

Er verstellt sich, spricht
  rheinisch statt sächsisch und
  infiltriert
meuchlings und nur
  hinterrücks.
Und wenn du bis heute ver-
  schont bliebst, ist das eine
Frage persönlichen Glücks.
Am Nachmittag platzt eine
  Bombe in Bonn,
aber da hat er sich geirrt!
Weil, wenn einer nur an KZs
  mitentworfen hat,
daraus kein Staatseklat
  wird.
Und wer ein Kommunist ist,
  kriegt man niemals richtig'
  raus;
so ein Krytokommunist sieht
  immer agitproper aus.
Huhuuuu . . .

4.

Zumeist kommunistet er dort in
  der Hütte,
die gleich hinterm Bahndamm
  versteckt liegt.
Da übt er sich heimlich in
  Philosophie,
Analyse sowie Dialektik.
Müd' kommt er nach Hause, er
  küßt seine Frau und
spielt mit den Kindern
  Verstecken.
Die Kinder sind auch durch und
  durch infiziert, denn
sie kennen im Haus alle
  Ecken.
Dann hört er sich die Platte mit
  der h-Moll-Messe an,

weil er nicht einmal privat mehr
    völlig unverstellt sein kann.
Dann zieht der Kommunist die
    Unterwanderstiefel aus,

und dann ruht er sich von
    seinem schweren
    Untertagwerk aus.
Huhuuu . . .

DREADFUL BALLAD OF THE CRYPTO-COMMUNIST

1.
When the sun, in the East, of
    course
and red, rises behind the clouds,
that's his time, when he arises as
    flat as a tiger
from his hairshirt bed.
He doesn't like to wash, just
    glances in the mirror
at his Mongolian face.
He brushes his teeth with
    brandy and drinks some
vodka—and that's all he has for
    breakfast.
Oooh, oooh . . .

2.
And when he bares his fangs, he
    covers his mouth with his
    hand,
for no one is ever supposed to
    see that.
At nine A.M. he devours the
    day's first baby,
A blue-eyed, blonde-haired
    kindergartener.
At eleven the church is on fire,
    and to the rescue rush
fire department, citizens, and
    Christians.
Meanwhile, he's chatting with
    Sister Theresa, until
she, too, is in favor of world
    peace.

The Communist is so clever, you
    just can't touch him!
And at noon he even writes a
    political poem.
Oooh, oooh . . .

3.
He disguises himself with a West
    German dialect, not an
    Eastern one,
and infiltrates sneakily, behind
    your back.
And if you've been spared thus
    far, it's
only a matter of your good luck.
In the afternoon, a bomb goes
    off in Bonn,
but he slipped up with this one!
Because if you've only helped
    design concentration camps,
that's no reason for a national
    scandal.
And who the real Communist is,
    you'll never find out for sure,
for a Crypto-Communist always
    looks quite agitproper.
Oooh, oooh . . .

4.
Mostly he just Commun-nests in
    his little shack
hidden away beyond the
    railroad tracks.

There he secretly practices
  philosophy,
analysis as well as dialects.
He comes home weary, kisses
  his wife and
plays hide-and-seek with his
  kids.
The kids themselves are infected
  too,
for they know all hiding places
  in the house.

Then he listens to a record of
  the B-Minor Mass,
Because even in private, he dare
  not be completely himself.
Then the Communist takes off
  his subversive boots
and rests from a difficult day of
  underground work.
Oooh's oooh?

Transalted by Richard J. Rundell

FRIEDEN IM LAND

Text: Konstantin Wecker, 1977
Music: Konstantin Wecker, 1977

1.

Das Land steht stolz im
  Feiertagsgewand.
Die Zollbeamten sind schön
  aufgeputzt.
Sogar die Penner haben
  Ausgang, und am Rand
sind ein paar Unverbesserliche
  noch verdutzt.
Die alten Ängste, pitoresk
  gepflanzt,
treiben sehr bunte neue Blüten.
Die Bullen beißen wieder, und
  der Landtag tanzt.
Endlich geschafft: Ein Volk von
  Phagozyten.
Jetzt ist es allen klar: Der Herr
  baut nie auf Sand.
Es herrscht wieder Frieden im
  Land.

2.

Vereinzelt springen Terroristen
  über Wiesen.

Wie chic. Die Fotoapparate sind
  gezückt.
Die alten Bürgerseligkeiten
  sprießen,
die Rettung, Freunde, ist
  geglückt.
Die Schüler schleimen wieder
  um die Wette.
Die Denker lassen Drachen
  steigen.
Utopia onaniert im Seidenbette,
die Zeiten stinken, und die
  Dichter schweigen.
Wie schön, daß sich das Recht
  zum Rechten fand:
Es herrscht wieder Frieden im
  Land.

3.

Ich will mich jetzt mit einem
  runden Weib begnügen,
drei Kinder zeugen, Eigenheime
  pflanzen und

die Menschheit einfach mal um
   mich betrügen.
Warum denn leiden—schließ
   mir, Herr, den Mund.

Wirf mir die Augenbinden runter
   und den Stirnverband:
Es herrscht wieder Frieden im
   Land.

PEACE IN THE LAND

1.

The land stands proudly in its
   best array.
The customs officials are trimly
   dressed.
The hobos even are on leave,
   and far away
some hopeless cases still
   stupefied and stressed.
The same old fears,
   picturesquely set,
The pigs are biting, and
   ministers do a minuet.
Achieved at last: Of phagocytes
   a nation.
Now all can clearly see: God
   doesn't build on sand.
Peace reigns again in the land.

2.

Sporadically terrorists skip
   across meadows.
How chic. The cameras are
   drawn in case one fell.
Bourgeois happiness raises from
   shadows,
the rescue, friends, did turn out
   well.

The pupils write nonsense from
   their heads.
The thinkers let their kites fly
   high.
Utopia masturbates on silken
   beds,
the times smell foul, and poets
   only sigh.
How nice that lawful right
   found the right band:
Peace reigns again in the land.

3.

I will resign myself now to a
   chubby wife,
beget three children, plant some
   houses and accord
humanity abstention from my
   life.
To what aim suffer—shut my
   mouth, O Lord.
Toss me down a blindfold for
   my eyes and a forehead
   band:
Peace reigns again in the land.

*Translated by
Dietmar Pieper*

FÜR M. THEODORAKIS

Text: Franz Josef Degenhardt, 1968
Music: Franz Josef Degenhardt

1.

Da sind sie, die Konzern- und
  Landbesitzer,
Generäle, Popen, Panzer,
die bekannte Kumpanei.
Immer wieder wollen sie die Zeit
  aufhalten
in Athen und Kapstadt, Bogótá,
Berlin und Quang Ngai.
Ihre greisen, kalten Hände suchen
jedes heiße Herz, Theodorakis,
und du weißt, wie kalt sie sind.
Doch wir wissen auch, daß sie
  zu kalt sind,
daß sie viel zu alt sind, daß sie
  tot sind
dann, wenn unser Tag beginnt.
Jener Tag,
an dem die Sonne tanzt.
Roter Tag der Freiheit in Athen.
Jener Tag,
an dem wir auf den Straßen
  tanzen
und uns wiedersehn.

2.

Die Feinde dieser Parasiten—es
  sind
deine Freunde. Sie sind zahlreich
und sie leben überall.
Deine Lieder sind auf ihrem
  langen Marsch
die kurze Rast in einem
  quellenkühlen Tal.

Darum hassen sie die Lieder,
  unsre Feinde.
Ihre wurmstichigen Ohren
trifft dein Name wie ein
  Schlag.
Und im Bellen ihrer
  Stimmen,
in den kurzsichtigen Augen
ist die Angst vor jenem Tag,
jenem Tag,
an dem die Sonne tanzt . . .

3.

Und sie frieren in den weißen
  Häusern,
diese alten Männer. Ihre
  tausendfache Angst
wird tausendfach bewacht.
Wie ihr großer weißer
  Vater,
dieser Völkermörder Johnson,
löschen sie das Licht nicht mehr
  bei Nacht.
Denn sie wissen, die die auf
  morgen
warten, sie sind überall
und sie sind wach.
Seht! die Nacht geht schon zu
  Ende.
Ihre Sterne, sie verlöschen.
Bald beginnt der Tag.
Jener Tag,
an dem die Sonne tanzt . . .

FOR M. THEODORAKIS

1.

There they are, the company
    owners and the land owners,
generals, bishops, tanks,
the usual bunch.
They keep trying to make time
    stand still
in Athens and Capetown,
    Bogota,
in Berlin and Quang Ngai.
Their cold, aged hands grasping
    for
every warm heart, Theodorakis,
and you know how cold they
    are.
But we also know that they are
    too cold
and much too old, that they are
    dead
now that our day is
    approaching.
That day,
when the sun will dance.
The red day of freedom in
    Athens.
That day,
when we'll dance in the streets
and get together again.

2.

The enemies of these parasites—
    they
are your friends. There are many
    of them
and they live everywhere.
On their long march, your songs
    are

a short rest in a cool, deep
    valley.
So they hate your songs, our
    enemies do.
Your name strikes
their worm-ridden ears like a
    blow.
And in the barking of their
    voices,
in their squinting eyes
is the fear of that day.
Of that day,
when the sun will dance . . .

3.

And they're freezing in their
    white houses,
these old men. Their thousand-
    fold fear
is being watched by thousands.
Like their great white father,
the nation-killer Johnson,
they never turn off the lights at
    night.
For they know that those who
    are waiting
for tomorrow are everywhere
and that they are vigilant.
Look! The night is ending
Their stars are growing
    dim.
Soon, day will begin.
That day,
when the sun will dance . . .

Translated by
Richard J. Rundell

Großes Gebet der alten Kommunistin
Oma Meume in Hamburg

Text: Wolf Biermann, 1968
Music: Wolf Biermann, 1968

1.

O Gott, lieber Gott im Himml,
   hör mich betn
Zu Dir schrei ich wie in der
   Kinderzeit
Warum hat mich mein armer
   Vater nicht zertretn
Als ich noch selig schlief in
   Mutters Leib
Nun bin ich alt, ein graues
   taubes Weib
Mein kurzes Leben lang war
   reichlich Not
Viel Kampf mein Gott,
   viel für das bißchen
   Brot
Nach Friedn schrie ich in die
   großn Kriege
Und was hab ich erreicht? Bald
   bin ich tot
O Gott, laß DU den
   Kommunismus siegn!

2.

Gott, glaube mir: Nie wird der
   Mensch das schaffn
Ich hab mich krumm gelegt für
   die Partei
Erinner Dich, wie ich Karl
   Scholz mit Waffn
Bei mir versteckt hab und
   bekocht dabei!
Auf Arbeit Tag für Tag die
   Schinderei

Dann dieser Hitler, das vergeß
   ich nie
Wie brach unsre Partei da in die
   Knie
Die Bestn starbn im KZ wie
   Fliegn
Die Andern sind verreckt im
   Krieg wie Vieh
O Gott, laß DU den
   Kommunismus siegn!

3.

Mensch, Gott! Wär uns bloß *der*
   erspart gebliebn
Der Stalin, meintwegen durch
   ein Attntat
Gott, dieser Teufel hat es fast
   getriebn
—verzeih—wie ein Faschist im
   Sowjetstaat
Und war doch selber
   Kommunist und hat
Millionen Kommunisten
   umgebracht
Und hat das Volk geknecht mit
   all der Macht
Und log das Aas, daß sich die
   Balkn biegn
Was hat der Hund uns aufn
   Hund gebracht
O Gott, laß DU den
   Kommunismus siegn!

4.

(STOSSGEBET)
Mach, daß mein herznslieber
    Wolf nicht endet
Wie schon sein Vater hinter
    Stachldraht!
Mach, daß sein wirrer Sinn sich
    wieder wendet
Zu der Partei, die ihn verstoßn hat
Und mach mir drüben unsern
    Friednsstaat

So reich und frei, daß kein
    Schwein mehr abhaut
Und wird dann auch die Mauer
    abgebaut
Kann Oma Meume selig auf
    zum Himml fliegn
Sie hat ja nicht umsonst auf
    Dich gebaut
Dann, lieber Gott, wird auch der
    Kommunismus siegn!

THE OLD COMMUNIST GRANDMA MEUME'S GREAT PRAYER IN HAMBURG

1.

GOD, dear God in Heaven, hear
    me praying
I call you now as when I was a kid.
Why did my poor old
    father not destroy me
While in my mother's womb I
    still lay hid?
Now that I'm old, a grey and
    deaf old woman,
The whole of my short life was
    plagued with need.
A lot of struggle, God, just for a
    little bread.
I strained my voice for peace in
    two great wars
And what did I achieve? Soon
    I'll be dead.
O GOD, can't YOU make
    communism triumph?!

I've bent my back to serve the
    party's good.
Remember how I hid Karl
    Scholz at my place,
His guns and all, and even his
    cooked food.
I've grafted day by day for the
    oppressor;
And then that Hitler, him I
    won't forget.
How then our party broke down
    on its knees;
The best all died in
    concentration camps,
The others snuffed it in the war
    like fleas.
O GOD, can't YOU make
    communism triumph?!

2.

God, believe me, man will never
    do it.

3.

Christ, God, if we'd only been
    spared Stalin.

To my mind there was one to
  assassinate;
God, that bastard carried on—
  forgive me—
Almost like a fascist in a Soviet
  state
And yet he was a communist
  himself
But still put tons of communists
  to death,
And put the screws on people
  with his might,
And lied, the sod, until the roof
  fell in.
The pig, he really had us on all
  right.
O GOD, can't YOU make
  communism triumph?!

4. [FINAL PRAYER]
God, please see my dearest Wolf
  don't end up

Like his father did behind
  barbed wire;
See his wayward mind is quickly
  reconciled
To the party which went and
  kicked him out.
And for my sake please make it
  over there
That peaceful state we want
  that's rich and free,
So that no bugger hops the wall
  and then
They can pull it down and I'll
  die happy
To know I didn't trust in you in
  vain,
Dear God, 'cos only then will
  communism triumph!

Translated by
Steve Gooch

DAS HÖLDERLIN-LIED

Text: Wolf Biermann, 1972
Music: Wolf Biermann, 1972
«*So kam ich unter die Deutschen*»

1.
In diesem Lande leben wir
wie Fremdlinge im eigenen Haus
Die eigne Sprache, wie sie uns
entgegenschlägt, verstehn wir
  nicht
noch verstehen, was wir sagen,
die unsre Sprache sprechen
In diesem Lande leben wir wie
  Fremdlinge.

2.
In diesem Lande leben wir
wie Fremdlinge im eigenen Haus
Durch die zugenagelten Fenster
  dringt nichts
nicht wie gut das ist, wenn
  draußen regnet
noch des Windes übertriebene
  Nachricht
vom Sturm

In diesem Lande leben wir wie
   Fremdlinge.

3.

In diesem Lande leben wir
wie Fremdlinge im eigenen Haus
Ausgebrannt sind die Öfen der
   Revolution

früherer Feuer Asche liegt uns
   auf den Lippen
kälter, immer kältre Kälten
   sinken in uns
Über uns ist hereingebrochen
solcher Friede! solcher
   Friede
Solcher Friede.

THE HÖLDERLIN SONG

"Thus I came among the Germans"

1.

In this land we live
like strangers in our own house.
We don't understand our own
   language
as it slaps us in the face
nor do those who speak our
   language
understand what we say.
In this land we live like
   strangers.

2.

In this land we live
like strangers in our own house.
Nothing gets through the
   boarded-up windows
neither the good news about
   the rain outside

nor the wind's excessive tidings
   of the storm.
In this land we live like strangers.

3.

In this land we live
like strangers in our own house.
The ovens of the Revolution
   have burned out.
the ashes of earlier fires lie on
   our lips
colder, ever colder coldness
   sinks in us
What peace breaks in upon us
   what peace!
   what peace!
   What peace.

Translator unknown

JA, DIESES DEUTSCHLAND MEINE ICH

Text: Franz Josef Degenhardt, 1972
Music: Franz Josef Degenhardt, 1972

1.

Da, wo die Arbeit und
die Frau, mit der du lebst,
dein Auto und der Lohn,
der Anzug, den du trägst,
und was du sonst noch gern
    hast,
liest und hörst und siehst,
nicht morgen schon der Schnee
vom vorigen Jahre ist,
und wo du sicher weißt,
daß auch in dreißig Jahrn
die Dinge, die du tatst,
die meisten, richtig warn,
wo man noch lernen kann,
wie man's dann richtig macht,
und wo man alt wird, ohne,
daß da einer lacht—
da ist nichts großartig,
das soll es auch nicht sein,
weil wo was groß ist,
ist es drumherum meist klein,
und wo ihr alles macht,
daß euch da niemand stört,
weil nämlich euch das Land
und niemand sonst gehört,
ja, dieses Deutschland meine ich,
wo wir uns finden
unter den Linden
und auch noch anderswo.

2.

Du machst mal blau 'n Tag,
das leistest du dir, Mann,
und ziehst herum und siehst
dir euren Laden an,
so über Land im Herbst,
wenn eingefahren ist
und du die Felder weit
und ohne Zäune siehst,
guckst in paar Ställe rein,
packst hier und da mit an,
ihr sagt, was gut ist,
was man besser machen kann,
und gehst auch in ein Werk,
wo deine Kumpel sind,
hörst hin, was man da so
in der Kantine spinnt,
und mischst dich ein und zeigst,
wie weit ihr drüben seid,
und nehmt paar Schluck dabei,
und ihr kriegt keinen Streit,
und riechst und hörst dich um,
was sich so alles tut,
und gehst nach Haus und
    denkst:
Im großen Ganzen gut,
ja, diese Deutschland . . .

3.

Ja, dieses Deutschland meine
    ich,
das endlich denen gehört,
die tausend Jahre lang
geschafft und produziert,
in Schlachten abgeschlacht'
zum Nutzen für paar Herrn
bis zu der letzten Schlacht,
da schlugen sie die Herrn,
wo dieser lange Weg
nur noch Geschichte ist

und auch Geschichte bleibt,
weil man sie nicht vergißt,
und darum liest du an
den Straßen, Plätzen dann
so Namen wie die
Rosa Luxemburg, Ernst
    Thälmann,
Lumumba, Ho-chi Minh

und Solidarität,
weil nämlich anderswo
der Kampf noch weitergeht,
und ist kein Traum das Land,
geträumt aus rotem Mohn,
nämlich ein Stück davon
das gibt es schon,
ja, dieses Deutschland . . .

THIS IS THE GERMANY I MEAN

1.
The place you've got your job,
Where you live with your wife,
Your car, your salary,
Whatever else you like,
The suit you've got on,
The books you like to read—
That place will not become
The snows of yesteryear,
It's where you're sure to know
Most of the things you did
Were right, and still will be
Some thirty years from now,
Where you can still bone up
On how things should be done,
Grow old with dignity,
Not laughed at or ignored.
It's not a great big place,
Nor was it meant to be,
For anything that's small
Tends to be great inside.
The place where you make sure
To guard your safety, for
This land belongs to you,
And not to someone else.
This is the Germany I mean,
Where we can congregate
Beneath the linden-trees
And other places too.

2.
You take a day off work,
You can afford to do that, man,
You walk and look around
At what your shop is like.
The countryside in fall,
When all the harvest's in,
You see the fields stretch wide,
No fences and no end,
You peek into some barns
And lend a hand sometimes,
You tell them all "good work!",
"This needs to be improved."
You visit some plant where
Your buddies have a job,
Sit in the dining-room
And listen to them talk,
Chime in and then show off,
We're way ahead of you!
Then everybody downs
A glass or two, no fights,
You sniff, you listen hard
To hear what's going on,
Then you go home and think
It's going pretty well.
This is the Germany I mean,
Where we can congregate
Beneath the linden-trees
And other places too.

3.

This is the Germany I mean,
Which finally belongs to those
Who worked and who produced
These thousand years or more,
Who died in battles fought
To benefit some lords—
But in the final fight,
We did defeat those lords!
It's where this winding road
Is only history,
And where it stays that way
So that we don't forget,
And that is why you read
The name-plates on the streets,
With names of heroes like
Rosa Luxemburg, Ernst
    Thaelmann,

Lumumba, Ho Chi Minh,
And worker solidarity,
The Revolution still
Needs to be won elsewhere.
The nation of red poppies
Is not an empty dream,
It really does exist,
We've got a piece right
    here.
This is the Germany I
    mean,
Where we can congregate
Beneath the linden-trees
And other places too.

Translated by
Alexandra Chciuk-Celt

KINDER

Text: Bettina Wegner, 1981
Music: Bettina Wegner, 1981

1.
Sind so kleine Hände
winzige Finger dran.
Darf man nie drauf schlagen
die zerbrechen dann.

2.
Sind so kleine Füße
mit so kleinen Zehn.
Darf man nie drauf treten
könn sie sonst nicht gehn.

3.
Sind so kleine Ohren
scharf, und ihr erlaubt.
Darf man nie zerbrüllen
werden davon taub.

4.
Sind so schöne Münder
sprechen alles aus.
Darf man nie verbieten
kommt sonst nichts mehr raus.

5.
Sind so klare Augen
die noch alles sehn.
Darf man nie verbinden
könn sie nichts verstehn.

6.
Sind so kleine Seelen
offen und ganz frei.
Darf man niemals quälen
gehn kaputt dabei.

7.
Ist son kleines Rückgrat
sieht man fast noch nicht.
Darf man niemals beugen
weil es sonst zerbricht.

8.
Grade, klare Menschen
wärn ein schönes Ziel.
Leute ohne Rückgrat
hab'n wir schon zuviel.

CHILDREN

1.
Hands, the hands so little,
tiny fingers there.
Shouldn't ever slap them,
that they cannot bear.

2.
Feet, the feet so little,
with each wee, tiny toe.
Shouldn't ever stomp them,
else they cannot go.

3.
Ears, the ears so little,
sharp, a little cat.
Shouldn't ever shut them,
else will nothing flow.

4.
Mouths, the mouths so
    lovely
utter all they know.
Shouldn't ever shut them,
else will nothing flow.

5.
Eyes, the eyes so limpid,
still see everything.
Shouldn't ever bind them,
can't see anything.

6.
Souls, the souls so little,
open, free, sincere.
Shouldn't ever torment,
get done with fear.

7.
Spine, the spine so little,
you can hardly see.
Shouldn't ever bend it,
breaks so easily.

8.
Tall, clear-headed people,
goal for those who care.
Folks who turn out spineless
we've more than our fair share.

Translated by Dietmar Pieper

KIRSCHEN AUF SAHNE

Text: Dieter Süverkrüp, 1967
Music: Dieter Süverkrüp, 1967

In dem klei-nen Café mit dem Kopfschmerzenlicht sitzt ein
Lie-bes-paar drin, so als wär's in Pa-ris, a-ber
da ist es nicht. In dem kleinen Ca-fé sitzt der
zitt-ri-ge Mann mit der Nar-be am Au-ge, das
blickt die Ver-lieb-ten so freundschaftlich an. Die-ses
Au-ge blieb heil in fünf Jah-ren Ka-zett und am
Ne-ben-tisch Sah-ne mit Kir-schen, die Da-me ist
schön __ a-ber fett. Kirschen auf Sah-ne
Blutspur im Schnee ei-ne Mark fünf-zig
sanf - - tes Kli-schee. __ schee. __

1.

In dem kleinen Café
mit dem Kopfschmerzenlicht
sitzt ein Liebespaar drin
so als wär's in Paris
aber da ist es nicht

in dem kleinen Café
sitzt der zittrige Mann
mit der Narbe am Auge
das blickt die Verliebten
so freundschaftlich an

dieses Auge blieb heil
in fünf Jahren Kazett
sieht am Nebentisch Sahne
mit Kirschen die Dame
ist schön aber fett

Kirschen auf Sahne
Blutspur im Schnee
eine Mark fünfzig
sanftes Klischee.

2.

In dem kleinen Café
Kriminalfernsehzeit
nur der Wilddieb in Öl
im Barockrahmen starrt
auf die Ewigkeit

und der alte Mann der
mal im Widerstand war
spricht nicht gerne davon
pro Tag Auschwitz fünf
   Mark
wieviel macht das im Jahr?

wenn die Liebenden gehn
   müssen
grüßen sie matt
zu dem Zittermann hin
weil er ihnen so auf-
merksam zugeschaut hat

manche warn' Juden
manche war'n rot'
dreißig Verletzte
schimmliges Brot.

3.

Und da denkt er es hat sich
vielleicht doch gelohnt
und die Schmerzen komm'n
   wieder
er setzt sich gerade
er ist es gewohnt

der Geschenkevertreter
trink unentwegt Bier
es nistet das Graun in
der Rokokovase
gleich neben der Tür

und der zitternde Mann
wird verlegen und geht
denn er schämt sich weil all
die verdammte Erinnerung
nicht mehr verweht

Leben ist Leben
wer hat das nicht
zehntausend Tote
Neon macht Licht.

CHERRIES AND CREAM

1.
In the little café
with the candlelit glare
sit a couple of lovers
as if it were Paris
but they aren't there

in the little café
sits the tremble-y man
a scar over the eye
who watches the lovers
so amiably

his eye stayed unscathed
through five years in a camp
on the table nearby cream
with cherries the lady seems
really quite plump.

Cherries with cream
blood in the snow in a way
just one mark fifty
a gentle cliché.

2.
In the little café
prime detective show time
only the poacher in oils
in the baroque frame stares
into eternity

and the old man who
once fought in the rear
now talks reluctantly of
Auschwitz at five marks a day
how much is that in a year?
When the lovers get up to leave

they nod with a weak smile
to the tremble-er there
since he had been watch-
ing so keen all the while

some of 'em were Jews
some of 'em were red
thirty of them wounded
had only mouldy bread.

3.
And he thinks that just maybe
it had been worthwhile
and the pains come anew
so he sits up quite straight
that's now part of his style

the gifts representative
incessantly drinks beer
he shoves all the horror
in the rococo vase
right near the door here

and the tremble-y man,
gets embarrassed and leaves
for he is ashamed 'cause all
of the damned memories
that have no reprieves

Living is living
it's been so for an eon
ten thousand dead men
light's made form neon.

Translated by
Marilya Veteto-Conrad

LIED VON DER GEDANKENFREIHEIT

Text: Walter Mossmann, 1980
Music: Walter Mossmann

1.
Ach, das waren finstre Zeiten
finstre Zeiten waren das
als man die Gedanken jagte
und dabei die Köpfe traf.
Wenn der Volksmund Lieder
    plärrte
gegen Papst und Königshaus
riß man ihm auch gleich die
    Zunge
mit den Lästerliedern aus.
Selbst die allergrößten Geister
litten unter der Zensur
und der dünne Straßensänger
saß im Knast zur Schweigekur.
Diese Zeiten sind vorbei
Die Gedanken sind frei

2.
Heute sind das helle
helle Zeiten sind das heut.
Ja, ich sag euch, daß mich heute
die Gedankenfreiheit freut.
Neulich schrieb ich meine wahre
Meinung von der Bundeswehr
und ich trug sie hin ins
    Funkhaus
hin zu meinem Redakteur.
Ach, der hat mich nicht
    erschlagen
nicht gefoltert, nicht gepfählt
—bloß die Sendung nicht
    gesendet
und jetzt mangelt mir das Geld.
Also bleibet es dabei:
Die Gedanken sind frei

3.
Meine Freundin die ist Lehrerin
hat einen blonden Schopf
außen blond und innen helle
und sehr hart ist auch der Kopf.
Sie erklärte ihren Schülern
«Auch der Papst ist bloß ein Mann
ohne Kinder, ohne Pille
und den geht mein Bauch nichts
    an.»
Der Direktor ist katholisch
kugelrund und gar nicht grob
und der schrieb ihr einen Brief
und heute hat sie keinen Job.
Also bleibet es dabei:
Die Gedanken sind frei

4.
Mein Freund Fritz schafft bei
    Mercedes
und er ist organisiert
ich weiß nicht, auf welcher Linie
weil mich so ein Strich verwirrt.
Jedenfalls bei der Betriebsver-
    sammlung
meckert er laut,
weil Mercedes die Arbeiter
um den Arbeitslohn beklaut.
Sein Chef hat ihm nicht das
    Maul gestopft
und auch keinen Strick gedreht
Nur daß Fritz jetzt auch im
    Arbeitsamt
alltäglich Schlange steht.
Also bleibet es dabei:
Die Gedanken sind frei

5.

Also sieht man, daß es die
     finstern
finstern Zeiten nicht mehr gibt.
Grad die höhere Kritik ist doch
in unserm Staat beliebt.
Doch man muß sie mächtig
     heben
aus dem grauen Alltags-Dunst
dann sagt auch mal ein Minister

«Schön und kritisch ist die
     Kunst!»
Und der große Künstler achte
daß er nur nach Beifall schielt
schielt er nämlich nach
     Veränderung
hat er bald ausgespielt
Also bleibet es dabei:
Nur die Gedanken sind frei.

FREEDOM OF THOUGHT SONG

1.

Ah, those were dark times,
dark times they were indeed;
when people hunted thoughts
but hit other people's heads.
When folks sang songs
against the Pope and the king,
they got their tongues ripped out
along with their heretical songs.
Even the greatest thinkers
suffered under censorship,
and the poor streetsinger
got sentenced to silence in jail.
Those times are past—
Our thoughts are free.

2.

Today we live in bright times;
Bright times are ours indeed.
Yes, I can happily tell you,
     today
freedom of thought is secure.
Recently I wrote my frank
opinion about the army
and took it to the radio station
to my friend the announcer.
Well, he didn't beat me up,

he didn't torture me or lynch me
—he just didnt' broadcast it,
and now I need the money.
So the fact remains—
Our thoughts are free.

3.

My girlfriend is a teacher
wiht short blonde hair;
blonde outside and bright inside,
and she's got a hard head, too.
One time she told her pupils
"Even the Pope is merely a man
with no kids not on the pill,
and my body is none of his
     business."
The principal is a Catholic,
chubby and not crude at all,
and he wrote her a letter—
and today she doesn't have a job.
So the fact remains—
Our thoughts are free.

4.

My friend Fritz works for
     Mercedes

and he belongs to the union;
I don't know his politics,
because that stuff just confuses
 me.
Anyway, at factory meetings
he complains a lot,
because Mercedes is cheating
workers out of their fair wages.
His boss didn't shut his mouth
or wring his neck—
but Fritz is now in line
at the unemployment office.
So the fact remains—
Our thoughts are free.

5.
So you can see that the dark,
dark times are past and gone.

Elevated criticism is truly
welcome throughout our
 land.
But you must raise it well
above the grey haze of
 everyday.
Then a politician will say
"Art is fine and critical!"
And a great artist sees to it
that he only cares about
 applause;
if he bothers about change
then he's soon washed up.
Therefore the fact remains—
Only our thoughts are free.

Translated by
Richard J. Rundell

Manchmal sagen die Kumpanen

Text: Franz Josef Degenhardt, 1968
Music: Franz Josef Degenhardt

1.
Manchmal sagen die Kumpanen
jetzt, was soll denn dieser
 Scheiß?
Wo sind deine Zwischentöne?
Du malst bloß noch schwarz
 und weiß.
Na schön, sag ich, das ist ja
 richtig,
aber das ist jetzt nicht wichtig.
Zwischentöne sind bloß
 Krampf
im Klassenkampf.

2.
Auch die alten Kunden klagen,

wo bleibt Ihre Poesie?
Dinge bilderreich umschreiben,
andeuten, das können Sie.
Na schön, sag ich, das ist ja
 richtig,
aber das ist jetzt nicht wichtig.
Schöne Poesie ist Krampf
im Klassenkampf.

3.
Einen Scheißhaufen zu malen,
das nutzt gar nichts. Der muß
 weg.
Und trotz aller schönen Künste
stinkt der Dreck nach Dreck.

Daß er daliegt, ist nicht richtig.
Daß er weg muß, das ist
　　wichtig.
Schöne Künste sind bloß
　　Krampf,
im Klassenkampf.

4.
Und um es genau zu sagen
ohne alle Poesie:
Weg muß der Kapitalismus,
her muß die Demokratie.
Ja, genau das ist jetzt richtig,
alles andre nicht so wichtig.

Alles andere ist Krampf
im Klassenkampf.

5.
Und der Dichter, der poetisch
protestiert in seinem Lied,
bringt den Herrschenden ein
　　Ständchen
und erhöht ihren (und seinen)
　　Profit.
Und genau das ist nicht richtig,
und genau das ist nicht wichtig.
Protestieren ist bloß Krampf
im Klassenkampf.

THESE DAYS THE GUYS MIGHT SAY

1.
These days the guys might say,
to me, what is this crap?
Where is your subtlety?
Black-white is all you tap.
Okay, I say, that may be so,
but it's the only way to go,
because when the classes fight,
subtlety is just not right.

2.
Old customers complain,
is your sense for poetics muted?
Figurative language, imagery,
allusions are what you're good
　　at.
Okay, I say, that may be so,
it's just not the way to go,
because when the classes fight,
allusions and imagery are not
　　right.
3.
The painting of a pile of shit

is useless and no cure,
and despite all the fine arts
manure stinks like manure.
Its mere existence is a no,
the point is that it has to go.
In the heat of the classes' fight
the use of fine arts is not right.

4.
And to be precise and plain,
void of all poetry:
The capitalist system has to go.
We need democracy.
Yes, that is the way to go,
everything else is far below,
because when the classes fight
nothing short of that is right.

5.
If the poet lyrically
protests in his song,
he simply serenades his rulers,

helping their (and his) profit
  along.
And to that I shout my no,
that's just not the way to go,

because when the classes fight,
poetic protest is not right.

Translated by
Sabine Tober

MARSCH DER MINDERHEIT

Text: Hanns Dieter Hüsch, 1968
Music: Hanns Dieter Hüsch

1.
Freunde, noch sind wir wenige
Doch täglich werden es mehr
Wir sind weder Playboy noch
  Könige
Und wir haben kein grausames
  Heer
Doch wir sind auf dem Marsch
Schon Jahrhunderte weit
Durch Flüsse und Dschungel,
  Gebirge und Eis
Auf dem Marsch der Minderheit

2.
Man kann uns verbieten
Man kann uns bespein
Man kann uns den Löwen
Zum Fraße hinstreun
Man kann uns in Katakomben
  treiben
Man kann uns in Ghettos
  zusammenfassen
Man kann uns die härteste
  Folter beschreiben
Und uns die Folter auch spüren
  lassen

3.
Man kann uns Nägel und
  tödliche Pfeile

Durch unsere freundlichen
  Hände schlagen
Man kann uns durch Sümpfe
  und faulende Wälder
Mit Wolfshunden jagen,
  Freunde
Wir sind auf dem Marsch
Schon jahrhundertelang
Trommel und Traum
Sind in unsrem Gesang

4.
Man kann uns in lieblichen
  Gärten
Als Vergnügungsfackeln
  verbrennen
Doch man kann unsre Herzen
Nicht von unsren Hoffnungen
  trennen
Doch wir sind auf dem
  Marsch
Schon jahrtausende lang
Von Peking bis Rom und von
  Rom bis Harlem
Und von Harlem bis Da Nang.

5.
Freunde, noch sind wir wenige
Aber täglich werden es mehr

Und wir haben kein
grausames Heer
Wir sind auf dem Marsch
Für eine bessere Welt
Für eine glücklichere Zeit

Sind wir auf dem Marsch
Auf dem Marsch der Minderheit
Auf dem Marsch der Minderheit

Auf dem Marsch der Minderheit

MARCH OF THE MINORITY

1.
Friends, few in number are we
But daily we increase
Neither playboy nor king are we
We have no grisly companies
But we've been on the march
For centuries already
Through far rivers, jungles,
    mountains, ice
On the march of the minority

2.
They can proscribe us
And spit on us cast [???]
They can throw us to lions
For daily repast
In catacombs they can drive us
Clap us in a ghetto and seal it
The deadliest of tortures
    contrive us
And torment us then so that we
    feel it

3.
Sharp nails and also most deadly
    arrows
They pound and drive through
    our friendly hands
With wolfhounds they hunt us
    through noisome swamps
And rotting woods, my friends
But we've been on the march
For centuries long

Drumbeat and dream
Are in our song

4.
They can hang us in sweet-
    smelling gardens
And torch us bound with ropes
But they cannot from our hearts
Cut out our invincible hopes
For we've been on a march
For centuries long
From Peking to Rome and from
    Rome to Harlem
And from Harlem on to
    DaNang

5.
Friends, few in number are we
But daily we increase
Neither playboy nor king
    are we
We have no grisly companies
But we are on the march
For a far better world
For a happier time are we
Now on the march
On the march of the minority
On the march of the minority

On the march of the minority

Translated by
A. Leslie Willson

MORITAT AUF BIERMANN SEINE OMA MEUME IN HAMBURG

Text: Wolf Biermann, 1968
Music: Wolf Biermann, 1968

1.
Als meine Oma ein Baby war
Vor achtundachzig Jahrn
Da ist ihre Mutter im
    Wochenbett
Mit Schwindsucht zum Himmel
    gefahrn
Als meine Oma ein Baby war
Ihr Vater war Maschinist
Bis gleich darauf die rechte
    Hand
Ihm abgerissen ist

2.
Das war an einem Montag früh
Da riß die Hand ihm ab
Er war noch froh, daß die
    Fabrik
Den Wochenlohn ihm gab
Als meine Oma ein Baby war
Mit ihrem Vater allein
Da fing der Vater das Saufen an
Und ließ das Baby schrein

3.
Dann ging er in die Küche rein
Und auf den Küchenschrank
Da stellte er ganz oben rauf
Die kleine Küchenbank
Und auf die Bank zwei Koffer
    noch
Und auf den schiefen Turm
Ganz oben rauf aufs Federbett
Das kleine Unglückswurm

4.
Dann ging er mit dem letzten
    Geld
IN MEYERS FREUDENHAUS
Und spülte mit Pfefferminz-
    Absinth
Sich das Gewissen raus
Und kam zurück im
    Morgengraun
Besoffen und beschissen
Und stellte fest: «Verflucht, das
    Wurm
Hat sich nicht totgeschmissen!»

5.
Das Kind lag friedlich da und
    schlief
Hoch oben auf dem Turm
Da packte er mit seiner Hand
Das kleine Unglückswurm
Nahm es behutsam in den Arm
Und weinte Rotz und Wasser
Und lallte ihm ein Wiegenlied
Vor Glück und Liebe fraß er

6.
Der Oma fast ein Öhrchen ab
Und schwor, nie mehr zu
    trinken
Und weil er Maschinist gewesen
    war
Schwor er das mit der Linken
Das ist ein Menschenalter her
Hätt sie sich totgeschmissen

Dann würde ich von alledem
Wahrscheinlich garnix wissen

7.
Die Alte lebt heut immer noch
Und kommst du mal nach
    Westen
Besuch sie mal und grüß sie schön
Vom Enkel, ihrem besten
Und wenn sie nach mir fragt
    und weint
Und auf die Mauer flucht
Dann sage ihr: Bevor sie stirbt
Wird sie noch mal besucht

8.
Und während du von mir
    erzählst
Schmiert sie dir, erster
    Klasse
Ein Schmalzbrot, dazu
    Muckefuck
In einer blauen Tasse
Vielleicht hat sie auch Lust, und
    sie
Erzählt dir paar
    Geschichten
Und wenn die schön sind, komm
    zurück
Die mußt du mir berichten

MORITAT FOR BIERMANN'S GRANDMA MEUME IN HAMBURG

1.
When my old Gran was just a
    babe
Eighty-eight years ago
Her mother got TB in labor
And to heaven she did go
When my old Gran was just a
    babe
Her father turned a machine
Until one day it turned on him
And took his hand off clean

2.
It was Monday morning
    when
His hand was whipped away
He thanked his lucky stars the
    firm
Gave him a full week's pay
When my old Gran was just a
    babe
She'd just her Dad, that's all

But then he took to boozing
    beer
And let the baby bawl

3.
He went into the scullery
And on the cabinet
He put right at the very top
Their tiny kitchen seat
And on the seat two suitcases
And on this wobbling castle
Lying on her featherbed
The poor unlucky parcel

4.
Then off to Meyer's Pleasure-
    House
He took his last week's
    pay
And downing peppermint-
    absinth

He came back at the break of
   day
With booze still on his breath
And cursed to see the kid had
   not
Fallen to her death

5.
The child lay there in peace and
   slept
High up on that castle
So then with his one hand he
   grabbed
The poor unlucky parcel
He took her gently in his arms
And slobbering snot and water
He hummed to her a lullaby
Of love and joy to his daughter

6.
He nearly chewed my Gran's ear
   off
He vowed to drink no more
he swore with his left hand
   because
He'd turned machines before
All this was many years ago
If she'd fallen then and there

I wouldn't now be here to sing
About the whole affair

7.
The old girl's still alive today
And if you're over in the West
Look her up and wish her from
Her grandson all the best
And if she asks about me, cries
And rages at The Wall
Please tell her that before she
   dies
I'll come to pay a call

8.
And while you're telling her my
   news
She'll make you soup, none finer
Bread and dripping too she'll do
All served on her best china
Perhaps the mood'll take her
   and
She'll tell a tale or two
And if they're good, when you
   get back
I'd like to hear them too.

Translated by Steve Gooch

OSTERMARSCHLIED 68

Text: Franz Josef Degenhardt, 1968
Music: Franz Josef Degenhardt

1.
Da habt ihr es, das Argument
   der Straße.
Sagt bloß jetzt nicht: nur ein
   Verrückter schießt.
Ihr kennt sie doch, die grinsende
   Grimasse,

die sagt, daß auch der Dutschke
   noch ein Mensch ist.
Ihr habt gewußt, wie man uns
   hetzt und jagt.
Ihr habt es Tag für Tag
   gesehen.

Es kotzt mich an, wie ihr jetzt
  laut beklagt
ein sogenanntes tragisches
  Geschehen.

2.
Was nützt Protest Entrüstung
  Klagen!
Ihr wißt genau, wer jene Mörder
  sind.
Die haben Liebknecht, Rosa
  Luxemburg erschlagen.
Die Hintermänner kennt doch
  jedes Kind.
Sie sind noch da. Und sie
  regieren hier,
die ihren dreckigen Profit aus
  allem schlagen.
Die legen jene einfach um, die das
Geschäft zu stören wagen.

3.
Macht endlich Schluß mit
  diesem faulen Frieden,
mit unserer Angst die Springer
  täglich schürt.
Sonst wird uns wieder mal ein
  sogenanntes Los
  beschieden,
das uns zum dritten Male an die
  Schlachtbank führt.

4.
Beginnt! sofort! die Zeit langt
  kaum noch hin,
die Zwischenhändler reiben sich
  die Hände
und rechnen auf den ganz
  großen Gewinn
und unser Ende.

EASTER MARCH SONG 1968

1.
There you have it, the argument
  of the streets
Now don't say, "Only a crazy
  man would shoot a gun."
You recognize it, that grinning
  grimace.
that says that even Dutschke's a
  human being.
You knew how to provoke us
  and pursue us.
You watched it day after
  day.
It makes me puke, the way you
  now loudly complain
about what you call a tragic
  occurrence.

2.
What good is protesting, or
  outrage, or complaining?
You know exactly who the
  killers are.
They beat Liebknecht and Rosa
  Luxemburg to death.
Every child knows who's behind
  it all.
They're still there. And they're
  running things here,
sucking their filthy profit out of
  everything.
They just wipe out anyone
  who
dares to get in the way of
  business.

3.

Let's finally end this phony truce
and end our fear which Springer stirs up daily.
Or else we'll once again get a raw deal
and get dragged to slaughter a third time.

4.

Begin! Right now! there isn't much time left,
the middlemen are rubbing their hands
and counting on really big profits
and the end of us.

Translation by
Richard J. Rundell

SIEBEN FRAGEN EINES SCHÜLERS UND SIEBEN FREIHEITLICH-DEMOKRATISCH-GRUNDORDENTLICHE ANTWORTEN

Text: Walter Mossmann, 1980
Music: Walter Mossmann

1.

Sag mal, sag mal, sag mal Herr Lehrer
Wie war das im Alten Rom
Cäsars Schlachten und Schlächtereien
die stehn mir schon bis hier oben
Was lehrt uns die Geschichte vom Spartacus
Wie macht man mit der Knechschaft Schluß
Still mein Junge sei still
Wenn ich sowas sagen will
Dann will ich doch schon viel zuviel.

2.

Sag mal, sag mal, sag mal Herr Lehrer
Wie war das in den Bauernkriegen

Warum war der Luther drauf scharf
daß die Bauernschinder siegen
Was hat der Thomas Müntzer gedacht
Wie haben die den bewaffneten Aufstand gemacht
O wei mein Junge o wei
Ich hab eine Zunge aus Blei
Und fühl mich doch dabei ganz frei.

3.

Sag mal, sag mal, sag mal Herr Lehrer
Was war Achtzehnachtundvierzig los
Die schwarz-rot-goldene Trauermesse
in der Paulskirche langweilt mich bloß

Waren da nicht auch rote
    Fahnen gewest
und das kommunistische
    Manifest
Nee mein Junge nee
Ich bin von Kopf bis Zeh
eingestellt als
Beamter in Spe.

4.
Sag mal, sag mal, sag mal Herr
    Lehrer
Achtzehneinundsiebzig in Paris
War die deutsche Fahne nicht in
    Blut getaucht
im Versailler Spiegel-Paradies
Wir lernen nur die Sprüche von
    der Kaiser-Tribüne
Was aber lehrt uns die Pariser
    Commune
O Schreck mein Junge o Schreck
Steck den «Bürgerkrieg in
    Frankreich» bloß weg
Ich flieg, wenn man den hier
    entdeckt
in Dreck.

5.
Sag mal, sag mal, sag mal Herr
    Lehrer
Was kam nach der deutschen
    Monarchie
War da nicht eine Revolution
Und wo verblieb denn die
Du denkst so frei wie Marquis
    Posa
und sagst kein Wort über Karl
    und Rosa.
Verdammt mein Junge
    verdammt

Mir sind leider von Amts-
wegen die Genann-
ten nicht bekannt.

6.
Sag mal, sag mal, sag mal Herr
    Lehrer
Der Hitler, der war doch kein
    Vampir
der kam doch nicht aus dem
    Gully gekrochen
der kam doch nicht mir nichts
    dir . . . nichts
Wer hat den gebraucht, wer hat
    den bezahlt
Die Bourgeoisie oders
    Proletariat
Mann Junge Mann
Wenn ich dir das sage, dann
sag du mir auch wie lang
ich hier noch Lehrer bleiben
    kann . . .

7.
Sag mal, sag mal, sag mal Herr
    Lehrer
das interessiert uns jetzt
wie führt man heute den
    Klassenkampf
trotz Klassenjustiz und -gesetz
Wie kämpft man gegen das
    Berufsverbot
das dich kastriert, weil es dich
    bedroht
Na und mein Junge na und
Ich verbrenn mir halt nicht den
    Mund
Ich schwör dreimal aufs Grund-
gesetz und komm gesund
auf'n Hund.

8.

Hör mal, hör mal, hör mal Herr Lehrer wir stecken dir jetzt ein Licht Einen Lehrer, der nicht aus der Geschichte lernt den brauchen wir nicht	Wir brauchen einen Lehrer, der dem Volke nützt und trotzdem nicht auf der Straße sitzt *Und wie man das organisiert* *Daß sich jeder solidarisiert* *Das wird jetzt diskutiert.*

SEVEN QUESTIONS FROM A SCHOOLBOY AND SEVEN FREE, DEMOCRATIC, CONSTITUTIONALLY APPROPRIATE ANSWERS

1.

Tell me, tell me, tell me, teacher:
what was it like in ancient
   Rome?
Caesar's battles and
   slaughters—
I'm already fed up with them.
What does Spartacus' story
   teach us?
How do we make an end of
   slavery?
Quiet, my boy, be quiet!
If I want to talk of things like
   that,
then I already want much
   too much.

2.

Tell me, tell me, tell me teacher:
what was it like in the Peasant
   Wars?
Why was Luther so eager
to see the peasants' killers win?
What did Thomas Meuntzer
   think?
How did they start an armed
   rebellion?
Oh dear, my boy, oh dear!

My tongue feels like lead;
but I consider myself to be
Completely free.

3.

Tell me, tell me, tell me, teacher:
what was going on in 1848?
The black-red-and-gold requiem
   mass
in St. Paul's church is just boring
Weren't there red flags too,
and the Communist Manifesto?
No, my boy, oh no!
I am from head to toe
a civil servant for life—
I hope.

4.

Tell me, tell me, tell me,
   teacher:
in 1871 in Paris—
wasn't the German flag dipped
   in blood
in Versailles' wondrous Hall of
   Mirrors?
We only learn the Kaiser's
   slogans,

but what can we learn from the
  paris Commune?
Oh, heavens, my boy, goodness!
Put away that "Civil War in
  France";
I'll get fired if they find
That around here.

5.
Tell me, tell me, tell me,
  teacher:
what came after the German
  monarchy?
Wasn't there a revolution?
And what became of it?
You think as freely as Marquis
  Posa,
but you don't say a thing about
  Karl and Rosa.
Damn it, my boy!
I'm afraid I just can't
  officially
recognize those names.

6.
Tell me, tell me, tell me,
  teacher:
Hitler wasn't just some
  vampire;
he didn't crawl up out of the
  sewer;
he didn't just show up one
  day.
Who needed him, who paid for
  him?
The bourgeoisie or the
  proletariat?
Man oh man, my body!
If I told you that, then

You can just imagine how
  long
I could keep on teaching around
  here.

7.
Tell me, tell me, tell me, teacher:
we're really interested now;
How does the class struggle
  work today
in spite of class justice and class
  laws?
How can we fight against this
  loss of jobs
which castrates you as it
  threatens you?
So what, my boy, so what?
I'm not going to burn my
  fingers.
I'll just swear a loyalty oath
And stay healthy and keep out
  of trouble.

8.
Listen here, listen here, listen
  here, teacher:
we're going to wise you up!
A teacher who doesn't learn
  from history
we can easily do without;
we need a teacher who's useful
  to people
but isn't out of a job.
And how to organize things
So that people will show their
  solidarity—
now we'd like to discuss that.

Translated by
Richard J. Rundell

SPIEL NICHT MIT DEN SCHMUDDELKINDERN

Text: Franz Josef Degenhardt, 1964
Music: Franz Josef Degenhardt

Spiel nicht mit den
    Schmuddelkindern.
sing nicht ihre Lieder.
Geh doch in die Oberstadt.
mach's wie deine Brüder.

1.
So sprach die Mutter, sprach der
    Vater, lehrte der Pastor.
Er schlich aber immer wieder
    durch das Gartentor
und in die Kaninchenställe,
wo sie Sechsundsechzig spielten
um Tabak und Rattenfelle,
Mädchen unter Röcke schielten.
Wo auf alten Bretterkisten
Katzen in der Sonne dösten.
Wo man, wenn der Regen
    rauschte,
Engelbert, dem Blöden, lauschte,
der auf einen Haarkamm biß,
Rattenfängerlieder blies.
Abends, am Familientisch, nach
    dem Gebet zum Mahl,
hieß es dann: Du riechst schon
    wieder nach Kaninchenstall.
Spiel nicht mit den
    Schmuddelkindern,
sing nicht ihre Lieder.
Geh doch in die Oberstadt,
mach's wie deine Brüder!

2.
Sie trieben ihn in eine Schule in
    der Oberstadt,
kämmten ihm die Haare und die
    krause Sprache glatt.
Lernte Rumpf und Wörter
    beugen.
Und statt Rattenfängerweisen
mußte er das Largo geigen
und vor dürren Tantengreisen
unter roten Rattenwimpern
par coeur Kinderszenen
    klimpern
und verklemmt in Viererreihen,
Knochen morsch und morscher
    schreien,
zwischen Fahnen aufgestellt
brüllen, daß man Freundschaft
    hält.
Schlich er manchmal abends
    zum Kaninchenstall davon,
hockten da die Schmuddelkinder,
    sangen voller Hohn:
Spiel nicht mit . . .

3.
Aus Rache ist er reich geworden.
    In der Oberstadt
hat er sich ein Haus gebaut.
    nahm jeden Tag ein Bad,
Roch wie bessre Leute riechen,
lachte fett, wenn alle Ratten
ängstlich in die Gullys wichen,
weil sie ihn gerochen hatten,
und Kaninschenställe riß er
ab. An ihre Stelle ließ er
Gärten für die Kinder bauen.
Liebte hochgestellte Frauen.

schnelle Wagen und Musik,
blond und laut und honigdick.
Kam sein Sohn, der Nägelbeißer,
abends spät zum Mahl, roch
er an ihm, schlug ihn, schrie:
Stinkst nach Kaninchenstall.
Spiel nicht mit . . .

4.
Und eines Tages hat er eine
    Kurve glatt verfehlt.
Man hat ihn aus einem Ei von
    Schrott herausgepellt.
Als er später durch die
    Straßen

hinkte, sah man ihn an Tagen
auf 'nem Haarkamm Lieder blasen.
Rattenfell am Kragen tragen.
Hinkte hüpfend hinter Kindern,
wollte sie am Schulgang hindern
und schlich um Kaninchenställe.
Eines Tags in aller Helle
hat er dann ein Kind betört
und in einen Stall gezerrt.
Seine Leiche fand man, die im
    Rattenteich rumschwamm.
Drum herum die Schmuddel-
    kinder bliesen auf dem
    Kamm:
Spiel nicht mit . . .

DON'T PLAY WITH THOSE FILTHY CHILDREN

*Don't play with those filthy
children,
Stop singing their ditties.
Take your brothers as examples:
Your place is in the city.*

1.
Mother kept saying that, as did
father, as did the pastor. But he
kept slinking through the garden-
gate into the rabbit-cage area
where they played sixty-six and
peeked under girl's skirts: cards,
tobacco, rat-pelts, cats dozing in
the sun on old wooden crates.
When the rain poured, they
would listen for Stupid Engelbert
playing Pied Piper songs on a
comb to catch the rats.
    The same story every eve-
ning, while saying grace for

dinner: you stink like a rabbit-
cage again.

Don't play, etc.

2.
They pushed him into a classy
city school, combed his hair,
smoothed his coarse language.
He learned to bow his body and
his words, and instead of Pied
Piper songs, he had to play the
Largo for Violin and tinkle
"scénes d'enfants" from
memory for desiccated aunts
with red eyelashes like rats.
Squashed stiffly four abreast
between two flags, rows of boys
had to holler gung-ho buddy-
slogans of camaraderie. If he
tried slinking into the rabbit-
barn at night, the filthy children

camaraderie. If he tried slinking into the rabbit-barn at night, the filthy children would squat there and sing at him sarcastically:

Don't play, etc.

3.
He got even by getting rich. He built himself a house in the City, took a bath every day, smelled like classy people do, and chuckled richly when all the rats scurried into the alleys because they had smelled him coming. He tore down the rabbit-cages and built gardens for the children instead. He loved high-status women, fast cars, and music: blonde and loud and sticky-sweet respectively. Whenever his son came late to dinner biting his nails, he would sniff him, hit him, and scream: You stink like a rabbit-cage.
Don't play, etc.

4.
And then one day he skidded clear off the road; they peeled him out of the twisted wreckage like an egg. Later, he was often seen limping through the streets, playing songs on a comb, wearing rat-pelt collars. Limping and hopping, he would follow children, try and stop them from going to school, and slink around rabbit-cages. Then one day, in broad daylight, he lured a child into a barn. They later found his body floating in a rat-ditch. The filthy children played this song on a comb:
Don't play etc.

Translated by
Alexandra Chciuk-Celt

UND ALS WIR ANS UFER KAMEN

Text: Wolf Biermann, 1979
Music: Wolf Biermann

1.
Und als wir ans Ufer kamen
Und saßen noch lang im Kahn
Da war es, daß wir den Himmel
Am schönsten im Wasser sahn
Und durch den Birnbaum flogen
Paar Fischlein. Das Flugzeug schwamm

Quer durch den See und zerschellte
Sachte am Weidenstamm
—am Weidenstamm

2.
Was wird bloß aus unsern Träumen
In diesem zerrissnen Land

Die Wunden wollen nicht
zugehn
Unter dem Dreckverband
Und was wird mit unsern
Freunden

Und was noch aus dir, aus mir—
Ich möchte am liebsten weg
sein
Und bleibe am liebsten hier
—am liebsten hier

AND WHEN WE REACHED THE LAKE SHORE

1.
And when we reached the lake
shore
and lingered long in the boat,
we saw sublimely in the water
the sky sublimely float.
And flying through the pear tree
were fish. The plane we could
see
swim in the lake and shatter
softly on the willow tree
—on the willow tree.

2.
And what about our dreams
now
in this divided land?
Under the filthy dressing
the wounds refuse to mend.
And what will become of our
friendships
and what of you and me, pray?
I wish so much to stay
—wish so much to stay.

Translated by Hans Zeisel

WENN DER SENATOR ERZÄHLT

Text: Franz Josef Degenhardt, 1967
Music: Franz Josef Degenhardt

1.
Ja, wenn der Senator erzählt,
der, dem das ganze
Wackelsteiner Ländchen
gehört
und alles, was darauf steht.
Wie der angefangen hat:
Sohn eines Tischlers,
der war mit 40 schon
Invalide,
alle Finger der rechten Hand
unter der Kreissäge.

Mit fünf Jahren schon ist der
Senator jeden Tag
von Wackerode nach
Hohentalholzheim gelaufen,
zwölf Kilometer hin
und zwölf Kilometer
zurück.
Und warum?
Weil in Wackelrode ein Liter
Milch zweieinhalf Pfennig
gekostet hat,

in Hohentalholzheim aber nur
zwei Pfenning,
und diesen halben Pfennig durfte
der Bub behalten.
Das hat er auch getan, zehn
Jahre lang—
von Wackelrode
nach Hohentalholzheim,
von Hohentalholzheim
nach Wackelrode.
Und nach zehn Jahren, da hat
sich der Senator gesagt:
«So.» Hat das ganze Geld
genommen
und das erste Hüttenwerk
auf das Wackelsteiner Ländchen
gestellt.
Ja, wenn der Senator erzählt.

2.
Dann 14/18, der Krieg.
Und hinterher, da hat sich der
Senator gesagt:
«So, der Krieg ist verloren,
was ist dabei rausgekommen?
Gar nichts.»
Und dann kam die Arbeitslosen-
zeit, dann Adolf.
Ja, und 34, da gehörte ihm
praktisch schon
das ganze Wackelsteiner
Ländchen.
Und dann hat er noch ein
Hüttenwerk
auf das Wackelsteiner Ländchen
gestellt.
Das waren dann schon zwei,
das alte Wackelsteiner
Hüttenwerk
und das neue Wackelsteiner
Hüttenwerk.

Und mitten im Krieg, in
schwerer Zeit,
hat er noch ein Hüttenwerk
auf das Wackelsteiner Ländchen
gestellt.
Ja, wenn der Seantor erzählt.

3.
Und dann 45, ausgebombt,
demontiert.
Da hat sich der Senator gesagt:
«So, er Krieg ist verloren.
Was ist dabei rausgekommen?
Gar nichts.»
Und er war froh,
daß er wenigstens noch sein
Wackelsteiner Ländchen
hatte
und seine treuen Bauern;
hier einen Schinken, dort einen
Liter Milch.
Und so konnte man ganz
langsam wieder anfangen.
Aber dann 48, Währungsreform.
Da stand der Senator
wie jeder von uns mit vierzig
Mark auf der Hand.
Und was hat er damit
gemacht?
Etwa ein viertes Hüttenwerk
auf das Wackelsteiner Ländchen
gestellt?
Nein. Er hat's auf den Kopf
gehauen
in einer Nacht.
Und als er dann morgens auf der
Straße stand,
neblig war's und kalt,
da mußte der Senator plötzlich
so richtig lachen.
Er hatte eine gute Idee:

«Wie wäre es», sagte sich der
  Senator,
«wenn man aus dem
  Wackelsteiner Ländchen
ein Ferienparadies machen
  würde?»
Gesagt, getan.
Verkehrsminister angerufen—
  alter Kumpel aus schwerer
  Zeit.
Ja, und dann ist aus dem
  Wackelsteiner Ländchen
das Wackelsteiner Ländchen
  geworden,
wie es jedermann heute kennt.
Und dann hat der Senator noch
  ein Hüttenwerk
auf das Wackelsteiner Ländchen
  gestellt.
Ja, wenn der Senator erzählt.

4.
Aber dann wird er traurig, der
  Senator.
«Und wissen Sie was», sagt er,
«die waren damals doch
  glücklicher,
die Leute.
Wie ich angefangen habe:
Sohn eines Tischlers,
der war mit 40 schon Invalide,
alle Finger der rechten Hand
  unter der Kreissäge.
Mit fünf Jahren schon bin ich
  jeden Tag
von Wackelrode nach
  Hohentalholzheim gelaufen,
zwölf Kilometer hin
und zwölf Kilometer zurück.
Und warum?»
Ja, wenn der Senator erzählt.

WHEN THE SENATOR TELLS HIS TALES

1.
Ah yes, when the Senator tells
  his tales,
(the fellow who owns all of
  Little Wackelstein
and everything in it)—
About how he got his start
as the son of a cabinetmaker.
an invalid by the age of forty,
lost all the fingers of his right
  hand in the buzz saw.
Even as a five-year-old, the
  senator walked
from Wackelrode to
  Hohentalholzheim every
  day:
ten miles there

and ten miles back.
And why?
Because a quart of milk cost two
  and a half cents in
  Wackelrode
but only two cents in
  Hohentalholzheim,
and this half penny the boy
  could keep for himself.
And he did, too, for ten years—
from Wackelrode
to Hohentalholzheim
from Hohentalholzheim
to Wackelrode
And after ten years, the Senator
  said,

"Now then." He took all that
 and built his first iron foundry
in Little Wackelstein
Ah, yes, when the Senator tells
  his tales.

2.
Then 1914-1918 and the war.
Afterward, the Senator said,
"Now then, the war's lost,
and what did we get out of it?
Not a single thing."
So he took his money
And bought real estate;
here a piece, there a piece.
And then came unemployment,
  then Adolf.
Yes, and by 1934, practically all of
Little Wackelstein belonged to
  him.
And then he built another iron
  foundry
and the new Little Wackelstein
  iron foundry.
And in the middle of the war, in
  hard times,
he put up another iron foundry
in Little Wackelstein.
Ah, yes, when the Senator tells
  his tales.

3.
And then 1945, bombed out,
  torn down.
So the Senator said to himself,
"Now then, the war's lost
and what did we get out of it?
Not a single thing."
And he was glad
that he at least had his Little
  Wackelstein

and his loyal farmers
with a ham here, a quart of milk
  there.
So he was slowly able to start all
  over again from scratch.
But then in 1948, the currency
  reform;
the Senator stood there
just like the rest of us, with forty
  marks in his hand,
and what did he do with it?
Perhaps build a fourth iron
  foundry
in Little Wackelstein?
No. He blew it all
in a single night.
And in the morning, while he
  was standing on the street,
and it was foggy and cold,
he just suddenly had to laugh
  out loud.
He had a good idea:
"How would it be," the Senator
  said to himself,
"if we made a vacation
  resort
our of Little Wackelstein?"
No sooner said than done.
He called the transport
  ministry—an old chum,
  from the hard times—
Yes, and then Little Wackelstein
  turned into
the Little Wackelstein
the one everyone knows
  today.
And then the Senator built
another iron foundry in Little
  Wackelstein.
Ah, yes, when the Senator tells
  his tales.

4.

But then he gets sad, the Senator
    does.
"And you know what?" he says,
"people used to be happier,
they really did.
Back when I was getting
    started,
as the son of a cabinet maker,
an invalid by the age of forty,
lost all the fingers of his right
    hand in the buzz saw,

Even as a five-year-old, the
    Senator walked
from Wackelrode to Hohental-
    holzheim every day;
ten miles there
and ten miles back
and why?"
Ah yes, when the Senator tells
    his tales.

Translated by
Richard J. Rundell

National Anthems of German-Speaking Countries

NATIONALHYMNE DER BUNDESREPUBLIK DEUTSCHLAND (1949)

Text: A. H. Hoffmann von Fallersleben, 1848
Music: Franz Joseph Haydn, 1797

Einigkeit und Recht und Freiheit
Für das deutsche Vaterland!
Danach laßt uns alle streben
Brüderlich mit Herz und Hand!
Einigkeit und Recht und Freiheit

Sind des Glückes Unterpfand.
Blüh im Glanze dieses Glückes,
Blühe, deutsches Vaterland!
Blüh im Glanze dieses Glückes,
Blühe, deutsches Vaterland!

NATIONAL ANTHEM OF WEST GERMANY

Unity and Right and Freedom
For the German Fatherland!
After these let us all strive
Brotherly with heart and hand!
Unity and Right and Freedom
Are the pledge of happiness.

Bloom in the splendor of this
  happiness,
Bloom, my German Fatherland!
(*Last two lines sung twice*)

Translator unknown

NATIONALHYMNE DER DEUTSCHEN DEMOKRATISCHEN REPUBLIK 1949

Text: Johannes R. Becher, 1949
Music: Hanns Eisler

1. Auf - er - stan - den aus Ru - i - nen Und der Zu - kunft zu - ge - wandt, Lass uns dir zum Gu - ten die - nen,

1.

Auferstanden aus Ruinen
Und der Zukunft zugewandt,
Laß uns dir zum Guten dienen,
Deutschland, einig Vaterland.
Alte Not gilt es zu zwingen,
Und wir zwingen sie vereint,
Denn es muß uns doch gelingen,
Daß die Sonne schön wie nie
Über Deutschland scheint, über
    Deutschland scheint.

2.

Glück und Friede sei beschieden
Deutschland, unsrem Vaterland.
Alle Welt sehnt sich nach Frieden,
Reicht den Völkern eure Hand.
Wenn wir brüderlich uns einen,
Schlagen wir des Volkes Feind.

Laßt das Licht des Friedens
    scheinen,
Daß nie eine Mutter mehr
Ihren Sohn beweint, ihren Sohn
    beweint!

3.

Laßt uns pflügen, laßt uns bauen,
Lernt und schafft wie nie zuvor,
Und der eigen Kraft vertrauend
Steigt ein frei' Geschlecht empor.
Deutsche Jugend, bestes Streben
Unsres Volks in dir vereint,
Wirst du Deutschlands neues
    Leben,
und die Sonne schön wie nie
Über Deutschland scheint, über
    Deutschland scheint.

NATIONAL ANTHEM OF THE GDR

1.

From the ruins risen newly
To the future turned we stand,
May we serve your good weal truly,
Germany, our motherland.
Triumph over bygone sorrow
Can in unity be won,
For we must attain a morrow,
When over our Germany
There is radiant sun. (*twice*)

2.

May both joy and peace inspire
Germany, our motherland.
Peace is all the world's desire.
To the peoples give your hand.
In fraternity united
We shall crush the peoples' foe.

May our path by peace be
    lighted
That no mother shall again
Mourn her son in woe. (twice)

3.

Let us till and build our nation,
Learn and work as never yet,
That a free new generation
Faith in its own strength beget.
German youth, for whom the
    striving
Of our people is at one,
You are Germany's reviving
And over our Germany
There is radiant sun. (*twice*)

Translated by Yvonne Kapp

Nationalhyymne der Schweiz (1961)

Text: Leonard Widmer, 1841
Music: Alberich Zwyssig (Otto Kreis)

Eu - re from-me See - le ahnt.
Au ciel mon-tent plus joy - eux,
Li - ber - tà, con - cor - dia, a-mor.
Ti has lu in sen - ti - ment,
Ti - a or - ma sain - ta ferm.

Eu - re from-me See - le ahnt
Au ciel mon-tent plus joy - eux,
Li - ber - tà, con - cor - dia, a-mor
Ti has lu in sen - ti - ment
Ti - a or - man sain - ta ferm.

Gott im heh - ren
Les ac - cents d'un
All' El - ve - zia
De tiu Bab sul
Dieu in tschêl, il

Va - ter - land,___ Gott, im heh - ren, teu - ren Va - ter - land!
cœur pi - eux,___ Les ac - cents é - mus d'un cœur___ pi - eux.
serba o - gnor,___ All' El - ve - zia ser - ba o - gnor.
fir - ma - ment,___ De tiu Bab, tiu Bab, sul fir - ma - ment.
Bap e - tern!___ Dieu in tschêl il Bap, il Bap___ e - tern!

1.

Trittst im Morgen rot daher,
Seh' ich dich im Stahlenmeer,
Dich, du Hocherhabener,
   Herrlicher!
Wenn der Alpen Firn sich rötet,
Betet, freie Schweizer, betet!
Eure fromme Seele ahnt,
Eure fromme Seele ahnt
Gott im hehren Vaterland,
Gott im hehren, teuren
   Vaterland!

2.

Kommst im Abendglüh'n daher,
Find' ich dich im Sternenheer,
Dich, du Menschenfreundlicher,
   Liebender!

In des Himmels lichten Räumen
Kann ich froh und selig
   träumen!
Denn die fromme Seele ahnt,
Denn die fromme Seele ahnt
Gott in hehren . . .

3.

Ziehst im Nebelflor daher,
Such' ich dich im Wolkenmeer,
Dich, du Unergründlicher,
   Ewiger!
Aus dem grauen Luftgebilde
Tritt die Sonne klar und milde,
Und die fromme Seele ahnt,
Und die fromme Seele ahnt
Gott im hehren . . .

4.

Fährst im wilden Sturm daher,
Bist du selbst uns Hort und
    Wehr,
Du, allmächtig Waltender,
    Rettender!
In Gewittermacht und Grauen

Laßt uns kindlich ihm
    vertrauen!
Ja, die fromme Seele ahnt,
Ja, die fromme Seele ahnt
Gott in hehren . . .

NATIONAL ANTHEM OF SWITZERLAND

1.

When the morning skies grow
    red
And o'er us their radiance shed,
Thou, glorious appeareth
In their light.
When the Alps glow bright with
    splendor,
Pray to God, to Him surrender,
For you feel and understand,
    (twice)
That He dwelleth in this land.
    (twice)

2.

In the sunset Thou art nigh
And beyond the starry sky,
Thou, O loving Father, ever
    near.
When to Heav'n we are
    departing.
Joy and bliss Thou'lt be
    imparting.
For we feel and understand
    (twice)
That Thou dwellest in this land.
    (twice)

3.

When dark clouds enshroud the
    hills
And grey mist the valley fills,
Yet Thou are not hidden from
    Thy sons.
Pierce the gloom in which we
    cower
With Thy sunshine's cleansing
    power;
Then we'll feel and understand
    (twice)
That God dwelleth in this land.
    (twice)

4.

Through raging storms o'er crag
    and field,
Thou art our stronghold and
    our redeemer and our rock.
'Midst crashing thunder, pelting
    hail,
Thy shelt'ring mercy shall prevail;
Yea, we feel and understand
    (twice)
That God dwelleth in this land.
    (twice)

Translator unknown

NATIONALHYMNE VON ÖSTERREICH (1949)

Text: Paula von Preradović
Music: Johann Holzer

1.

Land der Berge, Land am
  Strome,
Land der Äcker, Land der
  Dome,
Land der Hämmer,
  zukunftsreich!
Heimat bist du großer Söhne,
Volk, begnadet für das Schöne,
Vielgerühmtes Österreich.
Vielgerühmtes Österreich.

2.

Heiß umfehdet, wild umstritten,
liegst dem Erdteil du inmitten
einem starken Herzen gleich.

Hast seit frühen Ahnentagen
Hoher Sendung Last getragen,
Vielgeprüftes Österreich
Vielgeprüftes Österreich.

3.

Mutig in die neuen Zeiten,
Frei und gläubig sieh uns
  schreiten,
Arbeitsfroh und hoffnungs-
  reich.
Einig laß in Brüderchören,
Vaterland, dir Treue schwören,
Vielgeliebtes Österreich,
Vielgeliebtes Österreich.

NATIONAL ANTHEM OF AUSTRIA

1.
Land of mountains, land of
    streams,
Land of fields, land of spires,
Land of hammers, with a rich
    future,
You are the home of great sons,
A nation blessed by its sense of
    beauty,
Highly praised Austria, highly
    praised Austria.

2.
Strongly fought for, fiercely
    contested,
You are in the centre of the
    Continent
Like a strong heart,
You have borne since the
    earliest days

The burden of a high
mission,
Much tried Austria, much tried
    Austria.

3.
Watch us striding free and
    believing,
With courage, into new eras,
Working cheerfully and full of
    hope,
In fraternal chorus let us take in
    unity
The oath of allegiance to you,
    our country,
Our much beloved Austria, our
    much beloved Austria.

Translator unknown

Songs of the People
Religious Songs

Alle Jahre wieder

Text: Wilhelm Hey, 1837
Music: Traditional, C. H. Rinck; Friedrich Silcher, 1842

Al - le Jah - re wie - der kommt das Chri-stus-kind
auf die Er - de nie - der—, wo wir Men - schen sind.

1.
Alle Jahre wieder
    kommt das Christuskind
auf die Erde nieder—,
    wo wir Menschen sind.

2.
Kehrt mit seinem Segen
    ein in jedes Haus,

geht auf allen Wegen
    mit uns ein und aus.

3.
Steht auch mir zur Seite
    still und unerkannt,
daß es treu mich leite
    an der lieben Hand.

Another Year

1.
As each happy Christmas
Dawns on Earth again

Comes the holy Christ child
To the hearts of men.

2.
Enters with his blessing
into ev'ry home
guides and guards our
    footsteps
as we go and come.

3.
All unknown, beside me
He will ever stand,
and will safely lead me
With His own right hand.

Translator unknown

AUS TIEFER NOT SCHREI ICH ZU DIR

Text: Psalm 130; Martin Luther, 1530
Music: Martin Luther, 1530

1.
Aus tiefer Not schrei ich zu dir,
Herr Gott, erhör mein Rufen.
Dein gnädig Ohren kehr zu mir
Und meiner Bitt sie öffen. *offne*
Denn so du willst das sehen an,
Was Sünd und Unrecht ist getan,
Wer kann, Herr, vor dir bleiben?

2.
Bei dir gilt nichts denn Gnad und
    Gunst,
Die Sünden zu vergeben.
Es ist doch unser Tun umsonst
Auch in dem besten Leben.
Vor dir niemand sich rühmen
    kann,
des muß dich fürchten
    jedermann
Und deiner Gnade leben.

3.
Darum auf Gott will hoffen ich,
Auf mein Verdienst nicht bauen.
Auf ihn mein Herz soll lassen sich
Und seiner Güte trauen,
Die mir zusagt sein wertes Wort.
Das ist mein Trost und treuer
    Hort,
Des will ich allzeit harren.

4.
Und ob es währt bis in die Nacht
Und wieder an den Morgen,
Doch soll mein Herz an Gottes
    Macht
Verzweifeln nicht noch sorgen.
So tu Israel rechter Art,
Der aus dem Geist erzeuget ward
und seines Gotts erharre.

5.
Ob bei uns ist der Sünden viel,
Bei Gott ist viel mehr Gnaden.
Sein Hand zu helfen hat kein
    Ziel,
Wie groß auch sei der Schaden.
Er ist allein der gute Hirt,
Der Israel erlösen wird
Aus seinen Sünden allen.

FROM DEPTHS OF WOE I CRY TO YOU

1.
From depths of woe I cry to you.
O Lord, my voice is trying
To reach your heart and, Lord,
    Break through
With these my cries and sighing.
If you keep record of our sin
And hold against us what we've
    been,
Who then can stand before you?

2.
Your grace and love alone avail
To blot out sin with pardon.
In your gaze our best efforts pale,
Develop pride and harden.
Before your throne no one can
    coast.
Our haven is your mercy.

3.
In God I anchor all my trust,
Discarding my own merit.
His love holds firm; I therefore
    must
His fullest grace inherit.
He tells me, and my heart has
    heard,
The steadfast promise of his Word,
That he's my help and haven.

4.
Though help delays until the
    night
Or waits till morning waken,
My heart shall never doubt his
    might
Nor think itself forsaken.
All you who are God's own
    indeed,
Born of the Spirit's Gospel
    seed,
Await his promised rescue.

5.
Though sins arise like dunes of
    sand,
God's mercy-tides submerge
    them.
Like oceans pouring from his
    hand,
Strong flows the grace to purge
    them.
Our shepherd will his Israel
    lead
To uplands out of every
    need
And ransom us from sinning.

Translated by
F. Samuel Janow

Es ist ein Ros entsprungen

Text: Traditional, 1599

Music: Michael Praetorius, 1609

Es ist ein Ros ent - sprun - gen aus
Wie uns die Al - ten sun - gen, aus

ei - ner Wur - zel zart. und hat ein
Jes - se kam die Art

Blüm - lein bracht, mit - ten im kal - ten

Win - ter wohl zu der hal - ben Nacht.

1.
Es ist ein Ros entsprungen,
aus einer Wurzel zart.
Wie uns die Alten sungen,
aus Jesse kam die Art
und hat ein Blümlein bracht,
mitten im kalten Winter
wohl zu der halben Nacht.

2.
Das Röslein, das ich meine,
davon Isaias sagt:
Maria ist's, die Reine,
die uns das Blümlein bracht.
Aus Gottes ew'gem Rat
hat sie ein Kind geboren
und blieb doch reine Magd.

Lo, How a Rose is Growing

1.
Lo, how a rose is growing
A bloom of finest grace;
The prophets had foretold it:
A branch of Jesse's race
Would bear one perfect
     flow'r
Here in the cold of winter
And darkest midnight hour.

2.
The rose of which I'm singing
Isaiah had foretold.
He came to us through Mary,
Who sheltered him from cold.
Through God's eternal will
This child to us was given
At midnight calm and still.

Translated by Gracia Grindal

HÖRT, IHR HERRN, UND LAßT EUCH SAGEN

Text: Traditional, 16th century; 1821
Music: Traditional, 17th century

Hört, ihr Herrn, und laßt euch sa - gen:

uns - re Glock hat *zehn* ge - schla - gen. Zehn Ge - bo - te

setzt' Gott ein; gib, daß wir ge - hor - sam sein!

Men - schenwa - chen kann nichts nüt - zen; Gott muß

wa - chen, Gott muß schützen. Herr, durch dei - ne

Güt und Macht gib uns ei - ne gu - te Nacht!

1.
Hört, ihr Herrn, und laßt euch
    sagen:
unsre Glock hat *zehn*
    geschlagen.
Zehn Gebote setzt' Gott ein;
gib, daß wir gehorsam sein!
Menschenwachen kann nichts
    nützen;
Gott muß wachen, Gott muß
    schützen;

Herr, durch deine Güt und Macht
gib uns eine gute Nacht!

2.
Hört, ihr Herrn, und laßt euch
    sagen:
unsre Glock hat *elf* eschlagen!
Elf der Jünger blieben treu,
einer trieb Verräterei.
Menschenwachen, etc.

3.

Hört, ihr Herrn, und laßt euch
sagen:
unsre Glock hat *zwölf*
geschlagen!
Zwölf, das ist das Ziel der Zeit.
Mensch, bedenk die Ewigkeit!
Menschenwachen, etc.

4.

Hört, ihr Herrn, und laßt euch
sagen:
unsre Glock hat *eins* geschlagen!
Ist nur ein Gott in der Welt,
ihm sei all's anheimgestellt.
Menschenwachen, etc.

5.

Hört, ihr Herrn, und laßt euch
sagen:
unsre Glock hat *zwei*
geschlagen!
Zwei Weg' hat der Mensch vor
sich.

Herr, den rechten lehre mich!
Menschenwachen, etc.

6.

Hört, ihr Herrn, und laßt euch
sagen:
unsre Glock hat *drei* geschlagen!
Drei ist eins, was göttlich heißt:
Vater, Sohn und Heilger Geist.
Menschenwachen, etc.

7.

Hört, ihr Herrn, und laßt euch
sagen:
unsre Glock hat *vier* geschlagen!
Vierfach ist das Ackerfeld.
Mensch, wie ist dein Herz
bestellt?
Alle Sternlein müssen
schwinden,
und der Tag wird sich einfinden.
Danket Gott, der uns die Nacht
hat so väterlich bewacht!

Listen to Me, Gentlemen

1.

Listen to me, gentlemen.
Our bell has struck ten again.
Ten commandments gave us God,
That we might obey His law.
Vigilance is not enough,
God must watch and shelter us.
Lord, grant through Thy grace
and might,
That we have a peaceful night!

2.

Listen to me, gentlemen.

It's struck eleven o'clock again.
Eleven apostles true remained,
Let our death no guilt contain.
Vigilance . . .

3.

Listen to me, gentlemen.
The bell has now struck twelve
again.
That's the goal of time; may we
Contemplate eternity!
Vigilance . . .

4.

Listen to me, gentlemen,
Our bell has struck one again.
For there is just one God; may we
Place all our trust in Him,
     agreed?
Vigilance . . .

5.

Listen to me, gentlemen,
Our bell has struck two again.
We have two paths from which
     to choose,
Lord, make me pick right and
     not lose!
Vigilance . . .

6.

Listen to me, gentlemen,
Our bell has struck three again.

Three is one, say heaven's host:
Father, Son, and Holy Ghost.
Vigilance . . .

7.

Listen to me, gentlemen,
Our bell has struck four again.
Fields are ordered in four
     parts,
What's the order of your
     heart?
A new day will soon be here
and the star will disappear.
Like a father with his light,
God kept watch throughout the
     night.

Translated by Alexandra
Chciuk-Celt

ICH STEH AN DEINER KRIPPE HIER

Text: Paul Gerhardt, 1650
Music: Johann Sebastian Bach, 1736

1.

Ich steh an deiner Krippe hier,
O Jesulein, mein Leben.
Ich stehe, bring und schenke dir,
was du mir hast gegeben.
Nimm hin, es ist mein Geist und
     Sinn,
Herz, Seel und Mut, nimm alles
     hin,
Und laß dir's wohl gefallen.

2.

Ich lag in tiefster Todesnacht,
Du wurdest meine Sonne,
Die Sonne die mir zugebracht
Licht, Leben, Freud und
     Wonne.
O Sonne, die das werte Licht
Des Glaubens in mir zugericht,
Wie schön sind Deine
     Strahlen!

☯

I STAND BESIDE THY CRADLE HERE

1.
I stand beside Thy cradle here,
O Jesus-Child, to tender
Thee all which Thou hast given
  me,
Which I do Thee surrender.
Take then my spirit, take my
  soul,
My heart and mind in Thy
  control,
And graciously receive them.

2.
In darkness black, in death I lay,
Thou Sun, dispell'd my sadness.
Thou broughtest heav'nly light
  of day,
A life of joy and gladness.
O sun, how beautiful Thy rays,
The holy words of faith I praise.
O Lord, I do believe them.

Translator unknown

IHR KINDERLEIN, KOMMET

Text: Christoph von Schmid, 1811
Music: Johann Abraham Peter Schultz, 1794

Ihr Kin - der - lein, kom - met, o kom - met doch all! Zur Krip - pe her - kom - met in Beth - le - hems Stall. Und seht, was in die - ser hoch - hei - li - gen Nacht der Va - ter im Him - mel für Freu - de uns macht.

1.

Ihr Kinderlein, kommet, o
    kommet doch all!
Zur Krippe herkommet in
    Bethlehems Stall.
Und seht, was in dieser
    hochheiligen Nacht
der Vater im Himmel für Freude
uns macht.

2.

O seht in der Krippe im
    nächtlichen Stall,
seht hier bei des Lichtleins
    hellglänzendem Strahl

in reinlichen Windeln das
    himmlische Kind,
viel schöner und holder, als
    Engel es sind.

3.

Da liegt es, das Kindlein, auf
    Heu und auf Stroh;
Maria und Joseph betrachten es
    froh.
Die redlichen Hirten knien
    betend davor;
hoch oben schwebt jubelnd der
    Engelein Chor.

O COME, LITTLE CHILDREN

1.

O come, little children, O come,
    one and all!
O come to the cradle in
    Bethleham's stall!
And see what the father, from
    high heav'n above,
Has sent us tonight as a proof of
    His love.

2.

O see in the cradle this night in
    the stall,
See here wondrous light that is
    dazzling to all.

In clean lovely white lies the
    heavenly child.
Not even the angels are more
    sweet and mild.

3.

O see where He's lying, the
    heavenly Boy!
Here Joseph and Mary behold
    Him with Joy;
The shepherds have come, and
    are kneeling in pray'r,
While songs of the angels float
    over Him there.

Translator unknown

KOMMET, IHR HIRTEN

Text: Traditional, 1605; Carl Riedel, 1880
Music: Traditional, 1605

1.

Kommet, ihr Hirten,
ihr Männer und Fraun!
Kommet, das liebliche
Kindlein zu schaun!
Christus, der Herr,
ist heute geboren,
den Gott zum Heiland
euch hat erkoren.
Fürchtet euch nicht!

2.

Lasset uns sehen
in Bethlehems Stall,
was uns verheißen
der himmlische Schall!

Was wir dort finden,
lasset uns künden,
lasset uns preisen
in frommen Weisen:
Halleluja!

3.

Wahrlich, die Engel
verkündigen heut'
Bethlehems Hirtenvolk
gar große Freud'.
Nun soll es werden
Friede auf Erden,
Den Menschen allen
ein Wohlgefallen:
Ehre sei Gott!

COME, YE MEN AND WOMEN

1.

Come on, ye men and ye
women,
Come ye, behold the heavenly
Child.
Christ, our Lord, was born
today
Him whom God has chosen to
save us.
Oh, fear ye not.

2.

Let us see in Bethlehem's
manger,
Him whose coming has been
foretold.

Let us make known what here
we shall witness
Let us praise in holy strains:
Halleluja.

3.

Truly the angels proclaim
today,
Great joy has come to
Bethlehem's shepherds
For now there shall be peace on
earth,
And happiness come unto all
men.
The Lord be praised!

Translator unknown

LEISE RIESELT DER SCHNEE

Text: Eduard Ebel
Music: Eduard Ebel

1. Lei - se rie - selt der Schnee, still und starr
ruht der See; weih-nacht-lich glän - zet der
Wald: Freu - e dich, Christ-kind kommt bald!

1.
Leise rieselt der Schnee,
still und starr ruht der See;
weihnachtlich glänzet der Wald:
Freue dich, Christkind kommt
    bald!

2.
In dem Herzen ist's warm,
still schweigt Kummer und
    Harm,

Sorge des Lebens verhallt:
Freue dich, Christkind kommt
    bald!

3.
Bald ist heilige Nacht,
Chor der Engel erwacht,
hört nur wie lieblich es schallt:
Freue dich, Christkind kommt
    bald!

SOFTLY FLUTTERS THE SNOW

1.
Softly flutters the snow,
Forests festively glow.
Frozen and dark lies the
    pond.
Christmas is coming anon!

2.
Hearts are cordial and warm,
Cares and sorrows have
    flown.

Now our life's trouble are gone:
Christmas is coming anon!

3.
Christmas Eve's coming soon,
Choirs of angels will croon.
Listen to their lovely song!
Christmas is coming anon!

*Translated by
Alexandra Chciuk-Celt*

LOBE DEN HERREN

Text: Joachim Neander, 1679
Music: Traditional, 1665

Lo - be den Her - ren, den mäch - ti - gen Kö -
mei - ne ge - lie - be - te See - le, das ist

nig der Eh - ren,   Kom - met zu - hauf, Psal - ter und
mein Be - geh - ren.

Har - fe, wacht auf, las - set den Lob - ge - sang hö - ren!

1.
Lobe den Herren, den mächtigen
    König der Ehren,
Meine geliebte Seele, das ist
    mein Begehren;
Kommet zuhauf,
Psalter und Harfe, wacht
    auf,
Lasset den Lobgesang hören.

2.
Lobe den Herren, der alles so
    herrlich regieret,
Der dich auf Adelers Fittichen
    sicher geführet,
Der dich erhält,
Wie es dir selber gefällt;
Hast du nicht dieses verspüret?

3.
Lobe den Herren, der künstlich
    und fein dich bereitet,
Der dir Gesundheit verliehen,
    dich freundlich geleitet;

In wieviel Not
Hat nicht der gnädige Gott
Über dir Flügel gebreitet!

4.
Lobe den Herren, der deinen
    Stand sichtbar gesegnet,
Der aus dem Himmel mit
    Strömen der Liebe geregnet;
Denke daran,
Was der Allmächtige kann,
Der dir mit Liebe begegnet.

5.
Lobe den Herren; was in mir ist,
    lobe den Namen.
Alles was Odem hat, lobe mit
    Abrahams Samen.
Er ist dein Licht!
Seele, vergiß es ja nicht;
Lobende, schließe mit
    Amen.

PRAISE TO THE LORD

1.
Praise to the Lord, the Almighty,
    the King of creation;
O my soul, praise him, for he is
    thy health and salvation:
Come ye who hear,
Brothers and sisters draw
    near,
Praise him in glad adoration.

2.
Praise to the Lord, who o'er all
    things so wondrously
    reigneth,
Shelters thee under his wings,
    yea, so gently sustaineth:
hast thou not seen
All that is needful hath been
Granted in what he ordaineth?

3.
Praise to the Lord, who doth
    prosper thy work,
and defend thee;
Surely his goodness and mercy
    here daily attend thee:
Ponder anew
All the Almighty can do,

He who with love doth befriend
    thee.
4.
Praise to the Lord, who, when
    tempests their warfare and
    waging,
Who, when the elements madly
    around thee are raging,

Biddeth them cease,
Turneth their fury to peace,
Whirlwinds and waters
    assuaging.

5.
Praise to the Lord! O let all that
    is in me adore him!
All that hath life and breath
    come now with praises
    before him!
Let the amen
Sound from his people again:
Gladly for ay we adore him.

Translated by
Catherine Winkworth

MARIA DURCH EIN'N DORNWALD GING

Text: Traditional, 1608 (1850)
Music: Traditional

1.

Maria durch ein'n Dornwald
    ging,
Kyrie eleison!
Maria durch ein'n Dornwald
    ging,
der hat in siebn Jahrn kein Laub
    getragen.
Jesus und Maria!

2.

Was trug Maria unterm
    Herzen?
Kyrie eleison!

ein kleines Kindlein ohne
    Schmerzen,
das trug Maria unterm Herzen.
Jesus und Maria!

3.

Da haben die Dornen Rosen
    getragen,
Kyrie eleison!
Als das Kindlein durch den Wald
    getragen,
da haben die Dornen Rosen
    getragen.
Jesus und Maria!

MARY WALKS AMID THE THORN

1.

Maria walks amid the thorn,
Kyrie eleison.
Maria walks amid the thorn,
Which seven years no leaf has
    borne.
Jesus and Maria.

2.

What 'neath her heart doth
    Mary bear?
Kyrie Eleison
A little child doth Mary bear,

Beneath her heart He nestles
    there.
Jesus and Maria.

3.

And as the two are passing
    near,
Kyrie eleison,
Lo! roses on the thorns appear,
Lo! roses on the thorns appear.
Jesus and Maria.

Tranlator unknown

NUN DANKET ALLE GOTT

Text: M. Rinckart, 1630, 1638
Music: J. Crüger, 1648

Nun dan-ket al-le Gott mit Her-zen,
der gro-ße Din-ge tut an uns und

Mund und Hän-den,
al-len En-den, der uns von Mut-ter-

leib und Kin-des-bei-nen an un-zäh-lig

viel zu-gut und noch jetz-und ge-tan.

1.

Nun danket alle Gott
mit Herzen, Mund und
    Händen,
der große Dinge tut
an uns und allen Enden,
der uns von Mutterleib
und Kindesbeinen an
unzählig viel zugut
und noch jetzund getan.

2.

Der ewigreiche Gott
wollt uns bei unserm Leben
ein immer fröhlich Herz
und edlen Frieden geben
und uns in seiner Gnad
erhalten fort und fort
und uns aus aller Not
erlösen hier und dort.

3.

Lob, Ehr und Preis sei Gott,
dem Vater und dem Sohne
und dem, der beiden gleich
im höchsten Himmelsthrone,
dem dreimal einen Gott,
wie es ursprünglich war
und ist und bleiben wird
jetzund und immerdar.

NOW THANK WE ALL OUR GOD

1.

Now thank we all our God
With hearts and hands and
      voices,
Who wondrous things has done,
In whom his world rejoices;
Who from our mothers' arms
Has blest us on our way
With countless gifts of love
And still is ours today.

2.

Oh, may this bounteous God
Through all our life be near us,
With ever joyful hearts
And blessed peace to cheer us
And keep us in his grace

And guide us when perplexed
And free us from all harm
In this world and the next!

3.

All praise and thanks to God
The Father now be given,
The Son, and him who reigns
With them in highest heaven.
The one eternal God,
Whom earth and heaven adore;
For thus it was, is now,
And shall be evermore.

Translated in Lutheran
Book of Worship, 1978

O DU FRÖHLICHE

Text: Johannes Falk, 1816; J. G. Holzschuher, 1829
Music: Sicilian Folk Song

1.

O du fröhliche, o du selige,
Gnadenbringende
      Weihnachtszeit!
Welt ging verloren,
Christ ist geboren:
Freue, freue dich, o Christenheit!

2.

O du fröhliche, o du selige,
Gnadenbringende
      Weihnachtszeit!

Christ ist erschienen,
Uns zu versühnen:
Freue, freue dich, o Christenheit!

3.

O du fröhliche, o du selige,
Gnadenbringende
      Weihnachtszeit!
König der Ehren
Dich wolln dir hören.
Freue, freue dich, o Christenheit!

O YOU JOYFUL

1.

O you joyful, o you blissful,
Blessed grace-bearing
    Christmastime!
When the world was lost,
    forlorn,
Christ our Savior was born?
Christendom rejoice, rejoice
    with all mankind!

2.

O you joyful, o you blissful,
Blessed grace-bearing
    Christmastime!
Christ has come between us

Meaning to redeem us.
Christendom rejoice, rejoice
    with all mankind!

3.

O you joyful, o you blissful,
Blessed grace-bearing
    Christmastime!
King of all Eternity,
We'll henceforth obey Thee.
Christendom rejoice, rejoice
    with all mankind!

Translated by
Alexandra Chciuk-Celt

O HAUPT VOLL BLUT UND WUNDEN

Text: Arnulf von Löwen, 13th century; Paul Gerhardt, 1656
Music: "Herzlich tut mich verlangen";
Hans Leo Haßler, 1601

O Haupt voll Blut und Wun - den, voll
o Haupt, zum Spott ge - bun - den mit

Schmerz und vol-ler Hohn,
ei - ner Dor-nen-kron,   o Haupt, sonst schön ge -

zie - ret mit höch-ster Ehr und Zier,   jetzt a - ber

hoch schimp-fie - ret: ge - grü-ßet seist du mir!

1.

O Haupt voll Blut und Wunden,
Voll Schmerz und voller Hohn,
O Haupt, zum Spott gebunden
Mit einer Dornenkron!
O Haupt, sonst schön gezieret
Mit höchster Ehr und Zier,
Jetzt aber hoch schimpfieret,
Gegrüßet seist du mir!

2.

Die Farbe deiner Wangen,
Der roten Lippen Pracht
Ist hin und ganz vergangen,
Des blassen Todes Macht
hat alles hingenommen,
Hat alles hingerafft,
Und daher bist du kommen
Von deines Leibes Kraft.

3.

Nun, was du, Herr, erduldet,
Ist alles meine Last,
Ich hab es selbst verschuldet,
Was du getragen hast!
Schau her, hier steh ich Armer,
Der Zorn verdienet hat,
Gib mir, O mein Erbarmer,
Den Anblick deiner Gnad.

4.

Ich will hier bei dir stehen,
Verachte mich doch nicht!
Von dir will ich nicht gehen,
Wann dir dein Herze bricht.
Wann dein Haupt wird erblassen
Im letzten Todesstoß,
Alsdann will ich dich fassen
In meinen Arm und Schoß.

5.

Ich danke dir von Herzen,
O Jesu, liebster Freund,
Für deines Todes Schmerzen,
Da du's so gut gemeint.
Ach gib, daß ich mich halte
Zu dir und deiner Treu
und, wenn ich nun erkalte,
In dir mein Ende sei.

6.

Erscheine mir zum Schilde,
Zum Trost in meinem Tod
Und laß mich sehn dein Bilde
In deiner Kreuzenot.
Da will ich nach dir blicken,
Da will ich glaubensvoll
Dich fest an mein Herz drücken.
Wer so stirbt, der stirbt wohl.

O SACRED HEAD NOW WOUNDED

1.

O sacred head, now wounded,
With grief and shame weighed
      down,
Now scornfully surrounded
With thorns, your only
      crown.
O sacred head, what glory

And bliss did once combine;
Though now despised and gory,
I joy to call mine!

2.

How pale you are with anguish,
With sore abuse and scorn!

Your face, your eyes, now
   languish,
Which once were bright as
   morn.
Now from you cheeks has
   vanished
Their color once so fair;
From loving lips is banished
The splendor that was there.

3.
All this for my transgression,
My wayward soul to win;
This torment of your Passion,
To set me free from sin.

I cast myself before you,
Your wrath my rightful lot;
Have mercy, I implore you,
O Lord, condemn me not!

4.
Here will I stand beside you,
Your death for me my plea;
Let all the world deride you,
I clasp you close to me.
My awe cannot be spoken,

To see you crucified;
But in your body broken,
Redeemed, I safely hide!

5.
What language can I borrow
To thank you, dearest friend,
For this your dying sorrow,
You mercy without end?
Bind me to you forever,
Give courage from above;
Let not my weakness sever
your bond of lasting love.

6.
Lord, be my consolation,
My constant source of cheer;
Remind me of your Passion,
My shield when death is near.
I look in faith, believing
That you have died for me;
Your cross and crown
   receiving,
I live eternally.

Translated in Lutheran
Book of Worship, 1982

O TANNENBAUM

Text: Traditional, 16th century; August Zahneck, 1820;
Ernst Anschütz, 1824
Music: Traditional, 16th century; 1820

O Tannenbaum, o Tannen-baum, wie grün sind dei-ne

Blät-ter! Du grünst nicht nur zur Som-mers-zeit, nein,

auch im Win-ter, wenn es schneit. O Tan-nen-baum, o

Tan-nen-baum, wie grün sind dei-ne Blät-ter!

1.
O Tannenbaum, o Tannenbaum,
wie grün sind deine Blätter!
Du grünst nicht nur zur
    Sommerszeit,
nein, auch im Winter, wenn es
    schneit.
O Tannenbaum, o Tannenbaum,
wie grün sind deine Blätter!

2.
O Tannenbaum, o Tannenbaum,
du kannst mir sehr gefallen.
Wie oft hat nicht zur
    Weihnachtszeit

ein Baum von dir mich
    hocherfreut.
O Tannenbaum, o Tannenbaum,
du kannst mir sehr gefallen.

3.
O Tannenbaum, o Tannenbaum,
dein Kleid will mich was
    lehren:
Die Hoffnung und Beständigkeit
gibt Trost und Kraft zu jeder
    Zeit.
O Tannenbaum, o Tannenbaum,
dein Kleid will mich was lehren.

O CHRISTMAS TREE

1.
O Christmas tree, O Christmas
 tree,
With faithful leaves unchanging;
Not only green in summer's
 heat,
But also winter's snow and sleet,
O Christmas tree, O Christmas
 tree
With faithful leaves unchanging.

2.
O Christmas tree, O Christmas
 tree,
Of all the trees most lovely;
Each year, you bring to me
 delight
Gleaming in the Christmas
 night.

O Christmas tree, O Christmas
 tree,
Of all the trees most lovely.

3.
O Christmas tree, O Christmas
 tree,
Your leaves will teach me, also,
That hope and love and
 faithfulness
Are precious things I can
 possess.
O Christmas tree, O Christmas
 tree,
Your leaves will teach me,
 also.

Traditional translation

STILLE NACHT, HEILIGE NACHT

Text: Joseph Mohr, 1818
Music: Franz Xavier Gruber, 1818

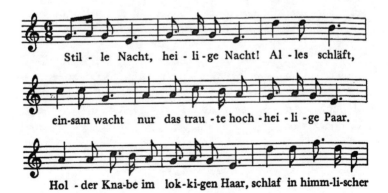

Stil - le Nacht, hei - li - ge Nacht! Al - les schläft,

ein-sam wacht nur das trau - te hoch - hei - li - ge Paar.

Hol - der Kna-be im lok-ki-gen Haar, schlaf in himm-li-scher

Ruh___, schlaf in himm - li - scher Ruh___!

1.
Stille Nacht, heilige Nacht!
Alles schläft, einsam wacht
nur das traute hochheilige Paar.
Holder Knabe im lockigen Haar,
schlaf in himmlischer Ruh,
schlaf in himmlischer Ruh!

2.
Stille Nacht, heilige Nacht!
Hirten erst kundgemacht;
durch der Engel Halleluja
tönt es laut von fern und nah:

Christ, der Retter ist da.
Christ, der Retter ist da.

3.
Stille Nacht, heilige Nacht!
Gottes Sohn, o wie lacht
Lieb aus deinem göttlichen
    Mund,
da uns schlägt die rettende
    Stund,
Christ, in deiner Geburt.
Christ, in deiner Geburt.

Silent Night

1.
Silent night, holy night!
All is calm, all is
    bright!
'Round yon Virgin Mother and
    Child,
Holy Infant so tender and mild,
Sleep in heavenly peace.

2.
Silent night, holy night!
Shepherds quake at the sight!
Glories stream from heaven afar,

Heav'nly host sing Alleluia,
Christ the Savior is born!

3.
Silent night, holy night!
Child of Heav'n, O how bright!
Thou dids't smile when Thou
    wast born!
Blessed be that happy morn,
Full of heavenly joy.

Traditional translation

TOCHTER ZION, FREUE DICH

Text: Heinrich Ranke, 1820
Music: Georg Friedrich Händel, 1747

1. Toch - ter___ Zi - on, freu - e dich,

jauch - ze laut, Je - ru - sa - lem.

Sieh,___ dein Kö - nig kommt___ zu dir,

ja,___ er kommt, der Frie - de - fürst.

Toch - ter___ Zi - on, freu - e dich,

jauch - ze laut, Je - ru - sa - lem.

1.
Tochter Zion, freue dich,
jauchze laut, Jerusalem.
Sieh, dein König kommt zu dir,
ja, er kommt, der Friedefürst.
Tochter Zion, freue dich,
jauchze laut, Jerusalem.

2.
Hosianna, Davids Sohn!
Sei gesegnet deinem Volk!
Gründe nun dein ewig Reich!

Hosianna in der Höh!
Hosianna, Davids Sohn!
Sei gesegnet deinem Volk!

3.
Hosianna, Davids Sohn!
Sei gegrüßet, König mild!
Ewig steht dein Friedensthron,
du, des ewgen Vaters Kind!
Hosianna, Davids Sohn!
Sei gegrüßet, König mild!

DAUGHTER OF ZION, COME REJOICE

1.
Daughter of Zion, come rejoice,
Jubilate, Jerusalem!
Here He comes, the Prince of
Peace,
Here He comes, He is your
king.
Daughter of Zion, come rejoice,
Jubilate, Jerusalem!

2.
Sing Hosanna, David's son!
May Thy kingdom never die!
Thou art blessed 'mong the
Jews.

Sing Hosanna up on high!
Sing Hosanna, David's son!
May thy kingdom never die!

3.
Sing Hosanna, David's son!
Blessed be Thou, King so mild!
May Thy throne of peace
remain,
Thou Eternal Father's child!
Sing Hosanna, David's son!
Blessed be Thou, King so mild!

Translated by
Alexandra Chciuk-Celt

VOM HIMMEL HOCH

Text: Traditional, 5th century; Martin Luther, 1535
Music: Traditional; Martin Luther

Vom Himmel hoch da komm ich her, ich bring euch gu - te neu - e Mär; der gu - ten Mär bring ich so viel, da - von ich singn und sa - gen will.

1.
Von Himmel hoch, da komm ich
   her.
Ich bring euch gute, neue Mär.
Der guten Mär bring ich so viel,
Davon ich sing'n und sagen will.

2.
Euch ist ein Kindlein heut geborn,
Von einer Jungfrau auserkorn,
Ein Kindelein so zart und fein,
Das soll eur Freud und Wonne
   sein.

3.
Es ist der Herr Christ, unser Gott.
Der will euch führn aus aller
   Not.
Es will eur Heiland selber sein,
Von allen Sünden machen rein.

4.
Er bringt euch alle Seligkeit,
Die Gott der Vater hat bereit't,
Daß ihr mit uns im Himmelreich
Sollt leben nun und ewiglich.

5.
So merket nun das Zeichen
   recht:
Die Krippen, Windelein so
   schlecht.
Da findet ihr das Kind gelegt,
Das alle Welt erhält und
   trägt.

6.
Des laßt uns alle fröhlich sein
Und mit den Hirten gehn
   hinein,
Zu sehn, was Gott uns hat
   beschert
Mit seinem lieben Sohn
   verehrt.

7.
Merk auf, mein Herz, und sieh
   dort hin.
Was liegt doch in dem
   Krippelein?
Wer ist das schöne
   Kindelein?
Es ist das liebe Jesulein.

FROM HEAVEN ABOVE TO EARTH I COME

1.
From Heaven above to earth I
   come
To bring good news to everyone!
Glad tidings of great joy I bring
To all the world and gladly sing:

2.
To you this night is born a
   child
Of Mary, chosen virgin mild;

This newborn child of lowly
   birth
Shall be the joy of all the earth.

3.
This is the Christ, God's Son
   most high,
Who hears your sad and bitter cry;
He will himself your Savior be
And from all sin will set you free.

4.

The blessing which the Father
  planned
The Son holds in his infant
  hand
That in his kingdom, bright and
  fair,
You may with us his glory share.

5.

These are the signs which you
  will see
To let you know that it is he:
In manger bed, in swaddling
  clothes
The child who all the earth
  upholds.

6.

How glad we'll be to find it is so!
Then with the shepherds let us go
To see what God for us had
  done
In sending us his own dear Son.

7.

Look, look, dear friends, look
  over there!
What lies within that manger
  Bare?
Who is that lovely little one?
The baby Jesus, God's dear Son.

Translated in Lutheran Book
of Worship, 1978

WAS SOLL DAS BEDEUTEN?

Text: Traditional, 1817
Music: Silesian Folk Song

Stern – lein, je   län – ger, je   mehr.

1.
Was soll das bedeuten?
Es taget ja schon?
Ich weiß wohl, es geht erst
um Mitternacht 'rum.
Schaut nur daher,
schaut nur daher!
Wie glänzen die Sternlein,
je länger, je mehr.

2.
Treibt zusammen, treibt
    zusammen
die Schäflein fürbaß!
Treibt zusammen, treibt
    zusammen!
Dort zeig' ich euch was!
Dort in dem Stall,
dort in dem Stall,
werdet Wunderding' sehen,
treibt zusammen einmal!

3.
Ich hab' nur ein wenig
von weitem geguckt,
da hat mir mein Herz
schon vor Freuden gehupft.
Ein schönes Kind,
ein schönes Kind,
liegt dort in der Krippen
bei Esel und Rind.

4.
Ein herziger Vater,
der steht auch dabei,
eine wunderschöne
    Jungfrau
kniet auch auf dem Heu.
Um und um singt's,
um und um klingt's,
man sieht ja kein Lichtlein,
so um und um brinnt's.

5.
Das Kindlein, das zittert
vor Kälte und Frost!
Ich dacht' mir »Wer hat es
denn also verstoßt,
daß man auch heut',
daß man auch heut'
ihm sonst keine andere Herberg'
    anbeut?«

6.
So gehet und nehmet ein
    Lämmlein vom Gras
und bringet dem schönen
Christkindlein etwas.
Geht nur fein sacht,
Geht nur fein sacht,
auf daß ihr dem Kindlein
kein' Unruh' nicht
    macht.

I KNOW IT'S JUST MIDNIGHT

1.
I know it's just midnight,
But daylight has come.
Does this have some meaning?
I'm wondering some.

Just look over yonder, just look
    over yonder,
The stars are aglitter,
You can't count them all.

2.
O shepherd, go gather
Your sheep into flocks.
Come see what I'm watching:
'Midst donkey and ox,
A miracle's happened
In this little manger, in this little
    manger,
'Midst donkey and ox.

3.
I just had a small peek
From quite far away,
But my heart was joyful
And frolicked all day.
A baby boy gorgeous,
a baby boy gorgeous
Lay there in the manger
Come see what I saw.

4.
It's glowing all over,
But I see no flame;
A beautiful virgin
Kneels there in the hay.
The bells are now ringing,

The people are singing.
The father so handsome
Is standing there too.

5.
The baby doth shiver
With frost and with cold!
I cannot help thinking,
"He's guiltless, behold!
How could they refuse Him,
    how could they refuse Him,
A better night's lodging,
Tonight of all nights?"

6.
The lamb goes a-strolling
And picks up some grass,
Then brings it to Jesus
To share its repast
Step softly, all! Step softly, all!
The Christ child is sleeping,
Don't wake him with noise!

Translated by Alexandra
Chciuk-Celt

Songs about Seasons
and the Times of the Day

ABEND WIRD ES WIEDER

Text: A. H. Hoffmann von Fallersleben, 1837
Music: Johann Christian Rinck, 1827

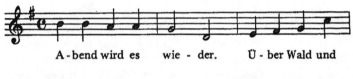

A - bend wird es wie - der. Ü - ber Wald und

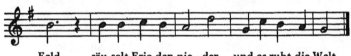

Feld säu-selt Frie-den nie - der, und es ruht die Welt.

1.
Abend wird es wieder.
Über Wald und Feld
säuselt Frieden nieder,
und es ruht die Welt.

2.
Nur der Bach ergießet
sich am Felsen dort,
und er braust und fließet
immer, immer fort.

3.
Und kein Abend bringet
Frieden ihm und Ruh',
keine Glocke klinget
ihm ein Rastlied zu.

4.
So in deinem Streben
bist, mein Herz, auch du:
Gott nur kann dir geben
wahre Abendruh'.

EVENTIDE'S RETURNING

1.
Eventide's returning, peace is
    settling down
Over fields and meadows, and
    the world's at calm.

2.
Yet the brook keeps flowing
    over yonder rock,
Rushing down the cliffside, it
    will never stop.

3.
No peace comes unto it 'neath
    the evening sky,
And no bell can sing the brook a
    lullaby.

4.
You are like that troubled
    brook, my heart;
You can get no evening peace
    except from God!

Translated by
Alexandra Chciuk-Celt

BUND SIND SCHON DIE WÄLDER

Text: Johann Gaudenz Freiherr von Salis-Seewis, 1782
Music: Joahann Friedrich Reichardt, 1799

Bunt sind schon die Wäl - der, gelb die Stop-pel-

fel - der, und der Herbst be - ginnt.

Ro - te Blät - ter fal - len, grau - e Ne - bel

wal - len, küh - ler weht der Wind.

1.
Bunt sind schon die Wälder,
gelb die Stoppelfelder
und der Herbst beginnt.
Rote Blätter fallen,
graue Nebel wallen,
kühler weht der Wind.

2.
Wie die volle Traube
aus dem Rebenlaube
purpurfarbig strahlt!
Am Geländer reifen
Pfirsiche, mit Streifen
rot und weiß bemalt.

3.
Flinke Träger springen,
und die Mädchen singen,
alles jubelt froh!
Bunte Bänder schweben
zwischen hohen Reben
auf dem Hut von Stroh.

4.
Geige tönt und Flöte
bei der Abendröte
und im Mondesglanz;
junge Winzerinnen
winken und beginnen
frohen Erntetanz.

ALL THE LEAVES ARE TURNING

1.
All the trees are turning,
Stubbled fields are yellow,
Fall is starting now.
Reddish leaves are falling,
Blue-gray fog is misting,
And the wind blows chill.

2.
How the ripened grapevine
Shows off perfect bunches
In a purple glow!
Peaches growing riper
Look like they've been painted
With stripes white and red.

3.
Messengers are fleeting
And the girls are singing,
All are merry here!
Bands of colored ribbon
Float atop straw hats here
Over fields of grapes.

4.
Fiddles play and flutes sing
In the rosy twilight
And in moonlit glow;
Grapevine harvest maidens
Beckon and begin a
Joyful harvest dance

Translated by
Alexandra Chciuk-Celt

DER MOND IST AUFGEGANGEN

Text: Matthias Claudius, 1778
Music: Johann Abraham Peter Schulz, 1790

Der Mond ist auf-ge-gan-gen, die gold-nen Sternlein pran-gen am Him-mel hell und klar; der Wald steht schwarz und schweiget, und aus den Wie-sen stei-get der wei-ße Ne-bel wun-der-bar.

1.
Der Mond ist aufgegangen,
Die goldnen Sternlein prangen
Am Himmel hell und klar;
Der Wald steht schwarz und schweiget,
Und aus den Wiesen steiget
Der weiße Nebel wunderbar.

2.
Wie ist die Welt so stille
Und in der Dämmrung Hülle
So traulich und so hold!
Als eine stille Kammer,
Wo ihr des Tages Jammer
Verschlafen und vergessen sollt.

3.
Seht ihr den Mond dort stehen?
Er ist nur halb zu sehen
Und ist doch rund und schön!
So sind wohl manche Sachen,
Die wir getrost belachen,
Weil unsre Augen sie nicht sehn.

4.
Wir stolzen Menschenkinder
Sind eitel arme Sünder
Und wissen gar nicht viel;
Wir spinnen Luftgespinste
Und suchen viele Künste
Und kommen weiter von dem
     Ziel.

5.

Gott, laß dein Heil uns schauen,
Auf nichts Vergänglichs trauen,
Nicht Eitelkeit uns freun!
Laß uns einfältig werden
Und vor dir hier auf Erden
Wie Kinder fromm und fröhlich
    sein!

6.

Wollst endlich sonder Grämen
Aus dieser Welt uns nehmen
Durch einen sanften Tod!

Und wenn du uns genommen,
Laß uns in Himmel kommen,
Du, unser Herr und unser Gott!

7.

So legt euch denn, ihr Brüder,
In Gottes Namen nieder!
Kalt ist der Abendhauch.
Verschon uns, Gott, mit Strafen
Und laß uns ruhig schlafen
Und unsern kranken Nachbarn
    auch!

EVENING SONG

1.

The silver moon has risen.
The starry heavens glisten
In golden splendor clear.
The woods stand mute and
    dreary,
And from the pastures weary
White fogs surge up afar and
    near.

2.

The world looks calm and
    rested,
In twilight shadows vested
So friendly and so warm.
Just like a quiet shelter
Where you forgot the welter
Of life's distress and every
    storm.

3.

The moon seems to be growing,
With half of it just showing,
Yet it is round and fair.
'Tis once again a matter

Of which we blithely chatter
Though it is not for us to bare.

4.

Prideful, yet mere beginners,
Poor souls we are and sinners,
We error-stricken souls.
We dream of building towers,
Seek ever greater powers
And yet stray farther from our goal.

5.

Lord, let us see salvation,
distrust our passing station
And earthly revelry.
Teach us the joys of meekness,
Of strength—beyond man's
    weakness—
In childlike trust and piety.

6.

And when the time is ready,
Grant that, serene and steady,
We heed death's gentle nod.

And let us—simple mortals—
Pass through the pearly portals,
You, our Lord and our God.

To rest, each in his room.
Save us, God, from disaster,
Bless our sleep, O Master,
And our ailing neighbor's, too.

7.
Go, brethren, to—God willing—
Your daily round fulfilling,

Translated by
Alexander God

Es tönen die Lieder

Text: Traditional, 19th century

Music: Traditional

Es tö-nen die Lie-der, der Früh-ling kehrt
wie-der, es spie-let der Hir-te auf
sei-ner Schal-mei: La la la la la la la
la___, la la la la la la la la.

Es tönen die Lieder
Der Frühling kehrt wieder:
es spielet der Hirte

auf seiner Schalmei
La -la-la-la-la-la-la-la-la
La -la-la-la-la-la-la-la.

Now Spring Is a-Springing

Now spring is a-springing,
Now songs are a-singing,
The shepherd is playing
On his shawm again.

La-la-la-la-la-la-la-la-la.
La-la-la-la-la-la-la-la.

Translated by
Alexandra Chciuk-Celt

GEH AUS, MEIN HERZ, UND SUCHE FREUD

Text: Nikolaus Herman, 1560; Paul Gerhardt, 1656
Music: Nikolaus Herman, 1560; Augustin Harder, 1813

Geh aus mein Herz und su - che Freud in
die - ser lie - ben Som - mers-zeit an dei - nes Got - tes
Ga - ben. Schau an der schö-nen Gär - ten Zier und
sie - he wie sie mir und dir sich aus - ge - schmük-ket
ha - ben, sich aus - ge - schmük-ket ha - ben.

1.
Geh aus mein Herz und suche
    Freud
In dieser lieben Sommerszeit
An deines Gottes Gaben.
Schau an der schönen Gärten
    Zier
Und siehe wie sie mir und dir
Sich ausgeschmücket haben,
Sich ausgeschmücket haben.

2.
Die Bäume stehen voller Laub,
Das Erdreich decket seinen
    Staub
Mit einem grünen Kleide:
Narzissus und die Tulipan,
Die ziehen sich viel schöner an
Als Salomonis Seide.

3.
Die Lerche schwingt sich in die
    Luft,
Das Täublein fleucht aus seiner
    Kluft
Und macht sich in die
    Wälder.
Die hochbegabte Nachtigall
Ergötzt und füllt mit ihrem
    Schall
Berg, Hügel, Tal und Felder.

4.
Die Glucke führt ihr Völklein
    aus,
Der Storch baut und bewohnt
    sein Haus.
Das Schwälblein speist die
    Jungen.

Der schnelle Hirsch, das leichte
Reh
Ist froh und kommt aus seiner Höh
Ins tiefe Gras gesprungen.

5.
Die Bächlein rauschen in dem Sand
Und malen sich und ihren Rand
Mit schattenreichen Myrthen.
Die Wiesen liegen hart dabei.
Und klingen ganz von
Lustgeschrei
Der Schaf und ihrer Hirten.

6.
Die unverdrossne Bienenschar
Fleucht hin und her, sucht hier
und da
Ihre edle Honigspeise.
Des süssen Weinstocks starker
Saft

Kriegt täglich neue Stärk und
Kraft
in seinem schwachen Reise.

7.
Der Weizen wächset mit Gewalt,
Darüber jauchzet Jung und Alt
Und rühmt die grosse Güte
Des, der so überflüssig labt
Und mit so machem Gut begabt
Das menschliche Gemüte.

8.
Ich selbsten kann und mag nicht
ruhn,
Des grossen Gottes grosses Tun
Erweckt mir alle Sinnen.
Ich singe mit, wenn alles singt,
Und lasse, was dem Höchsten
klingt,
Aus meinem Herze rinnen.

GO OUT, MY DEAR, AND FIND JOY

1.
Go out in this dear summertide
And seek to find the joys that
bide
In Heaven's gifts, of heart:
Befold the gardens' lovely hue,
And see how they for me and you
Are decked by fairest art.

2.
The trees in fullest leafage rise,
The earth, to give its dust
disguise,
Has put a green dress on.
Narcissus and the tulip-bloom
Far finer silks of Solomon.

3.
The lark soars high into the air,
The little dove departs its lair
And takes the woodland's way.
The sweetly gifted nightingale
Fills hill and mountain, field and
dale
With song, and makes them gay.

4.
The hen leads out her little
troop,
The stork does build and fill his
stoop,
Its young the swallow feeds.
The hasty stag, the agile doe

Are glad, and from their heights
do go
A-running through the reeds.

5.
The brooklets rustle in the sand
And o'er them and their banks a
band
Of shady myrtles keep.
The meadowlands lie close
thereby,
Resounding from the happy
cry
Of shepherds and their sheep.

6.
The bee-host back and forth has
made
Its trips, thus seeking unafraid
Its noble honey-food.
The goodly vine, with juice
grown big,
Gets daily in its weakest sprig
Its strength and force renewed.

7.
The wheat grows large with all
its might,
And does both young and old
delight:
They sing the bounteousness
Of Him Who soothes so
generously
And does such countless
property
Upon man's spirit press.

8.
Now I can neither rest, nor
will:
Great god's great manufactures
thrill
Awake my every sense.
I sing along, when all does sing,
And let what shall to Heaven
ring
From out my heart commence.

Translated by
George C. Schoolfield

GUTEN ABEND, GUT' NACHT

Text: Traditional, 18th century
Music: Johannes Brahms (op. 49, no. 4), 1868

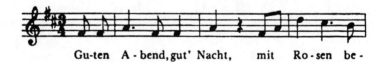

Gu-ten A - bend, gut' Nacht,   mit Ro - sen be -

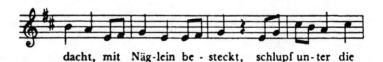

dacht, mit Näg-lein be - steckt, schlupf un - ter die

Deck. Mor-gen früh, wenn Gott will, wirst du wie-der ge -

weckt, morgen früh, wenn Gott will, wirst du wieder ge-weckt.

1.
Guten Abend, gut' Nacht,
mit Rosen bedacht,
mit Näglein besteckt,
schlupf unter die Deck.
Morgen früh, wenn Gott will,
wirst du wieder geweckt,
morgen früh, wenn Gott will,
wirst du wieder geweckt.

2.
Guten Abend, gut' Nacht,
von Englein bewacht,
die zeigen im Traum
dir Christkindleins Baum.
Schlaf nun selig und süß,
schau im Traum 's Paradies.
Schlaf nun selig und süß,
schau im Traum 's Paradies.

CRADLE SONG

1.
Good evening, good night,
Roofed with roses,
Trimmed with carnations,
Slip under the cover:
Tomorrow morning, if God
    wills,
You will wake up again.

2.
Good evening, good night,
watched over by angels.
They will show you in a dream
the Christchild's tree:
Sleep blessedly and sweetly,
in your dream look on paradise.

Translated by Philip Lieson Miller

JEDEN MORGEN GEHT DIE SONNE AUF

Text: Hermann Claudius, 1949
Music: Karl Marx, 1949

Je - den Mor - gen geht die Son - ne auf in der Wäl - der wun-der-sa- mer Run - de. Und die schö-ne scheu - e Schöp-fer - stun - de, je-den Mor-gen nimmt sie ih - ren Lauf.

1.
Jeden Morgen geht die Sonne auf
in der Wälder wundersamer
    Runde.
Und die schöne scheue
    Schöpferstunde,
jeden Morgen nimmt sie ihren
    Lauf.

2.
Jeden Morgen aus dem
    Wiesengrund
heben weiße Schleier sich ins
    Licht,
uns der Sonne Morgengang zu
    künden,
ehe sie das Wolkentor
    durchbricht.

3.
Jeden Morgen durch des Waldes
    Hall'n
hebt der Hirsch sein mächtiges
    Geweih,
der Pirol und dann die Vöglein
    alle
stimmen an die große Melodei.

4.
Jeden Morgen geht die Sonne
    auf
in der Wälder wundersamer
    Runde.
Und die schöne scheue
    Schöpferstunde,
jeden Morgen nimmt sie ihren
    Lauf.

EVERY MORNING

1.
Every morning the sun rises over
wondrous rounds of
forest.
Every morning this lovely
creative hour begins
anew.

2.
Every morning the meadow-
mists raise their veils unto
the sunlight,

Heralding the morning sun ere it
breaches walls of clouds.

3.
Every morning the elk raises
mighty antlers in vaulted
forest halls,
And all the birds join the oriole
in singing a great melody.

*Translated by
Alexandra Chciuk-Celt*

JETZT FÄNGT DAS SCHÖNE FRÜHJAHR AN

Text: Traditional, 19th century
Music: Traditional

1. Jetzt fängt das schö - ne Früh - jahr an, und
al - les fängt zu blü - hen an auf grü - ner
Heid ____ und ü - ber - all.

1.
Jetzt fängt das schöne Frühjahr
an,
und alles fängt zu blühen an
auf grüner Heid und
überall.

2.
Es wachsen Blümlein auf dem
Feld
sie blühen weiß, blau, rot und
gelb,
so wie es meinem Schatz gefällt.

3.

Wenn ich zu meinem Schätzlein
    geh',
da singt das Lerchlein in der Höh,
dweil ich zu meinem Schätzlein
    geh'.

4.

Hab ich dich nicht recht treu
    geliebt

und dir dein Herz niemals
    betrübt?
Doch du führst eine falsche
    Lieb?

5.

Nun geh ich in den grünen Wald,
zu suchen meinen Aufenthalt,
weil mir mein Schatz nicht mehr
    gefallt.

LOVELY SPRING

1.

Lovely spring has finally sprung,
And the blooming has begun
Here on the heath and
    everywhere.

2.

Flowers growing in the field,
Blooming white, blue, yellow,
    red,
Just the way my sweetheart
    likes.

3.

When I call on my ladylove,
The lark starts singing up above,

When I call on my ladylove.

4.

Have I not always worshiped
    you?
And have I ever made you blue?
So why is your love untrue?

5.

Into green woods I go away
To look for a new place to stay,
For I no longer like my love.

Translation by
Alexandra Chciuk-Celt

KEIN SCHÖNER LAND

Text: August Wilhelm Florentin von Zuccalmaglio, 1838
Music: Traditional, 18th century

Kein schö-ner Land in die-ser Zeit,
als hier das uns-re weit und breit,
wo wir uns fin-den wohl un-ter
Lin-den zur A-bend-zeit, A-bend-zeit.

1.
Kein schöner Land in dieser
    Zeit,
als hier das unsre weit und breit,
wo wir uns finden
wohl unter Linden
zur Abendzeit,
wo wir uns finden
wohl unter Linden
zur Abendzeit.

2.
Da haben wir so manche Stund'
gesessen wohl in froher Rund'
und taten singen;
die Lieder klingen
im Eichengrund.
Und taten . . .

3.
Daß wir uns hier in diesem Tal
noch treffen so viel
    hundertmal,
Gott mag es schenken,
Gott mag es lenken,
er hat die Gnad'.
Gott mag es . . .

4.
Nun, Brüder, eine gute
    Nacht,
der Herr im hohen Himmel
    wacht!
In seiner Güten
uns zu behüten
ist er bedacht.
In seiner . . .

THERE ARE NO OTHER LANDS

1.
There are no other lands as
    beautiful as these,
We feel so good at dusk beneath
    the linden trees,
We feel so good at dusk beneath
    the linden trees.

2.
We've spent many an hour in
    merry company,
Singing songs among the oaks so
    joyfully (*repeat*).

3.
Let's meet in this valley many
    hundred times.
God can grant this, He is
    merciful and kind (*repeat*)!

4.
Good night, brothers! The Lord
    in heaven is above.
He watches over and protects us
    with His love (*repeat*).

Translated by
Alexandra Chciuk-Celt

NUN WILL DER LENZ UNS GRÜßEN

Text: Neidhard von Reuenthal, 13th century;
A. Fischer, 1885
Music: Traditional, 17th century

Nun will der Lenz uns grü - ßen, von
aus al - len Ek - ken sprie - ßen die
Mit - tag weht es lau;
Blu - men rot und blau.
Draus wob die brau - ne
Hei - de sich ein Ge - wand gar fein und
lädt im Fest - tags - klei - de zum Mai - en - tan - ze ein.

1.
Nun will der Lenz uns grüßen,
von Mittag weht es lau;
aus allen Ecken sprießen
die Blumen rot und blau.
Draus wob die braune Heide
sich ein Gewand gar fein
und lädt im Festtagskleide
zum Maientanze ein.

2.
Waldvöglein Lieder singen,
wie ihr sie nur begehrt.
Drum auf zum frohen Springen,
die Reis' ist Goldes wert!
Hei, unter grünen Linden,
da leuchten weiße Kleid!
Heija, nun hat uns Kinden
ein End all Wintersleid.

SPRING SENDS US HEARTY GREETINGS

1.
Spring sends us hearty
    greetings,
Warm breezes blow at noon,
And blue and scarlet
    flowers
Are everywhere in bloom.
The drab heath has now
    woven
Herself a lovely gown
For May Day celebrations;
She says to come on down.

2.
The forest birds are chirping
Just like we want them to;
Let's gambol and let's frolic,
It's so much fun to do!
White dresses shine and sparkle
Beneath the linden trees;
We're free of all our worries,
For Winter's on his knees.

Translated by
Alexandra Chciuk-Celt

O, WIE WOHL IST MIR AM ABEND

Text: Traditional
Music: Traditional

O, wie wohl ist mir am Abend,
mir am Abend,
Wenn zur Ruh' die Glocken läuten,

Glocken läuten,
Bim, bam, bim,
    bam.

Oh, How Lovely Is the Evening

Oh, how lovely is the evening,
is the evening,
When to rest the bells are
ringing,

bells are ringing,
Bim, bam, bim, bam, bim, bam.

Translator unknown

So Treiben Wir Den Winter Aus

Text: Traditional, 1584
Music: Tradtional, 1548

So trei - ben wir den Win - ter aus durch
uns - re Stadt zum Tor hin - aus mit sein Be - trug und
Li - sten, den rech - ten An - ti - chri - sten.

1.
So treiben wir den Winter aus
durch unsre Stadt zum Tor
hinaus
mit sein Betrug und Listen,
den rechten Antichristen.

2.
Wir stürzen ihn von Berg zu Tal,
damit er sich zu Tode fall';
wir jagen ihn über die Heiden,

daß er den Tod muß leiden.

3.
Nun hab'n wir den Winter
ausgetrieben,
so bringen wir den Sommer
hernied'n,
den Sommer und den
Maien,
die Blümlein mancherleien.

LET'S DRIVE OUT OLD MAN WINTER!

1.

Let's drive out Old Man Winter
now!
Let's chase him through the city
gates!
He's Antichrist the Crafty,
Full of deceit and lies.

2.

Let's chase him down the
mountain slope
To make him fall unto his death.

That way he can't defraud us
And cheat us with his wiles.

3.

We've chased out Old Man
Winter now,
So Summer can come back again.
The month of May and Summer,
With flowers of all kinds.

Translated by
Alexandra Chciuk-Celt

WINTER, ADE!

Text: A. H. Hoffmann von Fallersleben, 1835
Music: "Schatzchen, ade!" 1816

1.

Winter, ade!
Scheiden tut weh;
aber dein Scheiden macht

daß mir das Herze lacht.
Winter, ade!
Scheiden tut weh!

2.
Winter, ade!
Scheiden tut weh;
gerne vergeß ich dein,
kannst immer ferne sein.
Winter, ade . . .

3.
Winter, ade!
Scheiden tut weh;
gehst du nicht bald nach Haus,
lacht dich der Kuckuck aus.
Winter, ade . . .

WINTER, GOOD-BYE!

1.
Winter, good-bye!
I'm going to cry.
Weeping with joy, I say,
Watching you go away!
Winter, good-bye!
I'm going to cry.

2.
Winter, good-bye!
I'm going to cry.
I would be glad, I say,
If you could stay away!

Winter, good-bye!
I'm going to cry.

3.
Winter, good-bye!
I'm going to cry.
If you don't go home soon,
Cuckoo will laugh at you!
Winter, good-bye!
I'm going to cry.

Translated by
Alexandra Chciuk-Celt

WEM GOTT WILL RECHTE GUNST ERWEISEN

Text: Joseph von Eichendorff, 1822
Music: Fr. Theodor Fröhlich (op. 13), 1834

Wem Gott will rech-te Gunst er-wei-sen, den

schickt er in die wei-te Welt, dem

will er sei-ne Wun-der wei-sen in

Berg und Wald und Strom und Feld.

1.
Wem Gott will rechte Gunst
   erweisen,
den schickt er in die weite Welt,
dem will er seine Wunder
   weisen
in Berg und Wald und Strom
   und Feld.

2.
Die Bächlein von den Bergen
   springen,
die Lerchen schwirren hoch vor
   Lust.

Was sollt' ich nicht mit ihnen
   singen
aus voller Kehl' und frischer
   Brust?

3.
Den lieben Gott laß ich nur
   walten.
Der Bächlein, Lerchen, Wald
   und Feld
und Erd' und Himmel will erhalten,
hat auch mein' Sach' aufs Best'
   bestellt.

WHOMEVER GOD DECIDES TO FAVOR

1.
Whomever God decides to favor
He sends into the world so
   wide
To view His miracles in
   mountains,
In streams and fields and ocean-
   tides.

2.
Larks fly rejoicing through the
   heavens
While brooks from mountain-
   cliffs do spring;

Full-throated joy is so contagious
I cannot possibly not sing.

3.
O God, the world is Thy
   dominion,
Its brooks and larks and fields
   and woods;
As Thou preservest earth and
   heaven,
My fate within Thy hands is good.

Translated by
Alexandra Chciuk-Celt

WOHLAUF IN GOTTES SCHÖNE WELT

Text: Julius Levy, 1908
Music: Traditional, 1820

1.
Wohlauf in Gottes schöne Welt,
lebe wohl, ade!
Die Luft ist blau und grün das
    Feld,
lebe wohl, ade (ade)!
Die Berge glühn wie
    Edelstein,
ich wandre mit dem
    Sonnenschein.
La (la la la) la (la la),
ins weite Land hinein.
La (la la la) la (la la),
ins weite Land hinein.

2.
Du traute Stadt am Bergeshang,
lebe wohl, ade!
Du hoher Turm, du
    Glockenklang,
lebe wohl, ade!
Ihr Häuser, alle wohlbekannt,
noch einmal wink ich mit der
    Hand,
La (la la la) la (la la),
und nun seitab
    gewandt!
La (la la la) la (la la),
und nun seitab gewandt!

3.

An meinem Wege fließt der
  Bach,
lebe wohl, ade!
Der ruft den letzten Gruß mir
  nach,
lebe wohl, ade!
Ach Gott, da wird's so eigen
  mir,
so milde wehn die Lüfte hier,
La (la la la) la (la la),
als wär's ein Gruß von dir!
La (la la la) la (la la),
als war's ein Gruß von dir!

4.

Ein Gruß von dir, du schönes
  Kind,
lebe wohl, ade!
Doch nun den Berg hinab
  geschwind,
lebe wohl, ade!
Wer wandern will, der darf nicht
  stehn,
der darf niemals nach hinten sehn,
La (la la la) la (la la),
muß immer weiter gehn!
La (la la la) la (la la),
muß immer weiter gehn!

GOD'S GORGEOUS WORLD

1.
God's gorgeous world I'm off to
  see. Farewell, adieu.
The air is blue, the fields are
  green. Farewell adieu.
Mountains glitter like precious
  stones,
Into the sunshine do I roam,
Lalalala, lalala, into the wide,
  wide world.

2.
Familiar towns on
  mountainsides. Farewell,
  adieu.
High towers with their bells that
  chime. Farewell, adeiu.
I know these houses, all of
  them,
And wave my hand adieu
  again,
Lalalala, lalala, I'm off into the
  world.

3.
A flowing brook is crossing nigh.
  Farewell, adieu.
It sees me off and calls goodbye.
  Farewell, adieu.
O God, I feel Thy presence here,
The breeze seems like Thy
  greeting dear,
Lalalala, lalala, God's made a
  gorgeous world.

4.
From yonder lovely child: hello!
  Farewell, adieu.
A roamer never should look
  back
Nor linger stopping in his tracks.
Lalalala, lalala, he sees God's
  gorgeous world.

Translated by
Alexandra Chciuk-Celt

NUN RUHEN ALLE WÄLDER

Text: Paul Gerhardt, 1647
Music: Traditional, 15th century

Nun ru - hen al - le Wäl - der, Vieh,

Men-schen, Städt und Fel - der, es schläft die gan - ze

Welt. Ihr a - ber mei-ne Sin -nen, auf, auf, ihr sollt be -

gin - nen, was eu - rem Schöp-fer wohl ge - fällt.

1.
Nun ruhen alle Wälder,
Vieh, Menschen, Städt und Felder,
Es schläft die ganze Welt.
Ihr aber meine Sinnen,
Auf, auf, ihr sollt beginnen,
Was eurem Schöpfer wohl
    gefällt.

2.
Wo bist du, Sonne, blieben?
Die Nacht hat dich vertrieben,
Die Nacht, des Tages Feind;
Fahr hin! Ein ander Sonne,
Mein Jesus, meine Wonne,

Gar hell in meinem Herzen
    scheint.

3.
Der Tag ist nun vergangen,
Die güldnen Sterne prangen
Am blauen Himmelssaal;
Also werd ich auch stehen,
Wenn dich wird heißen gehen
Mein Gott aus diesem
    Jammertal.

4.
Der Leib eilt nun zur Ruhe,

Legt ab das Kleid und Schuhe,
Das Bild der Sterblichkeit;
Die zieh ich aus. Dagegen
Wird Christus mir anlegen
Den Rock der Ehr und
    Herrlichkeit.

5.
Nun geht, ihr matten Glieder,
Geht hin und legt euch nieder,
Der Betten ihr begehrt;
Es kommen Stund und Zeiten,
Da man euch wird bereiten
Zur Ruh ein Bettlein in der Erd.

6.
Das Haupt, die Füß und Hände
Sind froh, daß nun zu Ende
Die Arbeit kommen sei;

Herz, freu dich, du sollst werden
Vom Elend dieser Erden
Und von der Sünden Arbeit frei.

7.
Breit aus die Flügel beide,
O Jesus, meine Freude,
und nimm dein Kücklein ein!
Will Satan mich verschlingen,
So laß die Engelein singen:
Dies Kind soll unverletzet sein.

8.
Auch euch, ihr meine Lieben,
Soll heute nicht betrüben
Ein Unfall noch Gefahr.
Gott laß euch selig schlafen,
Stell euch die güldnen Waffen
Ums Bett und seiner Engel Schar.

EVENSONG

1.
The woods sleep bathed in
    shadow,
Beast, borough, man, and
    meadow;
The whole world is at rest:
But you, my waking senses,
Up, up, your take commences:
Obedient to God's fond request.

2.
Lo sun, where have you
    vanished?
By night your light is banished;
The night your light is banished;
The night, dark foe of day:
Yet go! a sweeter sunlight,
My Jesus, souls' delight,
Inside my heart shines bright its ray.

3.
Now day has taken flight,
The golden stars, with light
Ignite the glimmering firmament:
I too will just as they,
My Lord's command obey
and pass beyond earth's sad
    lament.

4.
The body hastes to rest,
Casts off worn shoes and
    dress,
Mortality's token sign:
These gladly I'll lay down,
For Christ my soul will gown
In honor's robe of glorious
    design.

5.

My head and hands and feet,
Contented, gladly greet
The end of daily toil:
Heart, sing! rejoice to be
From earth's sad trials soon free,
Released from sin's oppressive
    moil.

6.

Weary limbs worn aching-raw,
Seek now rest; to sleep
    withdraw!
A bed is all you crave:
Yet comes the hour and day,
When deep in mortal clay,
God lays the cradle of your grave.

7.

Spread forth a sheltering wing,
Lord Jesus, joy's true spring,

This fledgling chick encompass!
When Satan hurls hell's fire
Then sing the angels' choir:
Keep safe this child from
    Lucifer's distress.

8.

And you, my kindred all,
Let not night's purple pall
Awaken thoughts of hazard's
    awful menace.
God grant you restful sleep,
And round your bedposts
    keep
His heavenly host with golden
    swords of grace.

Translated by
Ingrid Walsøe-Engel

KOMM, LIEBER MAI, UND MACHE

Text: Christian Adolf Overbeck, 1775
Music: Wolfgang Amadeus Mozart (KV 596), 1791

Komm, lie - ber Mai, und ma - che die Bäu-me wie - der

grün, und laß uns an dem Ba - che die

klei - nen Veil-chen blühn! Wie möch-ten wir so

ger - ne ein Veil-chen wie - der sehn, ach,

lie - ber Mai, wie ger - ne ein - mal spa - zie-ren gehn.

1.

Komm, lieber Mai, und mache
Die Bäume wieder grün,
Und laß uns an dem Bache
Die kleinen Veilchen blühn!
Wie möchten wir so gerne
Ein Veilchen wieder sehn,
Ach, lieber Mai, wie gerne
Einmal spazieren gehn.

2.

Zwar Wintertage haben
Wohl auch der Freuden viel;
Man kann im Schnee eins traben
Und treibt manch Abendspiel,
Baut Häuserchen von Karten,
Spielt Blindekuh und Pfand;
Auch gibt's wohl
  Schlittenfahrten
Aufs liebe freie Land.

3.

Doch wenn die Vögel singen
Und wir dann froh und flink
Auf grünen Rasen springen,
Das ist ein ander Ding!

Jetzt muß mein
  Steckenpferdchen
Dort in dem Winkel stehn;
Denn draußen in dem Gärtchen
kann man vor Kot nicht gehn.

4.

Am meisten aber dauert
Mich Lottchens Herzeleid;
Das arme Mädchen lauert
Recht auf die Blumenzeit;
Umsonst hol ich ihr Spielchen
Zum Zeitvertreib herbei,
Sie sitzt in ihrem Stühlchen
Wie's Hühnchen auf dem Ei.

5.

Ach wenn's doch erst gelinder
Und grüner draußen wär!
Komm, lieber Mai, wir Kinder,
Wir bitten dich gar sehr!
O komm und bring vor allen
Uns viele Veilchen mit,
Bring auch viel Nachtigallen
Und schöne Kuckucks mit!

YEARNING FOR SPRING

1.
Come, dear May, and make
the trees green again,
and for me by the brook let
the little violets bloom!
How much I would like
to see a voilet again,
ah, dear May, how I would like
sometime to go walking!

2.
True, the days of winter have
also many pleasures;
we can trot in the snow,
and in the evening games take
    over;
we build houses with cards,
play blind man's bluff and
    forfeits;
also there are sleighrides
into the open country.

3.
But when the birds sing
and we then, happy and agile,
leap on the green grass,
that is another thing!
Now my hobby horse
must stand in the corner,

for outside in the garden
we cannot walk, because of the
    mud.

4.
But most important reamains for
    me
Lotte's sorrow;
the poor girl waits in the garden
for the time of flowers.
In vain I bring her toys
to pass the time away;
she sits in her little chair
like a hen on her eggs.

5.
Ah, if it were only milder
and greener outside!
Come, dear May, we children
beg you so earnestly!
O come and above all bring
many violets for us:
bring also the nightingales
and beautiful cuckoos!

Translated by
Philip Lieson Miller

Songs of Wanderers

AM BRUNNEN VOR DEM TORE

Text: Wilhelm Müller, 1821
Music: Franz Schubert (op. 89, no. 5), 1828

Am Brun - nen vor dem To - re   da

steht ein Lin - den-baum,   ich träumt   in sei-nem

Schat-ten   so man-chen sü - ßen Traum.   Ich

schnitt in sei-ne Rin - de   so man-ches lie -be

Wort.   Es zog   in Freud und   Lei - de   zu

ihm mich im-mer fort,   zu ihm mich im - mer fort.

1.
Am Brunnen vor dem Tore
da steht ein Lindenbaum,
ich träumt in seinem Schatten
so manchen süßen Traum.
Ich schnitt in seine Rinde
so manches liebe Wort.
Es zog in Freud und Leide
zu ihm mich immer fort,
zu ihm mich immer fort.

2.
Ich mußt' auch heute wandern
vorbei in tiefer Nacht,
da hab' ich noch im Dunkeln
die Augen zugemacht.

Und seine Zweige rauschten,
als riefen sie mir zu:
Komm her zu mir, Geselle,
hier find'st du deine Ruh!

3.
Die kalten Winde bliesen
mir grad ins Angesicht,
der Hut flog mir vom Kopfe,
ich wendete mich nicht.
Nun bin ich manche Stunde
entfernt von jenem Ort,
und immer hör ich's rauschen:
du fändest Ruhe dort!

THE LINDEN TREE

1.
By the well in front of the gate
there stands a linden tree;
I have dreamed in its shade
many a sweet dream.
I have carved in its bark
many a fond word;
in joy and in sorrow
I have always felt drawn
    to it.

2.
I had to pass it again just now
in the deep night,
and even in the dark

I closed my eyes.
And its branches rustled,
as if they were calling to me:
"Come here, friend,
here you will find rest!"

3.
The cold winds blew
right into my face;
my hat flew off my head,
yet I always hear it rustling:
"you would find rest there!"

Translated by
Philip Lieson Miller

AUF, DU JUNGER WANDERSMANN

Text: Walther Hensel
Music: Traditional, 18th century

1.

Auf du junger Wandersmann,
Jetzo kommt die Zeit heran,
Die Wanderzeit, die gibt uns
    Freud.
Woll'n uns auf die Fahrt
    begeben,
Das ist unser schönstes Leben:
Große Wasser, Berg und Tal
Anzuschauen überall.

2.

An dem schönen Donaufluß
Findet man ja seine Lust
Und seine Freud auf grüner Heid,
Wo die Vöglein lieblich
    singen
Und die Hirschlein fröhlich
    springen,
Dann kommt man vor eine
    Stadt,
Wo man gut Arbeit hat.

3.

Mancher hinterm Ofen sitzt
Und gar fein die Ohren spitzt,
Kein Stund vor's Haus ist
    kommen aus;

Den soll man als G'sell
    erkennen,
Oder gar ein Meister nennen,
Der noch nirgend ist gewest,
Nur gesessen in sei'm Nest.

4.

Mancher hat auf seiner Reis
Ausgestanden Müh und Schweiß
Und Not und Pein, das muß so
    sein;
Trägt's Felleisen auf dem
    Rücken,
Trägt es über tausend Brücken,
Bis er kommt nach Innsbruck
    ein,
Wo man trinkt Tiroler Wein.

5.

Morgens, wenn der Tag angeht
Und die Sonn am Himmel steht
So herrlich rot wie Milch und
    Blut:
Auf, ihr Brüder, laßt uns reisen,
Unserm Herrgott Dank erweisen
Für die fröhlich Wanderzeit,
Hier und in die Ewigkeit!

UP, YOUNG TRAVELER, HI-HO

1.

Up, young traveler, hi-ho,
Journeys bring us joy, let's
    go.

For that time is nigh at hand,
Time for hiking through the
    land.

Mountains, valleys, lakes, and
    seas
To be viewed by you and me:
That's the beauty of our lives.

2.
Hiking near the Danube blue
—I like that, and so do you.
What a pleasure, heaths of
    green,
Where sweet birdies chirp and
    sing
And the fawns go frolicking.
Soon we will arrive in town,
Someplace where the jobs
    abound.

3.
Some folks simply sit at home,
Doing nothing, staying warm,
Pricking up their ears. Land's
    sakes,
That does not a master make—
Nor a journeyman, I say,
If you've never been away,
Never seen the world at all.

4.
Others travel near and far,
Sweating, suff'ring, working
    hard.
That's how you're supposed to
    act:
With a knapsack on your
    back,
Carry it without a frown
Till you reach fair Innsbruck
    town
Where you have a glass of wine.

5.
When the day dawns in the
    morn
And the sun has been
    reborn,
Crimson sky like milk and
    blood:
Brothers, let's get up and go,
God our gratitude we show
For our joyful travels free,
Here and in Eternity!

Translated by
Alexandra Chciuk-Celt

DAS WANDERN IST DES MÜLLERS LUST

Text: Wilhelm Müller, 1818

Music: Franz Schubert (op. D. 795, no. 1); C. Zöllner, 1844

Das Wan-dern ist des Mül-lers Lust, das Wan-dern ist des

Mül-lers Lust, das Wan - dern. Das muß ein schlechter

Mül-ler sein, dem nie-mals fiel das Wan-dern ein, dem
nie-mals fiel das Wan-dern ein, das Wan - dern.

1.

Das Wandern ist des Müllers Lust,
das Wandern ist des Müllers Lust,
das Wandern.
Das muß ein schlechter Müller
     sein,
dem niemals fiel das Wandern ein,
dem niemals fiel das Wandern
     ein,
das Wandern.

2.

Vom Wasser haben wir's gelernt,
vom Wasser haben wir's gelernt,
vom Wasser:
Das hat nicht Rast bei Tag und
     Nacht,
ist stets auf Wanderschaft
     bedacht,
das Wasser.

3.

Das sehn wir auch den Rädern ab,
das sehn wir auch den Rädern ab,
den Rädern:
Die gar nicht gerne stille stehn,

die sich mein Tag nicht müde
     drehn,
die Räder.

4.

Die Steine selbst, so schwer sie
     sind,
die Steine selbst, so schwer sie
     sind,
die Steine,
sie tanzen mit den muntern
     Reih'n
und wollen gar noch schneller
     sein,
die Steine.

5.

O Wandern, Wandern meine
     Lust,
O Wandern, Wandern meine Lust,
O Wandern!
Herr Meister und Frau
     Meisterin,
laßt mich in Frieden weiter ziehn
und wandern.

The Journeyman's Song

1.
Oh wandering is a miller's joy,
Oh wandering!
A sorry miller he must be
Who never wanted to be free
For wandering!

2.
The water taught us what to do,
The water!
For it rests not by night or day,
And always strains to be away,
The water!

3.
We learn it from the millwheels
     too,
The millwheels!
They're like the water down
     below,
I've never seen them weary grow,
The millwheels!

4.
The millstones too, though
     heavy they,
The millstones!
In merry circles round they
     dance,
Would like to faster race and
     prance,
The millstones!

5.
Oh, wandering, wandering, my
     delight,
Oh, wandering!
Oh, master, mistress miller,
     pray
Let me in peace now go my way
And wander!

Translated by
Francis Owen

Der Mai ist gekommen

Text: Emanuel Geibel, 1835
Music: Justus Wilhelm Lyra, 1843

1.
Der Mai ist gekommen,
die Bäume schlagen aus;
da bleibe wer Lust hat,
mit Sorgen zu Haus!
Wie die Wolken dort wandern
am himmlischen Zelt,
so steht auch mir der Sinn
in die weite, weite Welt!

2.
Herr Vater, Frau Mutter,
daß Gott euch behüt'!
Wer weiß, wo in der Ferne
mein Glück mir noch blüt.
Es gibt so manche Straße,
da nimmer ich marschiert;
es gibt so manchen Wein,
den ich nimmer noch probiert.

3.
Frisch auf drum, frisch auf,
im hellen Sonnenstrahl,
wohl über die Berge,
wohl durch das tiefe Tal!
Die Quellen erklingen,
die Bäume rauschen all—
mein Herz ist wie' ne Lerche
und stimmet ein mit Schall.

4.
Und abends im Städtchen,
da kehr' ich durstig ein:
Herr Wirt, mein Herr Wirt,
eine Kanne blanken Wein!
Ergreife die Fiedel,
du lustiger Spielmann du,
von meinem Schatz das Liedel,
das sing' ich dazu.

5.
Und find ich keine Herberg',
so lieg' ich zu Nacht
wohl unter blauem Himmel,
die Sterne halten Wacht.
Im Winde, die Linde,
die rauscht mich ein gemach,
es küsset in der Früh'
das Morgenrot mich wach.

6.
O Wandern, o Wandern,
du freie Burschenlust!
Da wehet Gottes Odem,
so frisch in der Brust;
da singet und jauchzet
das Herz zum Himmelszelt:
Wie bist du doch so schön,
o du weite, weite Welt!

Now May Is Arriving

1.
Now May is arriving,
Trees break into leaf;
Who wants to stay home now,
Alone with his grief?
Just like the clouds journey
The firmament sky,
I'd like to go trav'ling,
The world is so wide!

2.
O Father, O Mother,
May God be with you!
Somewhere in the distance
My luck is in bloom.
The paths are so many
I've not traveled yet,
Wines I haven't tasted,
Men I haven't met.

3.
So off I go hiking
In sun's golden rays,
Up over the mountains,
Through valleys, away!
The trees rustle softly,
The brook's murmuring,
My heart is a skylark
And gladly joins in!

4.
At night I am thirsty
And walk into town:
"Oh, barkeep, some wine please,
So smooth going down!
Oh, pick up your fiddle
To my sweetheart's song,
If you play the music,
I'll sing right along!"

5.
If I cannot find me
A bed in the inn,
The night sky protects me,
The stars twinkling.
The linden trees rustle
A lullaby great.
Then dawn in the
morning
Will kiss me awake.

6.
Adventurous travel,
O freedom, O zest!
God's breath wafts right
    through me
And freshens my breast.
My heart is rejoicing
To heavens on high:
The world is so gorgeous
Beneath this bright sky!

Translated by
Alexandra Chciuk-Celt

EIN HELLER UND EIN BATZEN

Text: Albert Schlippenbach, prior to 1830
Music: Traditional

1.
Ein Heller und ein Batzen,
die waren beide mein;
der Heller ward zu Wasser,
der Batzen ward zu Wein.
Juchheidi, juchheida,
valleri, juchheirassa,
juchheidi, juchheida,
valleri, juchhe.

2.
Die Wirtsleut und die
    Mädel,
die rufen beid: Oh weh!
Die Wirtsleut, wenn ich
    komme,
die Mädel, wenn ich geh.

3.
Meine Strümpfe sind zerrissen,
meine Stiefel sind entzwei,
und draußen auf der Heiden,
da singt der Vogel frei.

4.
Und gäb's kein Landstraß nirgend,
da säß ich still zu Haus,
und gäb's kein Loch im Fasse,
da tränk ich gar nicht draus.

5.
War das 'ne große Freude,
als ihn der Herrgott schuf,
ein Kerl, wie Samt und Seide,
nur schade, daß er suff.

ᘓᘔ

A PENNY AND A FORTUNE

1.

A penny and a fortune,
I've had both in my time;
The penny turned to water,
The fortune turned to wine.
Yoo-hie-dee, yoo-hie-dah,
Valleree, yoo-hie-ras-sah,
Yoo-hie-dee, yoo-hie-dah,
Valleree, yoo-hey!

2.

The wenches and the barkeeps
Both cry "Oh, no!" and grieve:
The barkeeps when I'm
    coming,
The wenches when I leave.
Yoo-hie-dee, etc.

3.

My boots are all in tatters,
My shoes are history,
And out there in the meadow
The bird is singing free.
Yoo-hie-dee, etc.

4.

And when He made Yours
    Truly,
God must have had a ball:
A smooth and polished fellow
Who's just a drunk, that's all.
Yoo-hie-dee, etc.

Translated by
Alexandra Chciuk-Celt

ES, ES, ES UND ES

Text: Traditional, 1826
Music: Traditional, 1826

Es, es, es und es, es ist ein har-ter
weil, weil, weil und weil, weil ich aus Frankfurt

Schluß, muß. Drum schlag ich Frank-furt

aus dem Sinn und wen-de mich, Gott weiß, wo-hin. Ich

will mein Glück pro - bie - - ren, mar - schie - ren.

1.

Es, es, es und es, es ist ein harter
Schluß,
weil, weil, weil und weil, weil ich
aus Frankfurt muß.
Drum schlag ich Frankfurt aus
dem Sinn
und wende mich, Gott weiß,
wohin.
Ich will mein Glück probieren,
marschieren.

2.

Er, er, er und er, Herr Meister,
leb er wohl!
Er, er, er und er, Herr Meister,
leb er wohl!
Ich sag's ihm grad frei ins
Gesicht:
Seine Arbeit und sein Lohn
gefällt mir nicht.
Ich will mein Glück probieren,
marschieren.

3.

Sie, sie, sie und sie, Frau
Meistrin, leb sie wohl!
Sie, sie, sie und sie, Frau
Meistrin, leb sie wohl!
Ihr Essen war so angericht't,
manchmal fraßen es die
Schweine nicht.
Ich will mein Glück probieren,
marschieren.

4.

Er, er, er und er, Herr Wirt, nun
leb er wohl!
Er, er, er und er, Herr Wirt, nun
leb er wohl!
Hätt' er die Kreid' nicht doppelt
geschrieben,
so wär ich noch länger
dageblieben.
Ich will mein Glück probieren,
marschieren.

5.

Und, und, und und und, und
wird auf mich zuletzt,
auch, auch, auch und auch, auch
mal ein Hund gehetzt:
Dem Kerl setz' auf den
Türenknauf
ich nachts 'was warmes Weiches
drauf.
ich will mein Glück probieren,
marschieren.

6.

Ihr, ihr, ihr und ihr, ihr Brüder
lebet wohl!
Ihr, ihr, ihr und ihr, ihr Brüder
lebet wohl!
Hab'ich euch was zuleid getan,
so bitt ich um Verzeihung
an.
Ich will mein Glück probieren,
marschieren.

IT, IT, IT, AND IT

1.
It, it, it, and it, it's sad it's ending
    so,
for, for, for, and for, for I must
    leave and go.
I've been in this town quite a bit,
and have it up to here with it.
I shall try my luck yonder,
and wander.

2.
He, he, he, and he, my master
    fare thee well,
he, he, he, and he, my master
    fare thee well,
I'll tell you now quite frank and
    free,
your work and wages don't
    please me.
I shall try my luck yonder,
and wander.

3.
She, she, she, and she, the
    master's wife farewell,
she, she, she, and she, the
    master's wife farewell,
The food she served was of that
    kind
that even pigs left it behind.
I shall try my luck yonder,
and wander.

4.
He, he, he, and he, innkeeper
    fare thee well,

he, he, he, and he, innkeeper fare
    thee well,
had he not doubled up the
    charge,
it might well be I wouldn't
    march.
I shall try my luck yonder,
and wander.
I shall try my luck yonder,
and wander.

5.
And, and, and, and and, if finally
    there went
some, some, some, and some,
    some dog for me they sent,
I'd take some warm soft stuff at
    night,
and decorate their door all
    right.
I shall try my luck yonder,
and wander.

6.
You, you, you, and you, my
    brothers fare you well,
you, you, you, and you, my
    brothers fare you well,
if I've hurt you in any way,
I beg your parden, if I may.
I shall try my luck yonder,
and wander.

Translated by
Sabine Tober

GLÜCK AUF! GLÜCK AUF!

Text: Traditional, 1730
Music: Traditional, 18th century

Glück auf! Glück auf! Der Stei-ger kommt, und er
hat sein hel - les Licht bei der Nacht und er
hat sein hel - les Licht bei der Nacht hat'r an - ge -
zündt ____, hat'r an - ge - - zündt.

1.
Glück auf! Glück auf!
Der Steiger kommt,
und er hat sein helles
    Licht
bei der Nacht,
und er hat sein helles Licht
bei der Nacht
hat'r angezündt,
hat'r angezündt.

2.
Schon angezündt,
es gibt ein' Schein,
damit fahren wir ins
Bergwerk 'nein,
damit fahren wir ins
Bergwerk 'nein,
ins Bergwerk 'nein
ins Bergwerk 'nein.

3.
Ins Bergwerk 'nein
wo Bergleut' sein;
und sie graben das Silber
aus Felsengestein,
und sie graben das Silber
aus Felsengestein,
aus Felsenstein,
aus Felsenstein.

4.
Aus Felsenstein
grab'n sie das Gold.
Und dem schwarzbraunen

Mägdlein, dem sein sie
   hold,
Und dem schwarzbraunen

Mägdlein, dem sein sie hold,
dem sein sie hold,
dem sein sie hold.

GOOD LUCK, GOOD LUCK!

1.
Good luck, good luck! The
   miner's here.
And he's got his headlamp
   lighting his way,
He's turned it on, he's turned it
   on.

2.
He's turned it on. The light
   shines forth.
We'll use it to ride right into the
   mines,
We'll use it to ride right into the
   mines,
Into the mines, into the
   mines.

3.
Into the mines, where miners work.
They mine silver, digging it out,
They mine silver, digging it out,
Out of this rock, out of this rock.

4.
Out of this rock they go mining
   gold.
And the swarthy- faced maiden
   here,
And the swarthy-face maiden here
Is their sweetheart, is their
   sweetheart.

Translated by Alexandra
Chciuk-Celt

HOCH AUF DEM GELBEN WAGEN

Text: Rudolf Baumbach, 1879
Music: Heinz Höhne, 1922

1.
Hoch auf dem gelben Wagen
sitz ich beim Schwager vorn.
Vorwärts die Rosse traben;
lustig schmettert das Horn.
Berge, Täler und Auen,
leuchtendes Ährengold.
Ich möchte in Ruhe gern schauen,
aber der Wagen, der rollt.

2.
Flöten hör ich und Geigen,
lustiges Baßgebrumm,
junges Volk im Reigen
tanzt um die Linde herum.
Wirbelnde Blätter im Winde,
es jauchzt und lacht und tollt,
ich bliebe so gern bei der Linde,
aber der Wagen, der rollt.

3.

Postillon in der Schenke
füttert die Rosse im Flug,
schäumendes Gerstengetränke
reicht uns der Wirt im Krug.
Hinter den Fensterscheiben
lacht ein Gesicht gar hold,
ich möchte so gerne noch
    bleiben,
aber der Wagen, der rollt.

4.

Sitzt einmal ein Gerippe
hoch auf dem Wagen vorn,
hält statt der Peitsche die
    Hippe,
Stundenglass statt Horn.
Sag ich: Ade, nun, ihr Lieben,
die ihr nicht mitfahren wollt,
ich wäre so gern noch geblieben,
aber der Wagen, der rollt.

ATOP THE YELLOW CARRIAGE

1.

I'm sitting here with my brother-
    in-law
On top of the carriage yellow.
The horses are trotting in front
    of the coach,
The horn blows so merry and
    mellow
The fields and the heaths and the
    meadows we pass
Gleam golden with grain 'mid
    the ponds.
I'd love to stay for a much better
    look,
But the carriage keeps rolling
    along.

2.

The mail-coach stops at the inn
    for a moment,
The horses are fed in a few.
The innkeeper hands me an
    earthenware mugful
Of foaming and barley-based
    brew.
Inside the window, a lovely face
    laughing,

Fringed with ringlets of blond.
I'd love to stay for a much better
    look,
But the carriage keeps rolling
    along.

3.

I hear some fiddles and flutes
    being played,
Young men and women join
    hands,
And to the tunes of the merry
    noise,
Around the linden they dance.
They whirl the leaves of the
    linden about
In merriment, laughter, and
    song.
I'd love to stay for a much better
    look,
But the carriage keeps rolling
    along.

4.

Someday my skeleton will be
    a-sitting

On the coach-top forlorn,
A scythe will be heard instead of
a horse-whip,
A funeral-march, not a horn.
Then I'll say good-bye to my
loved ones
Who won't join me beyond;

I'd love to stay here for just a
while longer,
But the carriage keeps rolling
along.

Translated by
Alexandra Chciuk-Celt

IM FRÜHTAU ZU BERGE

Text: (Swedish original) Olaf Thunman, 1905;
(German translation) G. Schulten, 1917
Music: Traditional (Swedish)

Im Früh-tau zu Ber-ge wir ziehn, fal-le-ra, es
grü-nen al-le Wäl-der, al-le Höh'n, fal-le-ra.
Wir wan-dern oh-ne Sor-gen sin-gend in den
Mor-gen, noch e-he im Ta-le die Häh-ne krähn.

1.
Im Frühtau zu Berge wir ziehn,
fallera,
es grünen alle Wälder, alle
Höh'n, fallera.
Wir wandern ohne Sorgen
singend in den Morgen,

noch ehe im Tale die Hähne krähn.
Wir wandern . . .

2.
Ihr alten und hochweisen Leut,
fallera,

ihr denkt wohl, wir sind nicht
    gescheit?
    Fallera.
Wer wollte aber singen,
wenn wir schon Grillen fingen
in dieser herrlichen
    Frühlingszeit?
Wer wollte . . .

3.
Werft ab alle Sorge und Qual,
    fallera,
und wandert mit uns aus dem Tal!
    Fallera.
Wir sind hinaus gegangen,
den Sonnenschein zu fangen:
Kommt mit und versucht es auch
    selbst einmal!
Wir sind . . .

HIKING IN THE MOUNTAIN DEW

1.
We hike in the mountain dew,
    fa-la-la,
Woods are green and skies are
    blue, fa-la-la.
We wander in the morning,
Free of worry, singing
So early roosters haven't even
    crowed.
We wander . . .

2.
All you wise and ancient men,
    fa-la-la,
Must think we're not very smart,
    fa-la-la.
But who would ever sing
This gorgeous day in spring

If we just sat and moped like
    you?
But who would . . .

3.
Just banish worries from your
    mind, fa-la-la,
And leave the valley far behind!
    Fa-la-la.
We're here so we can run
And gambo in the sun,
So why not come and join us
    too?
We're here so . . .

Translated by
Alexandra Chciuk-Celt

IM KRUG ZUM GRÜNEN KRANZE

Text: Wilhelm Müller, 1821
Music: Traditional, 1843

1.
Im Krug zum grünen Kranze,
da kehrt ich durstig ein;
da saß ein Wandrer drinnen,
ja drinnen am Tisch beim kühlen
     Wein,
da saß ein Wandrer drinnen,
ja drinnen am Tisch beim kühlen
     Wein.

2.
Ein Glas ward eingegossen,
das wurde nimmer leer;
sein Haupt ruht auf dem
     Bündel,
dem Bündel, als wär's ihm viel
     zu schwer,
sein Haupt ruht . . .

3.
Ich tat mich zu ihm setzen,
ich sah ihm ins Gesicht,
das schien mir gar befreundet,
befreundet und dennoch kannt
     ich's nicht,
das schien . . .

4.
Da sah auch mir ins Auge
der fremde Wandersmann
und füllte meinen Becher,
ja Becher und sah mich wieder an,
und füllte meinen. . .

5.
Hei! Wie die Becher klangen,
wie brannte Hand in Hand:

wie brannte Hand in Hand:
»Es leb' die Liebste
    deine,

ja deine, Herzbruder im
    Vaterland,
es leb' die . . .

THE EMERALD GARLAND

1.
I felt a little thirsty
And walked into an inn;
It was the Emerald Garland,
A traveler drank within.
It was the Emerald Garland,
A traveler drank within.

2.
His glass was never empty,
They poured the cool wine in.
He hung his head so heavy,
His chest was in his chin.
He hung his head , etc.

3.
I sat on down beside him
And looked into his face.
I thought he seemed familiar,
A look I couldn't place.
I thought, etc.

4.
This stranger then glanced
    at me
And filled his cup with wine,
And then this trav'ling
    stranger
Looked right into my eyes.
And then this, etc.

5.
I recognized my buddy,
We drank glass after glass:
Long live our lovely
    homeland,
Long live your loving lass!
Long live our lovely
    homeland,
Long live your loving lass!

Translated by
Alexandra Chciuk-Celt

IM MÄRZEN DER BAUER

Text: Traditional, 19th century; Walther Hensel, 1923
Music: Traditional

1.
Im Märzen der Bauer die
    Rößlein einspannt;
er setzt seine Felder und Wiesen
    instand,

er pflüget den Boden, er egget
    und sät
und rührt seine Hände
    frühmorgens und spät.

2.

Die Bäurin, die Mägde, sie
	dürfen nicht ruhn:
sie haben im Haus und im
	Garten zu tun;
sie freun sich, wenn alles
	schön
	grünet und blüht.

3.

So geht unter Arbeit das
	Frühjahr vorbei;
da erntet der Bauer das duftende
	Heu;
er mäht das Getreide, dann
	drischt er es aus:
im Winter da gibt es manch
	fröhlichen Schmaus.

FARMWORK SONG

1.

The farmer now yokes up his
	horses in March,
His fields and his meadows he
	means to maintain.
He plows up his soil, and he
	harrows and sows,
His hands never idle, no
	movement in vain.

2.

No rest for his hard-working
	wife or the girls,
The house and the garden need
	tending all day.

They hoe and they rake while
	they're singing a song,
Look forward to seeing things
	blooming in May.

3.

Because of the work that took
	up all of Spring,
The farmer will harvest sweet
	hay in the Fall.
He mows and he threshes the
	grain he will need
So Winter's abundant and joyful
	for all.

Translated by
Alexandra Chciuk-Celt

৩৫

INNSBRUCK, ICH MUß DICH LASSEN

Text: Traditional, 15th century
Music: Heinrich Isaac, late 15th century

Inns-bruck, ich muß dich las - sen, ich fahr da-hin mein Stra - ßen, in frem-de Land da - hin. Mein Freud ist mir ge-nom - men, die ich nit weiß be-kom-men, wo ich in E - - - lend bin.

1.
Innsbruck, ich muß dich lassen,
ich fahr dahin mein Straßen,
in fremde Land dahin.
Mein Freud ist mir genommen,
die ich nit weiß bekommen,
wo ich in Elend bin.

2.
Groß Leid muß ich jetzt tragen,
das ich allein tu klagen
dem liebsten Buhlen mein.

Ach Lieb, nun laß mich Armen
im Herzen dein erbarmen,
daß ich muß dannen sein.

3.
Mein Trost ob allen Weiben,
dein tu ich ewig bleiben,
stät, treu, der Ehren fromm.
Nun müß dich Gott bewahren,
in aller Tugend sparen,
bis daß ich wiederkomm.

INNSBRUCK, NOW I MUST DEPART

1.
Innsbruck, now I must depart,
My journey's road I'm forced to
    start,
To foreign lands I'll roam.
Sweet happiness has vanished,
Joy stolen, ever banished,
In climes so far from home.

2.
Great sorrow now weighs on
    me,
Yet I'll ask pity only
From my heart's true delight.

All wretched, I entreat thee,
My love, show thy heart's
    mercy,
For I must leave tonight.

3.
No other girl will cheer me,
And ever will I love thee,
Your true and steadfast swain.
Now God alone shall guard
    thee.

Translated by
Ingrid Walsøe-Engel

NUN ADE, DU MEIN LIEB HEIMATLAND

Text: August Disselhoff, 1851
Music: Traditional, 19th century

1.
Nun ade, du mein lieb
        Heimatland,
lieb Heimatland, ade.
Es geht nun fort zum fremden
        Strand,
lieb Heimatland, ade.
Und so sing ich denn mit frohem
        Mut,
wie man singet, wenn man
        wandern tut,
lieb Heimatland, ade!

2.
Wie du lachst mit deines
        Himmels Blau,
lieb Heimatland, ade.
Wie du grüßest mich mit Feld
        und Au',
lieb Heimatland, ade.
Gott weiß, zu dir steht stets mein
        Sinn,
doch jetzt zur Ferne zieht's mich
        hin:
Lieb Heimatland, ade!

3.

Begleitest mich, du lieber Fluß,
lieb Heimatland, ade.
Bist traurig, daß ich wandern
   muß;
lieb Heimatland, ade.

Vom moos'gen Stein, vom
   wald'gen Tal,
da grüß' ich dich zum
   letztenmal:
Lieb Heimatland, ade!

SWEET HOMELAND, FAREWELL!

1.

Sweet homeland, farewell! I now must travel to other shores, so I sing loudly and heartily, the way a person does when taking off somewhere. Sweet homeland, farewell!

2.

Sweet homeland, farewell! I'll miss the laughter of your blue skies, the greetings from your meadows, God knows, but now I must leave. Sweet homeland, farewell!

3.

Sweet homeland, farewell! You're sad to see me go, the river follows me to see me off. My final greetings to mossy stones and wooded valleys. Sweet homeland, farewell!

Translated by
Alexandra Chciuk-Celt

SCHÖN IST DIE WELT

Text: Traditional, late 19th century
Music: Traditional

Schön ist die Welt, drum Brü - der, laßt uns
rei - sen wohl in die wei - te
Welt, wohl in die wei - te Welt.

1.
Schön ist die Welt,
drum Brüder, laßt uns reisen
wohl in die weite Welt,
wohl in die weite Welt.

2.
Wir sind nicht stolz,
wir brauchen keine Pferde,
die uns von dannen ziehn,
die uns von dannen ziehn.

3.
Wir steig'n hinauf
auf Berge und auf Hügel,

wo uns die Sonne sticht,
wo uns die Sonne sticht.

4.
Wir laben uns
an jeder Felsenquelle,
wo frisches Wasser fließt.
wo frisches Wasser fließt.

5.
Wir reisen fort
von einer Stadt zur andern,
wo uns die Luft gefällt,
wo uns die Luft gefällt.

THE WORLD IS BEAUTIFUL

1.
The world is beautiful, so brethren, let's roam it!

2.
We're not too proud, we don't need horses in order to travel.

3.
We'll climb up hills and mountains and feel the stinging sun.

4.
We'll seek refreshment at every brook where pristine water flows.

5.
We'll travel from town to town, wherever we please.

*Translated by
Alexandra Chciuk-Celt*

ÜB IMMER TREU UND REDLICHKEIT

Text: Ludwig Christoph Heinrich Hölty, 1775
Music: Wolfgang Amadeus Mozart, 1791

1.
Üb immer Treu und Redlichkeit
Bis an dein kühles Grab
Und weiche keinen Finger breit

Von Gottes Wegen ab;
Dann wirst du wie auf grünen
    Aun,

Durchs Pilgerleben gehn,
Dann kannst du sonder Furch
    und Graun
Dem Tod ins Auge sehn.

2.
Dann wird die Sichel und der
    Pflug
In deiner Hand so leicht,
Dann singest du beim
    Wasserkrug,
Als warst du Wein gereicht.
Dem Bösewicht wird alles
    schwer,
Er tue, was er tu.
Der Teufel treibt ihn hin und her
Und läßt ihm keine Ruh.

3.
Der schöne Frühling lacht ihm
    nicht,
Ihm lacht kein Ährenfeld:
Er ist auf Lug und Trug erpicht
Und wünscht sich nichts als
    Geld,
Der Wind im Hain, das Laub am
    Baum
Saust ihm Entsetzen zu:
Er findet nach des Lebens Traum
Im Grabe keine Ruh.

4.
Dann muß er in der Geisterstund
Aus seinem Grabe gehn
Und oft als schwarzer
    Kettenhund
Vor seiner Haustür stehn.
Die Spinnerinnen die, das Rad
Im Arm, nach Hause gehn
Erzittern wie ein Espenblatt,
Wenn sie ihn gehen sehn.

5.
Und jede Spinnestube spricht
Von diesem Abenteur
Und wünscht den toten
    Bösewicht
Ins tiefste Höllenfeur.
Der alte Kunz war bis
    ans Grab
Ein richter Höllenbrand;
Er pfügte seinem Nachbar ab
Und stahl ihm vieles Land.

6.
Nun pflügt er als ein
    Feuermann
Auf seines Nachbars Flur
Und mißt das Feld hinab,
    hinan
Mit einer glühnden Schnur;
Er brennet wie ein Schober
    Stroh
Dem glühnden Pfluge nach
Und pflügt und brennet
    lichterloh
Bis an den hellen Tag.

7.
Der Amtmann, der im Weine
    floß,
Den Bauern schlug
    halbkrumm,
Trabt nun auf einem glühnden
    Roß
In jenem Wald herum.
Der Pfarrer, der aufs Tanzen
    schalt
Und Filz und Wurchrer
    war,
Steht nun als schwarze
    Spukgestalt
Am nächtlichen Altar.

8.

Üb immer Treu und Redlichkeit
Bis an dein kühles Grab,
Und weiche keinen Finger
    breit
Von Gottes Wegen ab:

Dann suchen Enkel deine Gruft
Und weinen Tränen drauf
Und Sommerblumen, voll von
    Duft,
Blühn aus den Tränen auf.

BE ALWAYS TRUE AND RIGHTEOUS

1.

Be always true and righteous
Until your dying day,
Stay on God's straight and
    narrow path,
And never go astray;
Then you shall stroll in
    meadows green
And have a pilgrim's life,
And never fear nor cringe when
    you
Look Death straight in the eye.

2.

The sickle and the plough will
    feel
So light unto your tug,
Instead of water you will think
There's wine inside the jug.
For evil men cannot succeed,
No matter how they try;
The devil won't let them
    alone,
He leaves them high and dry.

3.

An evil man will never hear
The laughter of the spring;
He's full of lies, full of deceit,
And gold is everything.

He's filled with horror when he
    hears
A sweet and leafy breeze;
And even when life's dream is o'er,
The grave brings him no peace.

4.

He's often forced to leave his
    grave
At every witching hour,
Becoming some black dog that's
    chained
Before his own front door.
The spinning-women going
    home,
Their spindles in their arms,
They see him lying there, and
    they
Just shudder with alarm.

5.

And when they gossip while they
    spin
About this strange affair, off
And pilfer it, the thief.
They curse this monster into hell
And hope he's roasting there.
Until he died, old What's-His-
    Name

Was bad beyond belief:
He'd plow his neighbor's
topsoil off
And pilfer it, the thief.

6.

And now he plows his
neighbor's land
With brimstone and with fire,
Surveying fields with molten
ropes,
And trudging till he's tired;
He has turned into burning
straw,
A trail of haystack blaze
That's following the burning
plow
And flaming into day.

7.

The bureaucrat who swam in
wine
And beat the serfs half-dead

Is erring through the forest on
A fiery steed of red.
The priest, that userer corrupt,
Who scolded when we danced,
Has lost his belly-fat and haunts
The church in nighttime trance.

8.

Be always true and righteous
Until your dying day,
Stay on God's straight and
narrow path,
And never go astray;
your children's children will then
come
And weep upon your grave,
Their tears will make the
summer earth
Bloom fragrant with bouquets.

Translated by Alexandra
Chciuk-Celt

WAS NOCH FRISCH UND JUNG AN JAHREN

Text: Traditional, 18th century
Music: Traditional

Was noch frisch und jung an Jah-ren,
um was Neu-es zu er-fah-ren,
das geht jetzt auf Wan-der-schaft,
keck zu pro-ben sei-ne Kraft.
Bleib nicht sit-zen
in dem Nest: Rei-sen ist das Al-ler-best!

1.

Was noch frisch und jung an
    Jahren,
das geht jetzt auf Wanderschaft,
um was Neues zu erfahren,
keck zu proben seine Kraft.
Bleib nicht sitzen in dein'm Nest,
Reisen ist das Allerbest.

2.

Fröhlich klingen unsre Lieder,

und es grüßt der Amsel Schlag,
auf, so laßt uns reisen, Brüder,
in den hellen, jungen Tag!

3.

Also gehn wir auf die Reise
in viel Stadt und fremde
    Land,
machen uns mit ihrer Weise,
ihren Künsten wohl bekannt!

ANYONE WHO'S SPRY AND YOUTHFUL

1.

Anyone who's spry and
    youthful
Will go hiking now at length,
Hoping to experience new
    things,
Hoping to prove his own
    strength.
Don't go sitting in your nest,
Traveling is simply best!

2.

Merry calls the blackbird's
    greeting,

Gaily sound the songs we sing,
Come into the bright young new
    day,
Let us all go traveling!

3.

Off we go to see new places,
Many foreign towns and lands,
Studying their art and customs,
Learning culture at first hand.

Translated by
Alexandra Chciuk-Celt

Love Songs

ÄNNCHEN VON THARAU

Text: Simon Dach, 1637;
Johann Gottfried von Herder, 1778
Music: Freidrich Silcher, 1825

Änn-chen von Tha-rau ist's, die mir ge - fällt.
Änn-chen von Tha-rau hat wie-der ihr Herz

Sie ist mein Reich-tum, mein Gut und mein Geld.
auf mich ge - rich - tet in Lieb und in Schmerz.

Änn-chen von Tha-rau, mein Reich-tum, mein Gut,

du mei - ne See - le, mein Fleisch und mein Blut.

1.
Ännchen von Tharau ist's, die
mir gefällt.
Sie ist mein Reichtum, mein Gut
und mein Geld.
Ännchen von Tharau, mein
Reichtum, mein Gut,
du meine Seele, mein Fleisch und
mein Blut.

2.
Ännchen von Tharau hat
wieder ihr Herz
auf mich gerichtet in Lieb und in
Schmerz.
Ännchen von Tharau, etc.

3.
Ännchen von Tharau,
mein Reichtum, mein Gut,

Du meine Seele,
mein Fleisch und mein Blut.

4.
Käm' alles Wetter gleich auf uns
	zu schlahn,
Wir sind gesinnet beieinander zu
	stahn.
Ännchen von Tharau, etc.

5.
Krankheit, Verfolgung,
	Betrübniß und Pein
Soll unsrer Liebe Verknotigung
	seyn.
Ännchen von Tharau, etc.

6.
Recht als ein Palmenbaum über
	sich steigt,
Je mehr ihn Hagel und Regen
	anficht;
Ännchen von Tharau, etc.

7.
So wird die Lieb' in uns mächtig
	und groß
Durch Kreuz, durch Leiden,
	durch allerlei Noth.
Ännchen von Tharau, etc.

8.
Würdest du gleich einmal von
	mir getrennt,
Lebtest da, wo man die Sonne
	kaum kennt;
Ännchen von Tharau, etc.

9.
Ich will dir folgen durch Wälder,
	durch Meer,
Durch Eis, durch Eisen, durch
	feindliches Heer.
Ännchen von Tharau, etc.

10.
Ännchen von Tharau, mein
	Licht, meine Sonn,
Mein Leben schließ ich um
	deines herum.
Ännchen von Tharau, etc.

11.
Was ich gebiete, wird von dir
	gethan,
Was ich verbiete, das läßt du
	mir stahn.
Ännchen von Tharau, etc.

12.
Was hat die Liebe doch für ein
	Bestand,
Wo nicht ein Herz ist, ein
	Mund, eine Hand?
Ännchen von Tharau, etc.

13.
Wo man sich peiniget, zanket
	und schlägt,
Und gleich den Hunden und
	Katzen beträgt?
Ännchen von Tharau, etc.

14.
Ännchen von Tharau , das
	woll'n wir nicht thun;
Du bist mein Täubchen, mein
	Schäfchen, mein Huhn.

15.

Was ich begehre, ist lieb dir und
   gut;
Ich laß den Rock dir, du läß mir
   den Hut!
Ännchen von Tharau etc.

16.

Dies ist uns, Ännchen, die
   süsseste Ruh.

Ein Leib und Seele wird aus Ich
   und Du.
Ännchen von Tharau, etc.

17.

Dies macht das Leben zum
   himmlischen Reich,
Durch Zanken wird es der Hölle
   gleich.
Ännchen von Tharau etc.

ANNIE OF THARAW

1.

Annie of Tharaw, my true love
   of old,
She is my life, and my goods,
   and my gold.

2.

Annie of Tharaw her heart once
   again
To me has surrendered in joy
   and in pain.

3.

Annie of Tharaw, my riches, my
   good,
Thou, O my soul, my flesh, and
   my blood!

4.

Then come the wild weather,
   come sleet or come snow,
We will stand by each other,
   however it blow.

5.

Oppression, and sickness, and
   sorrow, and pain
Shall be to our true love as links
   to the chain.

6.

As the palm-tree standeth so
   straight and so tall,
The more the hail beats, and the
   more the rains fall,—

7.

So love in our hearts shall grow
   mighty and strong,
Through crosses, through sorrows,
   through manifold wrong.

8.

Shouldst thou be torn from me
   to wander alone
In a desolate land where the sun
   is scarce known,—

9.
Through forests I'll follow, and
    where the sea flows,
Through ice, and through iron,
    through armies of foes.

10.
Annie of Tharaw, my light and
    my sun.
The threads of our two lives are
    woven in one.

11.
Whate'er I have bidden thee
    thou hast obeyed,
Whatever forbidden thou hast
    not gainsaid.

12.
How in the turmoil of life can
    love stand,
Where there is not one heart,
    and one mouth, and one
    hand?

13.
Some seek for dissension, and
    trouble, and strife;

Like a dog and a cat live such
    man and wife.

14.
Annie of Tharaw, such is not
    our love;
Thou art my lambkin, my chick,
    my dove.

15.
Whate'er my desire is, in thine
    may be seen;
I am king of the household, and
    thou art its queen.

16.
It is this, O my Annie, my
    heart's sweetest rest,
That makes of us twain but one
    soul in one breast.

17.
This turns to a heaven the hut
    where we dwell;
While wrangling soon changes a
    home to a hell.

Translated by
Henry Wadsworth Longfellow

Du, du, liegst mir im Herzen

Text: Traditional, 1820
Music: Traditional, 1820

Du, du, liegst mir im Her - zen, du, du,

liegst mir im Sinn. Du, du, machst mir viel Schmerzen,

weißt nicht, wie gut ich dir bin. Ja, ja,

ja, ja, weißt nicht, wie gut ich dir bin!

1.
Du, du, liegst mir im Herzen,
du, du, liegst mir im Sinn.
Du, du, machst mir viel
   Schmerzen,
weißt nicht, wie gut ich dir bin.
Ja, ja, ja, ja,
weißt nicht, wie gut ich dir bin!

2.
So, so, wie ich dich liebe,
so, so, liebe auch mich!
Die, die zärtlichsten Triebe
fühl' ich allein nur für dich!
Ja, Ja, ...

3.
Doch, doch, darf ich dir trauen,
dir, dir mit leichtem Sinn?
Du, du kannst auf mich
   bauen,
weißt ja, wie gut ich dir bin.
Ja, ja, . . .

4.
Und, und wenn in der Ferne
mir, mir dein Herz erscheint,
dann, dann wünsch ich so
   gerne,
daß uns die Liebe vereint.
Ja, ja, . . .

You, You Are My True Love

1.
You, you are my true love,
You, you are my whole life,
You, you make my heart
    ache.

2.
You don't know how much I
    love you.
Yes, yes, yes, yes,
You don't know how much I
    love you.

3.
Please, please do try to love me
As much as I love you.
All, all my deepest feelings
Go out only to you.
Yes, yes, yes, yes
Go out only to you.

4.
But, but may I trust you,
You, you of fickle heart?
You, you can build on my
    love,
You know how I feel about you.
Yes, yes, yes, yes,
You know how I feel about you.

5.
And, and when we're apart,
Your, your image appears,
Oh, oh how I shall wish then
That true love do join us till
    death;
Yes, yes, yes, yes,
That true love do join us till
    death.

Translator unknown

Es dunkelt schon in der Heide

Text: Traditional, 1471
Music: Traditional, 1802

Es dun-kelt schon in ___ der Hei-de, nach
Hau - se laßt uns gehn. Wir ha-ben das Korn ge -
schnit - ten mit un - serm blan - ken Schwert.

1.

Es dunkelt schon in der Heide,
nach Hause laßt uns gehn.
Wir haben das Korn geschnitten
mit unserm blanken Schwert.

2.

Ich hörte die Sichel rauschen,
wohl rauschen durch das Korn.
Ich hört mein Feinslieb klagen,
sie hätte ihr Lieb verloren.

3.

Hast du dein Lieb verloren,
so hab ich noch das mein,
So wollen wir beide mitnander
uns winden ein Kränzelein.

4.

Ein Kränzelein von Rosen,
ein Sträußelein von Klee.

Zu Frankfurt auf der Brücke
da liegt ein tiefer Schnee.

5.

Der Schnee, der ist zerschmolzen,
das Wasser läuft dahin.
Kommst du mir aus den Augen,
kommst mir nicht aus dem Sinn.

6.

In meines Vaters Garten,
da stehn zwei Bäumelein.
Das eine trägt Muskaten,
das andere Braunnägelein.

7.

Muskaten, die sind süße,
Braunnägelein sind schön.
Wir beide, wir müssen uns scheiden,
ja scheiden, das tut weh.

DARK IN THE HEATH

1.

It's growing dark in the heath
    now,
Let us all go home!
We have cut down the grain-
fields
With our naked swords.
We have cut down the grainfields
With our naked swords.

2.

I heard the swishing sickle
Swishing through the grain;
"I've lost my darling lover,"
I heard my love complain.
(Repeat)

3.

You may have lost you lover,
But I have not lost mine.
Let's weave a flower-garland
Together, dear, sometime.
(Repeat)

4.

A garland made of roses,
A bunch of clover true.
And on the bridge at Frankfurt,
The snow is piled up too.
(Repeat)

5.

The snow has gone a-melting,
The water flows away;

memory is waning,
You're hared to see today.
(Repeat)

6.
And in my father's garden
Two tiny trees you'll see;
The first of them bears cloves, and
The other's a nutmeg-tree.
(Repeat)

7.
The nutmeg is so sweet, and
The cloves are pretty too.
We must part; it hurts me
To say farewell to you.
(Repeat)

*Translated by
Alexandra Chciuk-Celt*

Es waren zwei Königskinder

Text: Traditional, 12th century; A. H. Hoffmann
von Fallersleben, 1819
Music: Traditional, 1807

1.
Es waren zwei Königskinder,
die hatten einander so lieb,
sie konnten beisammen nicht
    kommen,
das Wasser war viel zu tief,
das Wasser war viel zu tief.

2.
»Ach Schätzchen, ach könntest
    du schwimmen,
So schwimm doch herüber zu
    mir!
Drei Kerzchen will ich
    anzünden,
Und die solln leuchten zu dir,
Und die solln leuchten zu dir.«

3.
Das hört ein falsches Nönnchen,
Die tat, als wenn sie schlief;
Sie tät die Kerzlein auslöschen,

Der Jüngling ertrank so tief,
Der Jungling ertrank so tief.—

4.
»Ach Fischer, lieber Fischer,
Willst dir verdienen Lohn,
So senk deine Netze ins
    Wasser,
Fisch' mir den Königssohn!
Fisch' mir den Königssohn!«

5.
Sie faßt ihn in ihre Arme
Und küßt seinen roten
    Mund:
»Ach Mündlein, könntest du
    sprechen,
So wär mein jung Herze
    gesund,
So wär mein jung Herze
    gesund.«

6.

Sie schwang sich um ihren
    Mantel
Und sprang wohl in die See:
»Gut Nacht, mein Vater und
    Mutter,
Ihr seht mich nimmermeh,
Ihr seht mich nimmermeh!«

7.

Da hört man Glockenläuten,
Da hört man Jammer und
    Not:
Hier liegen zwei Königs-
    kinder,
Die sind alle beide tot,
Die sind alle beide tot.

TWO ROYAL CHILDREN

1.

There were two royal children,
They loved one another so true,
Yet they could not come to each
    other,
'Cross waters so deep and so blue.

2.

"Oh darling, if only you'd swim
    to me,
Just swim right across to my
    arms,
Three candles will I light for
    you.
And their light will keep you
    from harm."

3.

A wicked nun heard their
    scheming,
She pretended to be asleep,
And so she extinguished the
    candles,
And the royal youth drowned in
    the deep.

4.

"Oh Fisherman, dear Fisherman,
There's fair reward to be won,

Just cast your nets in the water
And fetch me the king's royal son."

5.

Into her arms she gathered him,
And she kissed his mouth so red,
"Oh mouth, could you but
    speak to me,
My young heart would not be
    dead."

6.

She wrapped her cloak tight
    about her,
And jumped straight into the sea:
"Good night, my mother and
    father,
Never more I'll dwell with thee."

7.

And the bells rang out their
    sorrow,
There was mourning and bitter
    dread,
Here lie those two royal children,
And both of them dead.

Translated by
Ingrid Walsøe-Engel

SAH EIN KNAB EIN RÖSLEIN STEHN

Text: Traditional, 1602; Johann Wolfgang von Goethe, 1771
Music: Franz Schubert, 1815; H. Werner, 1827

Sah ein Knab ein Rös-lein stehn, Rös-lein auf der Hei - den, war so jung und mor -gen-schön, lief er schnell, es nah zu sehn, sah's mit vie - len Freu-den. Rös-lein, Rös-lein, Rös-lein rot, Rös-lein auf der Hei - den.

1.
Sah ein Knab ein Röslein stehn,
Röslein auf der Heiden,
war so jung und morgenschön,
lief er schnell, es nah zu sehn,
sah's mit vielen Freuden,
Röslein, Röslein, Röslein rot,
Röslein auf der Heiden.

2.
Knabe sprach: Ich breche dich,
Röslein auf der Heiden!
Röslein sprach: Ich steche dich,
daß du ewig denkst an mich,
und ich will's nicht leiden.

Röslein, Röslein, Röslein rot,
Röslein auf der Heiden.

3.
Und der wilde Knabe brach's
    Röslein auf der Heiden;
Röslein wehrte sich und
    stach,
half ihm doch kein Weh und
    Ach,
mußt' es eben leiden.
Röslein, Röslein, Röslein rot,
Röslein auf der Heiden.

THE WILD ROSEBUD

1.

A lad saw a rosebud,
Rosebud on the heath;
it was so young in its morning
    beauty
that he ran to look at it more
    closely.
He gazed at it with great pleasure.
Rosebud red,
rosebud on the heath.

2.

The lad said: "I'll pick you,
rosebud on the heath!"
The rosebud said: "I'll prick you,
so that you will always think of
    me,

and I will not stand for it."
Rosebud red,
rosebud on the heath.

3.

And the brutal lad picked
the rosebud on the heath;
the rosebud defended itself and
    pricked,
yet no grief and lamentation
    helped it:
it simply had to suffer.
Rosebud red,
rosebud on the heath.

Translator unknown

HORCH, WAS KOMMT VON DRAUßEN 'REIN?

Text: Traditional, 1870
Music: Traditional, 1870

Horch, was kommt von drau-ßen 'rein? Hol - la - hi,

hol - la - ho! Wird wohl mein Feins - lieb - chen sein;

hol - la - hi - ha - ho! Geht vorbei und kommt nicht 'rein,

hol - la - hi, hol - la - ho! Wird's wohl nicht ge -

we - sen sein! hol - la - hi - ha - ho!

1.
Horch, was kommt von draußen
   'rein?
Hollahi, hollaho!
Wird wohl mein Feinsliebchen
   sein;
hollahihaho!
Geht vorbei und kommt nicht
   'rein,
hollahi, hollaho!
Wird's wohl nicht gewesen sein!
Hollahihaho!

2.
D'Leute haben's oft gesagt,
hollahi, hollaho!
Daß ich kein Feinsliebchen hab',
hollahihaho!
Laß sie red'n, ich schweig' fein
   still,
hollahi, hollaho!
Kann doch lieben, wen ich will,
hollahihaho!

3.
Leutchen, sagt mir's ganz gewiß,
hollahi, hollaho!
Was das für ein Lieben ist,
hollahihaho!

Die man will, die kriegt man
   nicht,
hollahi, hollaho!
Und 'ne andre will ich nicht,
hollahihahao!

4.
Wenn mein Liebchen Hochzeit
   hat,
hollahi, hollaho!
Hab' ich meinen Trauertag,
hollahihaho!
Gehe in mein Kämmerlein,
hollahi, hollaho!
Trage meinen Schmerz
   allein,
hollahihaho!

5.
Wenn ich dann gestorben bin,
hollahi, hollaho!
Trägt man mich zum Grabe
   hin,
hollahihaho!
Setzt mir einen Leichenstein,
hollahi, hollaho!
Blühn bald da Vergißnichtmein,
hollahihaho!

HARK, WHO'S COMING INSIDE HERE?

1.
Hark, who's coming inside here?
Ho-la-hee, ho-la-ho.
That must be my darling dear.
Ho-la-hee, ho-la-ho.
Didn't stop, but went right by,
Ho-la-hee etc.
Must be someone else, that's why.
Ho-la-hee- etc.

2.
People often say that I
have a sweetheart. But, oh my,
I say nothing. Let them talk.
I can love whome'er I want.

3.
Tell me, people, what is love?
What stuff can it be made of?
The girl I love I cannot get,
    don't want anybody else.

4.
On my darling's wedding-day,
Ho-la-hee, ho-la-ho.
I'll be grieving far away,
Ho-la-hee, ho-la-ho.
I'll hide in my little room,
Ho-la-hee, ho-la-ho.
with my painful lonely gloom,
Ho-la-hee, ho-la-ho.

5.
When I die, then carry me,
Ho-la-hee, ho-la-ho.
To my grave, and hear my pleas,
Ho-la-hee, ho-la-ho.
Forget-me-nots I want to bloom,
Ho-la-hee, ho-la-ho.
At my gravestone every June,
Ho-la-hee, ho-la-ho.

Translated by
Alexandra Chciuk-Celt

IN EINEM KÜHLEN GRUNDE

Text: Joseph von Eichendorff, 1809
Music: Friedrich Glück, 1814

In ei-nem küh-len Grun-de, da geht ein Müh-len-

rad; mein Lieb-chen ist ver-schwun-den, das

dort ge-woh-net hat.   Mein   Lieb-chen ist   ver-

schwun-den,   das   dort ge-woh-net   hat.

1.
In einem kühlen Grunde,
da geht ein Mühlenrad
mein Liebchen ist verschwunden,
das dort gewohnet hat.
Mein Leibchen ist verschwunden,
das dort gewohnet hat.

2.
Sie hat mir Treu' versprochen,
gab mir ein' Ring dabei,
sie hat die Treu gebrochen:
Das Ringlein sprang entzwei.
Sie hat die Treu . . .

3.
Ich möcht' als Spielmann reisen
weit in die Welt hinaus

und singen meine Weisen
und gehn von Haus zu Haus.
Und singen . . .

4.
Ich möcht' als Reiter fliegen
wohl in die blut'ge Schlacht,
um stille Feuer liegen
im Feld bei stiller Nacht.
Um stille . . .

5.
Hör' ich das Mühl'rad gehen,
ich weiß nicht, was ich will—
ich möcht' am liebsten sterben,
dann wär's auf einmal still.
Ich möcht' . . .

THE BROKEN RING

1.
Within a watered valley
A mill turns night and day;
And there my love was dwelling
Before she went away.

2.
A little ring she gave me,
A pledge to bind her heart;

But since her troth she's broken,
My ring has come apart.

3.
I fain would go as minstrel
And wander far away,
And earn my bread by singing
My songs from day to day.

4.
I fain would mount a
    charger
And glory seek in fight,
By silent camp-fires lying,
When falls the dark of
    night.

5.
For when I hear the mill-wheel,
I know not what I will.—
I fain would die, then surely
It would at last be still!

Translated by
Geoffrey Herbert Chase

KEIN FEUER, KEINE KOHLE

Text: Traditional, 1786
Music: Traditional; Friedrich Silcher, 1825

1.
Kein Feuer, keine Kohle
kann brennen so heiß,
als heimliche Liebe,
von der niemand nichts weiß,
von der niemand nichts weiß.

2.
Kein Rose, keine Nelke
kann blühen so schön,

als wenn zwei verliebte Seelen
beieinander tun stehn,
beieinander tun stehn.

3.
Setze du mir einen Spiegel
ins Herze hinein,
damit du kannst sehen,
wie so treu ich es mein,
wie so treu ich es mein.

SECRET LOVE

1.

No wood-fire and no coal-
flame
So burningly glows
As love that is hidden,
And that nobody knows.

2.

No clove pink and no roses
Can blossom so fair

As when two true lovers
Their troth plight shall swear.

3.

In my heart pray set a mirror
And therein you'll see
My faith and my worship
Are only for thee

Translated by Babette Deutsch

KOMMT EIN VOGEL GEFLOGEN

Text: Adolf Bäuerle, 1822
Music: Wenzel Müller, 1822

1.

Kommt ein Vogel geflogen,
setzt sich nieder auf mein'n
    Fuß,
hat ein Briefchen im
    Schnabel,
von der Liebsten einen Gruß.

2.

Lieber Vogel, flieg' weiter,
bring' ein'n Gruß mit, einen
    Kuß;
denn ich kann dich nicht
    begleiten,
weil ich hier bleiben muß.

LITTLE BIRD

1.
Little bird flies through the
    window
Flutters down onto my
    knee.
Has a letter in his little
    beak
From my darling to me.

2.
Little bird, fly back again
Bring my love from me a kiss
    today.
For, alas, I can't fly with you,
For it's here I must stay.

Translated by Daniel Theisen

DIE LORELEY

Text: Heinrich Heine, 1823
Music: Friedrich Silcher, 1838

Ich weiß nicht, was soll es be - deu - ten, daß ich so trau - rig bin ___; ein Mär - chen aus al - ten Zei - ten, das kommt mir nicht aus dem Sinn ___. Die Luft ist kühl, und es dun - kelt, und ru - hig fließt der Rhein, der Gip - fel des Ber - ges fun - kelt im A - bend - son - nen - schein.

1.

Ich weiß nicht, was soll es
    bedeuten,
Daß ich so traurig bin;
Ein Märchen aus alten
    Zeiten,
Das kommt mir nicht aus dem
    Sinn.
Die Luft ist kühl, und es
    dunkelt,
Und ruhig fließt der Rhein,
Der Gipfel des Berges funkelt
Im Abendsonnenschein.

2.

Die schönste Jungfrau sitzet
Dort oben wunderbar,
Ihr goldnes Geschmeide
    blitzet,
Sie kämmt ihr goldenes Haar.

3.

Sie kämmt es mit goldenem
    Kamme
Und singt ein Lied dabei;
Das hat eine wundersame
Gewaltige Melodei.

4.

Den Schiffer im kleinen Schiffe
Ergreift es mit wildem Weh;
Er schaut nicht die Felsenriffe,
Er schaut nur hinauf in die
    Höh'.

5.

Ich glaube, die Wellen
    verschlingen
Am Ende Schiffer und Kahn;
Und das hat mit ihrem Singen
Die Loreley getan.

The Lorelei

1.

I do not know what it means
that I am so sad;
a tale of the olden times
will not go from my mind.

2.

The air is cool and it is growing
    dark,
and the Rhine flows peacefully;
the peak of the mountain
    sparkles
in the evening sunlight.

3.

The most beautiful girl is sitting
up over there;
her golden jewels shine,
she is combing her golden hair.

4.

She is combing it with a golden
    comb
and singing a song
that has a miraculously
powerful melody.

5.

The boatman in his little boat
is seized with sore distress;
he does not look at the rocky
    reef,
he only looks upward.

6.

I believe the waves
in the end devour the boatman
and the boat;

and this, with her singing,
the Loreley has done.

Translator unknown

Muß I Denn

Text: Traditional, 1800; Heinrich Wagner, 1824
Music: Traditional, 1800; Friedrich Silcher, 1825

Muß i denn, muß i denn zum Städ - te - le naus,

Städ-te - le naus, und du, mein Schatz, bleibst hier. Wenn i

komm, wenn i komm, wenn i wied - rum komm,

wied-rum komm, kehr i ein, mein Schatz, bei dir. Kann i

gleich net all-weil bei dir sein, han i doch mein Freud an

dir; wenn i komm, wenn i komm, wenn i wied-rum komm,

wied - rum komm, kehr i ein, mein Schatz, bei dir.

1.

Muß i denn , muß i denn zum
  Städtele naus,
Städtele naus, und du, mein
  Schatz, bleibst hier.
Wenn i komm, wenn i komm,
  wenn i wiedrum
  komm,
wiedrum komm, kehr i ein, mein
  Schatz, bei dir.
Kann i gleich net allweil bei dir
  sein,
han i doch mein Freud an dir;
wenn i komm, wenn i komm,
  wenn i wiedrum komm,
wiedrum komm, kehr i en, mein
  Schatz, bei dir.

2.

Wie du weinst, wie du weinst,
  daß i wandere muß,
wie wenn d' Lieb jetzt wär
  vorbei!

Sind au drauß, sind au drauß
  der Mädele viel,
lieber Schatz, i bleib dir treu.
Denk du net, wen i a andre sieh,
no sei mein' Lieb vorbei;
sind au drauß, sind au drauß der
  Mädele viel,
lieber Schatz, i bleib dir treu.

3.

Übers Jahr, übers Jahr, wenn
  mer Träuble schneid't,
stell i hier mi wiedrum ein;
bin i dann, bin i dann dein
  Schätzele noch,
so soll die Hochzeit sein.
Übers Jahr, do ist mein Zeit
  vorbei,
do g'hör i mein und dein,
bin i dann, bin i dann dein
  Schätzele noch,
so soll die Hochzeit sein.

Since I Must . . .

1.

Since I must, since I must go
  forth from this town,
Forth from this town, and you,
  my love, stay here.
When I come, when I come,
  when I come back again,
Come back again, I'll return to
  you, my dear.
If I cannot always be with you,
I know you're my only joy.
When I come, when I come,
  when I come back again,

Come back again, I'll return to
  you, my dear.

2.

How you cry, how you cry, that
  I must now set forth,
Must now set forth, as though
  our love were past.
Though everywhere, everywhere,
  there are girls galore,
Girls galore, to you my dear, I'm
  true.

Don't think if I see another lass,
My love for you is past.
Though everywhere, everywhere,
    there are girls galore,
Girls galore, to you, my dear,
    I'm true.

3.
In a year, in a year, when the
    grapes are ripe again,
Grapes are ripe again, I'll be
    with you once more.

If you still, if you still, want me
    then to be your love,
Then to be your love, our
    wedding shall be held.
In another year, when my time
    is up,
You'll be mine and I'll be yours.
If you still, if you still, want me
    then to be your love,
Then to be your love, our
    wedding shall be held.

Translator unknown

WENN ALLE BRÜNNLEIN FLIEßEN

Text: Leonhard Kleber, 1520
Music: Traditional, Friedrich Silcher, 1855

1.
Wenn alle Brünnlein fließen,
so soll man trinken,
wenn ich mein Schatz nicht
    rufen darf,
tu ich ihm winken.

Wenn ich mein Schatz
nicht rufen darf,
ju ja rufen darf,
tu ich ihm winken.

2.

Ja winken mit den Äugelein
und treten auf den Fuß:
Ist eine in der Stube drin,
die mir noch werden muß.
Ist eine . . .

3.

Warum soll sie's nicht werden?
Ich seh sie gar zu gern.
Sie hat zwei schwarzbraun
   Äugelein,

sind heller als der Stern.
Sie hat zwei . . .

4.

Sie hat zwei rote
   Bäckelein,
sind röter als der Wein.
Ein solches Mädchen findt man
   nicht,
wohl unterm Sonnenschein.
Ein solches . . .

THE FLOWING BROOKS

1.

When all the brooks are flowing,
   we must drink.
When I can't call my love, I
   wave and wink.
   (Repeat)

2.

I wave and wink and step our
   secret sign,
That girl in there, I've got to
   make her mine.
   (Repeat)

3.

Why should she not be mine?
   I'm so in love.
Her blue eyes sparkle like two
   stars above. (Repeat)

4.

She's got red cheeks, too, redder
   than red wine.
Another girl like that you just
   can't find! (Repeat)

Translated by
Alexandra Chciuk-Celt

WENN ICH EIN VÖGLEIN WÄR

Text: Traditional, 1778
Music: Traditional, 1784

Wenn ich ein Vög-lein wär und auch zwei Flü-gel hätt,

flög ich zu dir. Weils a-ber nicht kann sein,

weils a-ber nicht kann sein, bleib ich all-hier.

1.
Wenn ich ein Vöglein wär
und auch zwei Flügel hätt,
flög ich zu dir.
Weils aber nicht kann sein,
weils aber nicht kann sein,
bleib ich allhier.

2.
Bin ich gleich weit von dir,
bin ich doch im Traum bei dir
und red mit dir;

wenn ich erwachen tu,
wenn ich erwachen tu,
bin ich allein.

3.
Es vergeth kein' Stund in der
    Nacht,
da nicht mein Herz erwacht
und an dich denkt,
daß du mir viel tausendmal,
daß du mir viel tausendmal,
dein Herz geschenkt.

IF I WERE BUT A BIRD

1.
If I were but a bird,
And two small wings had I,
To thee I'd fly.
But as that cannot be,
Here must I lie.

2.
Though I am far from thee,
In sleep I cleave to thee,
and speak with thee.

But when my dreams depart,
I am alone.

3.
With every hour of night,
My heart awakes, my light,
And thinks of thee,
That thousandfold, thy love,
Thou gavest me.

Translated by
Ingrid Walsøe-Engel

Children's Songs

ALLE VÖGEL SIND SCHON DA

Text: A. H. Hoffmann von Fallersleben, 1835
Music: Traditional, 18th century

Al-le Vö-gel sind schon da, al-le Vö-gel, al-le! Welch ein Sin-gen, Mu-si-ziern, Pfei-fen, Zwit-schern, Ti-ri-liern! Früh-ling will nun ein-mar-schiern, kommt mit Sang und Schal-le.

1.
Alle Vögel sind schon da, alle
  Vögel, alle!
Welch ein Singen, Musiziern,
  Pfeifen, Zwitschern,
  Tiriliern!
Frühling will nun einmarschiern,
kommt mit Sang und Schalle.
2.
Wie sie alle lustig sind, flink und
  froh sich regen!
Amsel, Drossel, Fink und Star

und die ganze Vogelschar
wünschen dir ein frohes Jahr,
lauter Heil und Segen.

3.
Was sie uns verkünden nun,
  nehmen wir zu Herzen:
alle wollen wir lustig sein,
lustig wie die Vögelein,
hier und dort, feldhaus, feldein,
singen, springen, scherzen.

ALL THE BIRDIES HAVE RETURNED

1.
All the birdies have returned,
All the birds are here.
Listen to the birdies sing,
Chirping, trilling, and whistling!
Now it's time to welcome
    Spring,
Full of song and cheer.

2.
Look how joyful they all are,
Flitting quick and merry!
Blackbird, finch, and thrush are
    here,

And the starling full of cheer,
Wishing you a happy year,
Full of health and caring!

3.
Let us now all take to heart
What the birds are saying!
Let's be happy, just like them,
Frolicking in field and glen,
Joyful carefree kids again,
Gamboling and playing.

Translated by
Alexandra Chciuk-Celt

AUF EINEM BAUM EIN KUCKUCK

Text: Traditional, 18th century
Music: Traditional, 18th century

Auf ei - nem Baum ein Kuk - kuck --
sim sa-la-dim bam-ba sa-la-du sa-la-dim — auf
ei - nem Baum ein Kuk - kuck saß.

1.
Auf einem Baum ein Kuckuck,
Sim-sa-la-dim bam-ba sa-la-du
  sa-la-dim,
Auf einem Baum ein Kuckuck saß.

2.
Da kam ein junger Jäger
Sim-sa-la-dim bam-ba sa-la-du
  sa-la-dim,
da kam ein junger Jägersmann.

3.
Der schoß den armen Kuckuck,
Sim-sa-la-dim bam-ba sa-la-du
  sa-la-dim,
der schoß den armen Kuckuck tot.

4.
Und als ein Jahr vergangen,
Sim-sa-la-dim bam-ba sa-la-du
  sa-la-dim,
und als ein Jahr vergangen war:

5.
Da war der Kuckuck wieder,
Sim-sa-la-dim bam-ba sa-la-du
  sa-la-dim,
da war der Kuckuck wieder da.

6.
Da freuten sich die Leute,
Sim-sa-la-dim bam-ba sa-la-du
  sa-la-dim,
da freuten sich die Leute sehr.

A Cuckoo Sitting in a Tree

1.
A cuckoo on a tree-branch,
Sim-sa-la-dim bam-ba-sa-la-du
  sa-la-dim,
A cuckoo sitting in a tree.

2.
Young hunter came a-riding,
Sim-sa-la-dim bam-ba-sa-la-du
  sa-la-dim,
Young hunter came a-riding by.

3.
He shot the poor old cukoo,
Sim-sa-la-dim bam-ba-sa-la-du
  sa-la-dim,
He shot the poor old cuckoo
  dead.

4.
And when a year was over,

Sim-sa-la-dim bam-ba-sa-la-du
  sa-la-dim,
And when a whole year had
  passed by:

5.
The cuckoo had come back,
Sim-sa-la-dim bam-ba-sa-la-du
  sa-la-dim,
The cuckoo had come back again.

6.
The folks were glad to see him,
Sim-sa-la-dim bam-ba-sa-la-du
  sa-la-dim,
The folks were glad to see him
  back.

Translated by
Alexandra Chciuk-Celt

DER KUCKUCK UND DER ESEL

Text: A. H. Hoffmann von Fallersleben, 1835
Music: Karl Friedrich Zelter, 1810

Der Kuk-kuck und der E-sel, die hat-ten ein-mal Streit: wer wohl am be-sten sän-ge, wer wohl am be-sten sän-ge zur schö-nen Mai-en-zeit, zur schö-nen Mai-en-zeit.

1.
Der Kuckuck und der Esel,
die hatten einmal Streit:
wer wohl am besten sänge,
wer wohl am besten sänge
zur schönen Maienzeit,
zur schönen Maienzeit.

2.
Der Kuckuck sprach: Das kann
 ich
und fing gleich an zu schrein.

Ich aber kann es besser,
Ich aber kann es besser,
fiel gleich der Esel ein,
fiel gleich der Esel ein.

3.
Das klang so schön und lieblich,
so schön von fern und nah.
Sie sangen alle beide,
Sie sangen alle beide,
«Kuckuck, Kuckuck, ia,
Kuckuck, Kuckuck, ia.»

A CUCKOO AND THE DONKEY

1.

The cuckoo and the donkey,
They had a dreadful fight:
Which one would sing the
    sweetest,
Which one would sing the
    sweetest,
When lovely May arrived,
When lovely May arrived.

2.

The cuckoo said "I'll do that,"
And started screaming song.
"But I can do it better!"

"But I can do it better!"
The donkey brayed along,
The donkey brayed along.

3.

How sweet and how melodious
That sounded wide and far:
For both of them were singing,
"Cuckoo," and then "Hee-hah!"
For both of them were singing,
"Cuckoo," and then "Hee-hah!"

Translated by
Alexandra Chciuk-Celt

EIN JÄGER AUS KURPFALZ

Text: Traditional, 1763
Music: Traditional, 1807

Ein Jä-ger aus Kur-pfalz, der rei-tet durch den
grü-nen Wald und schießt sein Wild da-her, gleich
wie es ihm ge-fällt. Ju ja, ju
ja! Gar lu-stig ist die Jä-ge-rei allhier auf grü-ner Heid, all-hier auf grü-ner Heid.

1.
Ein Jäger aus Kurpfalz,
der reitet durch den grünen
    Wald
und schießt sein Wild daher,
gleich wie es ihm gefällt.
Ju ja, ju ja! Gar lustig ist die
    Jägerei
allhier auf grüner Heid,
allhier auf grüner Heid.

2.
Auf, sattelt mir mein Pferd
und legt darauf den Mantel-
    sack,
so reit ich weit umher
als Jäger von Kurpfalz.
Ju ja, ju ja, gar lustig ist die
    Jägerei
allhier auf grüner Heid,
allhier auf grüner Heid.

A HUNTER FROM KURPFALZ

1.
A hunter from Kurpfalz
Who gallops through the forest
    green,
He shoots with perfect aim
All wildlife he has seen.
Ju ja, ju ja,
for hunting is a merry game
O'er meadow all around.
O'er meadow all around.

2.
Go saddle me my horse,
And tighten the leather bag,
I boldly ride about,
The hunter from Kurpfalz.
Ju ja, ju ja,
for hunting is a merry game
O'er meadow all around.
O'er meadow all around.

Translator unknown

EIN MÄNNLEIN STEHT IM WALDE

Text: A. H. Hoffmann von Fallersleben, 1843
Music: Traditional, 1800

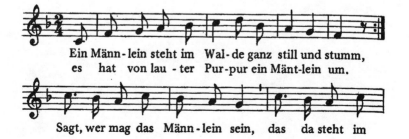

Ein Männ-lein steht im Wal-de ganz still und stumm,
es hat von lau-ter Pur-pur ein Mänt-lein um.

Sagt, wer mag das Männ-lein sein, das da steht im

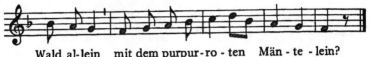

Wald al-lein   mit dem purpur-ro-ten   Män-te-lein?

1.

Ein Männlein steht im Walde
ganz still und stumm,
es hat von lauter Purpur
ein Mäntlein um.
Sagt, wer mag das Männlein
    sein,
das da steht im Wald allein
mit dem purpurroten
    Mäntelein?

2.

Das Männlein steht im Walde
auf einem Bein
und hat auf seinem Haupte
schwarz Käpplein klein.
Sagt, wer mag das Männlein
    sein,
das da steht im Wald allein
mit dem kleinen schwarzen
    Käppelein?

A LITTLE MAN STANDS IN THE WOODS

1.

A little man stands in the
    woods,
quiet and mute,
The coat he is wearing is a deep,
    deep purple.
Tell me who could the little man
    be
Standing there so
    quietly
With his coat such a deep, deep
    purple.

2.

The little man stands in the
    woods
on only one leg;
And on his head he wears a
    hood so black.
Tell me who could the little man
    be
Standing there so quietly
With his coat a deep, deep
    purple.

Translator unknown

EIN VOGEL WOLLTE HOCHZEIT MACHEN

Text: Traditional, 16th century
Music: Traditional, 16th century

1.

Ein Vogel wollte Hochzeit
machen in dem grünen Walde,
Fi-de-ral-la-la, fi-de-ral-la-la,
fi-de-ral-la-la-la-la.

2.

Die Drossel war der Bräutigam,
die Amsel war die Braute.
Fi-de-ral-la-la, etc.

3.

Der Sperber, der Sperber,
der war der Hochzeitswerber.
Fi-de-ral-la-la, etc.

4.

Der Stare, der Stare,
der flocht der Braut die Haare.
Fi-de-ral-la-la, etc.

5.

Der Seidenschwanz, der
    Seidenschwanz,

der bracht der Braut den
    Hochzeitskranz.
Fi-de-ral-la-la, etc.

6.

Die Lerche, die Lerche,
die führt die Braut zur Kerche.
Fi-de-ral-la-la, etc.

7.

Der Auerhahn, der Auerhahn,
der ist der Küster und Kaplan.
Fi-de-ral-la-la, etc.

8.

Die Meise, die Meise,
die sang das Kyrieleise.
Fi-de-ral-la-la, etc.

9.

Der Kuckuck kocht das
    Hochzeitsmahl,

fraß selbst die besten Brocken all.
Fi-de-ral-la-la, etc.

10.
Die Eule, die Eule,
die bracht die Hammelkeule.
Fi-de-ral-la-la, etc.

11.
Der Zeisig, der Zeisig,
der futtert gar fleißig.
Fi-de-ral-la-la, etc.

12.
Die Puten, die Puten,
die machten breite Schnuten.
Fi-de-ral-la-la, etc.

12.
Die Gänse und die Anten,
die war'n die Musikanten.
Fi-de-ral-la-la, etc.

14.
Der Wiedehopf, der Wiedehopf
bracht' nach dem Mahl den
 Kaffeetopf.
Fi-de-ral-la-la, etc.

15.
Der Pinguin, nicht spröde,
der hielt die Hochzeitsrede.
Fi-de-ral-la-la, etc.

16.
Der Rabe, der Rabe,
der bracht' die erste Gabe.
Fi-de-ral-la-la, etc.

17.
Der Rotschwanz, der
 Rotschwanz,

macht mit der Braut den ersten
 Tanz.
Fi-de-ral-la-la, etc.

18.
Der Papagei, der Papagei,
der macht' darob ein groß
 Geschrei.
Fi-de-ral-la-la, etc.

19.
Der Seidenschwanz, der
 Seidenschwanz,
der sang das Lied vom
 Jungfernkranz.
Fi-de-ral-la-la, etc.

20.
Der Marabu, der Marabu
hielt sich dabei die Ohren zu.
Fi-de-ral-la-la, etc.

21.
Rotkehlchen klein, Rotkehlchen
 klein,
das führt' die Braut ins
 Kämmerlein.
Fi-de-ral-la-la, etc.

22.
Der Uhu, der Uhu,
der schlug die Fensterläden zu.
Fi-de-ral-la-la, etc.

23.
Brautmutter war die Henne,
nahm Abschied mit Geflenne.
Fi-de-ral-la-la, etc.

24.
Das Haselhuhn, das Haselhuhn,

das sagt: »Wünsche wohl zu
ruh'n!«
Fi-de-ral-la-la, etc.

25.
Der Hahn, der krähet: »Gute
Nacht!«,
da wird die Lampe
ausgemacht.
Fi-de-ral-la-la, etc.

26.
Frau Kratzefuß, Frau Kratzefuß
gibt allen einen Abschiedskuß.
Fi-de-ral-la-la, etc.

27.
Nun ist die Vogelhochzeit aus,
und alle ziehn vergnügt nach
Haus.
Fi-de-ral-la-la, etc.

THE BIRD WEDDING

1.
A bird arranged a wedding in
the green forest,
di-di-ral-la-la, di-di-ral-la-la, di-
di-ral-la-la!

2.
The thrush was the groom, the
blackbird the bride.
Di-di-ral-la-la, etc.

3.
The sparrow-hawk was the go-
between.
Di-di-ral-la-la, etc.

4.
The starling braided the bride's
hair.
Di-di-ral-la-la, etc.

5.
The silktail brought the bride
her bouquet.
Di-di-ral-la-la, etc.

6.
The lark took her to church.

Di-di-ral-la-la, etc.

7.
The wood-grouse played curate
and sexton.
Di-di-ral-la-la, etc.

8.
The titmouse sang the Kyrie
Eleison.
Di-di-ral-la-la, etc.

9.
The cuckoo prepared the
wedding feast and ate all
the best pieces himself.
Di-di-ral-la-la, etc.

10.
The owl brought the leg of
lamb.
Di-di-ral-la-la, etc.

11.
The siskin really shovelled it in.
Di-di-ral-la-la, etc.

12.
The turkey-hens made faces.
Di-di-ral-la-la, etc.

13.
The geese and ducks made music.
Di-di-ral-la-la, etc.

14.
The hoopoe brought the coffee
    pot after the main course.
Di-di-ral-la-la, etc.

15.
The penguin, not one to be coy,
    gave the wedding speech.
Di-di-ral-la-la, etc.

16.
The raven brought the first
    wedding present.
Di-di-ral-la-la, etc.

17.
The redstart danced the first
    dance with the bride.
Di-di-ral-la-la, etc.

18.
The parrot made a noisy to-do
    about that.
Di-di-ral-la-la, etc.

19.
The silktail sang the song about
    the wedding wreath.
Di-di-ral-la-la, etc.

20.
The marabou-stork held his ears
    shut for that.
Di-di-ral-la-la, etc.

21.
Little robin red-breast led the
    bride into the alcove.
Di-di-ral-la-la, etc.

22.
The Eagle-Owl closed the
    shutters tight.
Di-di-ral-la-la, etc.

23.
The hen was the mother of the
    bride; she bade a tearful
    farewell.
Di-di-ral-la-la, etc.

24.
The grouse said, "My very best
    wishes for a good rest."
Di-di-ral-la-la, etc.

25.
The rooster crowed, "Good
    night!" and the lamp was
    extinguished.
Di-di-ral-la-la, etc.

26.
Lady Scrape-Grub gave
    everyone a goodnight
    kiss.
Di-di-ral-la-la, etc.

27.
So now the bird wedding's over,
    and everybody's going home
    happy.
Di-di-ral-la-la, etc.

Translated by
Alexandra Chiuck-Celt

Es klappert die Mühle am rauschenden Bach

Text: Ernst Anschütz, 1824
Music: Traditional, 18th century

Es klap-pert die Müh-le am rau-schen-den Bach: Klipp, klapp! Bei Tag und bei Nacht ist der Mül-ler stets wach: Klipp, klapp! Er mah-let uns Korn zu dem kräf-ti-gen Brot, und ha-ben wir die-ses, so hat's kei-ne Not! Klipp, klapp, klipp, klapp, klipp, klapp!

1.
Es klappert die Mühle am
   rauschenden Bach:
Klipp, klapp!
Bei Tag und bei Nacht ist der
   Müller stets wach:
Klipp, klapp!
Er mahlet uns Korn zu dem
   kräftigen Brot,
und haben wir dieses, so hat's
   keine Not!

Klipp, klapp, klipp, klapp,
   klipp, klapp!

2.
Flink laufen die Räder und
   drehen den Stein:
Klipp, klapp!
Und mahlen den Weizen zu
   Mehl uns so fein:
Klipp, klapp!

Der Bäcker dann Kuchen und
    Zwieback draus bäckt,
der immer den Kindern
    besonders gut schmeckt.
Klipp, klapp, klipp, klapp,
    klipp, klapp!

3.
Wenn reichliche Körner das
    Ackerfeld trägt:

Klipp, klapp!
Die Mühle dann flink ihre Räder
    bewegt:
Klipp, klapp!
Und schenkt uns der Himmel
    nur immerdar Brot,
so sind wir geborgen und leiden
    nicht Not.
Klipp, klapp, klipp, klapp,
    klipp, klapp!

THE RATTLING WATER MILL

1.
The water mill rattles atop
    raging streams,
Rat-tat, rat-tat.
The miller is never asleep, so it
    seems.
Rat-tat, rat-tat.
He grinds up the grain into
    heartiest bread,
So we won't go hungry, so we'll
    be well-fed.
Rat-tat, rat-tat, rat-tat.

2.
The wheels circle quickly and
    turn the great stone,
(Rat-tat, etc.)
Which grinds into flour the
    grain that was mown.

The baker turns that into
    cookies and cakes
So tasty that children insist they
    can't wait.

3.
When wheatfields produce a rich
    harvest of grain,
The millwheels start busily
    grinding again.
When heaven keeps giving us
    plenty of bread,
We're safe and protected and
    always well fed.

Translated by
Alexandra Chciuk-Celt

FUCHS, DU HAST DIE GANS GESTOHLEN

Text: Ernst Anschütz, 1824
Music: Traditional

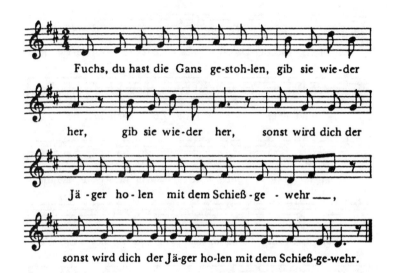

Fuchs, du hast die Gans ge-stoh-len, gib sie wie-der her, gib sie wie-der her, sonst wird dich der Jä-ger ho-len mit dem Schieß-ge-wehr___, sonst wird dich der Jä-ger ho-len mit dem Schieß-ge-wehr.

Fuchs, du hast die Gans
  gestohlen,
gib sie wieder her,
gib sie wieder her,

sonst wird dich der Jäger holen
mit dem Schießgewehr,
sonst wird dich der Jäger holen
mit dem Schießgewehr.

FOX, YOU'VE STOLEN THE GOOSE

Fox, you've stolen the goose,
Oh, give it back,
Oh, give it back.
Or surely the hunter will get you

With his shotgun,
Or surely the hunter will get you
With his shotgun.

Translator unknown

ICH BIN DER DOKTOR EISENBART

Text: Traditional, 1745
Music: Traditional, 1745

Ich bin der Dok-tor Ei-sen-bart, val-le-val-le-ri juch-he! Ku-rier die Leut nach mei-ner Art, val-le-val-le-ri juch-he! Kann ma-chen, daß die Blin-den gehn, val-le-ral-le-ri juch-hei-ra-sa, und die Lah-men wie-der sehn, val-le-ral-le-ri juch-he!

1.

Ich bin der Doktor Eisenbart,
vallevalleri juchhe!
Kurier die Leut nach meiner Art,
vallevalleri juchhe!
Kann machen, daß die Blinden
    gehn,
valleralleri juchheirassa,
und die Lahmen wieder sehn,
valleralleri juche!

2.

Des Küsters Sohn zu Dideldum,
widewidewitt, bum, bum.
Dem gab ich zehn Pfund Opium,
widewidewitt, bum, bum.
Drauf schlief er Jahre tag und
    nacht,
widewidewitt, juchheirassa,
und ist bis heut noch nicht
    erwacht,
widewidewitt, bum, bum.

3.

Zu Wien kuriert ich einen
    Mann,
widewidewitt, bum, bum.
Der hatte einen hohlen Zahn,
widewidewitt, bum, bum.

Ich schoß ihn raus mit der Pistol,
widewidewitt, juchheirassa.
O je, wie ist dem Mann so wohl,
widewidewitt, bum, bum.

4.
Das ist die Art, wie ich kurier,
widewidewitt, bum, bum.

Sie ist probat, ich bürg dafür,
widewidewitt, bum, bum.
Daß jedes Mittel Wirkung
    tut,
widewidewitt, juchheirassa,
schwör ich bei meinem
    Doktorhut,
widewidewitt, bum, bum.

I AM DOCTOR IRONBEARD

1.
I am Doctor Ironbeard, veedee-
    veedee-veet boom boom,
I treat my patients sort of weird,
    veedee-veedee-veet boom
    boom.
I can make a mute man walk,
    veedee-veedee-veet ya-hoo,
    ya-hey,
I can make a blind man talk,
    veedee-veedee-veet boom
    boom.

2.
I gave the sexton's only son,
    veedee-veedee-veet boom
    boom,
About ten pounds of opium,
    veedee-veedee-veet boom
    boom,
For nights he slept, for days he
    slept,
veedee-veedee-veet ya-hoo, ya-
    hey,
And he has not awakened yet,
    veedee-veedee-veet boom
    boom.

3.
I cured a man in Linz, forsooth,
    veedee-veedee-veet boom
    boom,
By taking out his hollow tooth,
    veedee-veedee-veet boom
    boom,
I shot it out with this here gun,
    veedee-veedee-veet ya-hoo,
    ya-hey,
Now he's as fine as anyone, veedee-
    veedee-veet boom boom.

4.
You know my treatment-
    method now, veedee-veedee-
    veet boom boom,
I stand behind my work, and how!
    Veedee-veedee-veet boom boom.
And by my doctor's cap I swear,
    veedee-veedee-veet ya-hoo,
    ya-hey,
That all my treatments work, so
    there, veedee-veedee-veet
    boom boom!

Translated by
Alexandra Chciuk-Celt

KUCKUCK, KUCKUCK

Text: A. H. Hoffmann von Fallersleben, 1817
Music: Traditional (Austrian)

Kuk-kuck, Kuk-kuck ruft aus dem Wald.

Las - set uns sin - gen, tan - zen und sprin - gen.

Früh - ling, Früh - ling wird es nun bald.

1.
Kuckuck, Kuckuck, ruft aus
    dem Wald.
Lasset uns singen, tanzen und
    springen.
Frühling, Frühling, wird es nun
    bald.

2.
Kuckuck, Kuckuck läßt nicht
    sein Schrei'n:

Komm' in die Felder,
Wiesen und Wälder!
Frühling, Frühling, stelle dich
    ein!

3.
Kuckuck, Kuckuck, trefflicher
    Held!
Was du gesungen,
ist dir gelungen:
Winter, Winter, räumet das Feld.

CUCKOO, CUCKOO

1.
Cuckoo's calling out of the woods:
Let us start dancing,
Singing and prancing.
Spring is coming soon, that feels
    good.

2.
Cuckoo won't stop calling cuckoo:
Come to the woods, the

fields and the meadows!
Springtime, we wait for you!

3.
Cuckoo, Cuckoo, hero of mine!
First you have sung it,
Then you have done it:
Old man winter's gone for a
    time.

LATERNE, LATERNE

Text: Traditional, 1740
Music: Traditional, 1740

Laterne, Laterne,
Sonne, Mond und
   Sterne,
Brenne auf, mein Licht,

brenne auf, mein
   Licht,
aber nur meine liebe Laterne
   nicht.

LANTERN, LANTERN

My lantern, my lantern,
Sun and moon and starlight,
Friendly little lantern bright,
Be my sun and shield the night.

Be my moon and star so high
When no light is in the sky.

Translator unknown

Notes

(Songs in Alphabetical Order)

ABEND WIRD ES WIEDER/EVENTIDE'S RETURNING: In 1837, Hoffmann von Fallersleben wrote this text for a melody that Johann Christian Rinck had composed in 1827.

ACH, DU MEIN SCHAURIGES VATERLAND/OH, MY GRUESOME FATHERLAND: Konstantin Wecker was born in Munich in 1947. Most of his songs and poems are written in Bavarian dialect. He had his artistic breakthrough in 1967 with the song "Willy," in which he viciously criticized the fascist past and the continuation of vestiges of that ideology in the Federal Republic of the present. This song, in which Wecker attacked conditions in the FRG that he saw as undemocratic, can be seen in that context.

ACHTZEHNTER MÄRZ/MARCH 18: Georg Herwegh wrote the text in 1873; the melody is from Josef Scheu. The song documents the disappointment over the failed Revolution of 1848.

ÄNNCHEN VON THARAU/ANNIE OF THARAW: The text was written in Low German in 1637 by the Königsberg cathedral-school rector Simon Dach for a wedding. More than 140 years later, Herder translated it into High German as a wedding song for the minister's daughter Anke Neander from Tharau (a village near Königsberg). Forty-seven years later Friedrich Silcher composed the melody for four-part men's choir.

ALLE JAHRE WIEDER/ANOTHER YEAR: This song was originally a Christian children's song and only gradually became a Christmas song, i.e. a folk song. The senior minister and fable writer Wilhelm Hey (1782–1854) adapted C. H. Rinck's text. The version of the melody known today was composed by Friedrich Silcher in 1842.

ALLE VÖGEL SIND SCHON DA/ALL THE BIRDIES HAVE RETURNED: While a professor at the University of Breslau, Hoffmann von Fallersleben wrote the text to this Silesian melody, which originally accompanied another song, in 1835. It was first published in 1843.

AM BRUNNEN VOR DEM TORE/THE LINDEN TREE: This ballad was already well known in the sixteenth century. This text from the series of poems *Winterreise* (*Winter Journey*) was written in 1821 by the teacher and librarian Wilhelm Müller and first published in 1823. The first musical arrangement, by Franz Schubert, was published in 1828 by the Vienna publishing house of Tobias Haslinger as "Lindenbaum" ("Linden Tree"), (op. 89, no. 5). Today's folk song version is from Friedrich Silcher, who left out the very difficult piano accompaniment and thereby produced a much simplified melody.

AUF, AUF, ZUM KAMPF/ON TO THE BATTLE, TO THE BATTLE: This song is a reworking of a song by the same name for August Bebel; this version was written in reaction to the murder of Rosa Luxemburg and Karl Liebknecht in 1919 and to the bloody suppression of the Spartacus Revolt. The song gained great popularity and was often sung in the Federal Republic in 1968 at demonstrations against the Emergency Laws.

AUF, DU JUNGER WANDERSMANN/UP, YOUNG TRAVELER, HI-HO: Walther Hensel wrote the text of this song from Franconia, which dates from the eighteenth century.

AUF EINEM BAUM EIN KUCKUCK/A CUCKOO SITTING IN A TREE: This folk song was sketched in Bergisch Land and first published in 1838 by Elk-Irmer. The incantation in the middle section recalls ancient Germanic sagas.

AUS TIEFER NOT SCHREI ICH ZU DIR /FROM DEPTHS OF WOE I CRY TO YOU: The text of the song is based on Psalm 130. In 1530, Martin Luther wrote his first version, but another version was written in Strasburg that same year. Besides the German-language Bible (New Testament in 1522, the entire Bible in 1534), Luther also produced a German-language songbook to which he contributed texts and melodies.

BADISCHES WIEGENLIED/LULLABY OF BADEN: The text was written in 1848 by Ludwig Pfau, a publisher and participant in the Revolution of 1848. Dieter Süverkrüp sang a variation of this song during the time of the German student movement in the Federal Republic.

BALLADE VON DER "JUDENHURE" MARIE SANDERS/BALLAD OF MARIE SANDERS, THE JEW'S WHORE: This 1935 ballad is a part of the "Svendborg Poems," which were written between 1933 and 1938. Brecht named the poems after the small Danish port city near where he lived in exile.

BRÜDER, ZUR SONNE, ZUR FREIHEIT/GO TO THE SUN, INTO FREEDOM: This song was originally written by the Russian scientist Leonid P. Radin in a czarist prison in 1897. In 1917, the conductor Herrmann Scherchen wrote the German version during his own Russian imprisonment. When Scherchen returned to Germany in 1918, the song quickly became very popular.

BUCHENWALDLIED/THE BUCHENWALD SONG: Fritz Böda-Löhner wrote the words; the music is by Herrmann Leopoldi (1938).

BUNDESLIED/SAID WEALTH TO TOIL: When the General German Workers' Union was founded in 1863, its first president, Ferdinand Lassalle, asked the poet Georg Herwegh for a revolutionary song. There have been various musical versions of this first "hymn of the proletariat," such as that by the famous composer and conductor Hans von Bülow (alias Solinger). The song was banned by the Berlin district court in 1910. The text of the song drew heavily from the poem "Men of England" by the English poet P. B. Shelley.

BUNT SIND SCHON DIE WÄLDER/ALL THE LEAVES ARE TURNING: The poet and Swiss politician Baron Johann Gaudenz Freiherr von Salis-Seewis wrote the text in 1782 as an "autumn song" during his days as a student; it was published in 1786. The Königsberg composer Johann Friedrich Reichardt, court conductor of Frederick the Great, wrote the melody. It was first published in 1799 in Leipzig as a part of the collection *Lieder für die Jugend* (*Songs for Young People*).

BÜRGERLIED/THE CITIZENS' SONG: This song called for carrying out the ideals of the French Revolution of 1789: freedom, equality, and brotherhood. It also made a basic demand to do away with arbitrary rule by the German nobility and to dissolve German feudalism by bourgeois democracy. The song is considered a herald of the German bourgeois revolution of 1848, during which it was very popular. The author was president of the Naumburg Court of Appeals; he first presented it in 1845 at a meeting of the Proletarian Friends. The melody is from the song "Prinz Eugen, der edle Ritter" ("Prince Eugene, the Noble Knight").

BÜRGERLIED DER MAINZER/THE MAINZ CITIZENS' SONG: This song quickly became known in 1792 during the short period of the Mainz Republic; the authors of the text are unknown.

DAS BARLACH-LIED/THE BARLACH SONG: Wolf Biermann was born in Hamburg in 1936 and moved to East Berlin in 1953; most of his numerous books and songs were initially published in the Federal Republic since almost from the beginning the GDR banned his publications and personal appearances. Adapting the term "Stückemacher" (art maker), coined by Brecht, he originated the term "Liedermacher" (songmaker). After a concert in Cologne in 1976, he was "expatriated" against his will by the GDR and was not allowed to return to East Berlin, a reaction by the regime against his critical texts and remarks during this public appearance. Biermann is one of the most popular songmakers from the GDR; he frequently uses ideas or quotes from historical texts and personalities and gives them small twists in order to fit current events.

DAS BLUTGERICHT/THE BLOOD COURT: Zwanziger and Dierig are the names of textile producers whose methods of exploitation caused the 1844 Silesian weavers' revolt, which was violently put down. There were many injured, several dead; although the song was immediately officially banned, it caught on. Wilke Wolff's "Das Elend und der Aufruhr in Schlesien" ("The Misery and the Uprising in Silesia"), which appeared in Darmstadt in 1844, is among the earliest published versions. The song has been passed on primarily by word of mouth and was sung to the melody of "Es liegt ein Schloß in Österreich" ("There Is a Castle in Austria"). Dieter Süverkrüp has reworked the song.

DAS HECKERLIED/THE SONG OF THE HECKER: Ludwig Schanz wrote this text in 1848. After the failed revolution in 1848–49, Friedrich Hecker (1811–81) led the armed uprising in Baden and the Palatinate in order to proclaim the republic. Workers and apprentice craftsmen had formed guerrilla groups. The Prussian military put down the popular revolt. Hecker and the rest of the guerrillas fled to Switzerland. The term "Hecker" later became a term of derision.

DAS HÖLDERLIN-LIED/THE HOELDERLIN SONG: (See "Das Barlach-Lied")

DAS PROLETARIAT/THE PROLETARIAT: The text was written by Lüchow during the Revolution of 1848; Dieter Süverkrüp composed the melody more than one hundred years later.

DAS WANDERN IST DES MÜLLERS LUST/THE JOURNEYMAN'S SONG: In 1818, Dessau lyricist Wilhelm Müller wrote the lyric circle "Die schöne Müllerin" ("The Beautiful Miller's Wife"), which Franz Schubert and others set to music. Yet it was the 1844 song version by the Thuringian choir director Carl Friedrich Zöllner that became popular.

DER ARBEITSMANN/THE WORKING MAN: Richard Strauss, in op. 39, no. 3, set Richard Dehmel's text to music in 1897–98, and there is a version (op. 30, no. 4) by Hans Pfitzer from 1922.

DER BAGGERFÜHRER WILLIBALD/THE BALLAD OF WILLIBALD THE POWER SHOVEL OPERATOR: Dieter Süverkrüp was born in Düsseldorf in 1934 and was already popular for the satirical texts of his songs and cabaret appearances in the early 1950s; he belongs to the first generation of song makers in the Federal Republic. The "Baggerführer" is without doubt the most popular political children's song since the 1970s in the Federal Republic. It proved to be so effective in street and hall gatherings that it also became a subject of instruction. Soon after its appearance in 1975, this song became the subject of two state parliament debates in Lower Saxony and North Rhine/Westphalia, as representatives of conservative parties and certain interest groups saw in it a "school smear song against private home ownership."

DER GUTE BÜRGER/THE SOLID CITIZEN: During the student movement in the Federal Republic, Jürgen Rohland took up, set to music, and sang many older texts, such as the one here by Ferdinand Freiligrath.

DER KUCKUCK UND DER ESEL/A CUCKOO AND THE DONKEY: The text was written by Hoffmann von Fallersleben in 1835. The melody was originally written in 1810 for the text of "Es ist ein Schuß gefallen" ("A Shot Has Been Fired").

DER MAI IST GEKOMMEN/NOW MAY IS ARRIVING: Lübeck poet Emanuel Geibel wrote this poem in 1835 while a student in Bonn; it was then reworked and put in its final form in 1841 in Lübeck. In 1843, Justus Wilhelm Lyra, a student fraternity member in Bonn and later a minister in Hanover, set it to music in the form of a Polish mazurka in accordance with the taste of the time. Today's popular simplified melody evolved only gradually.

DER MOND IST AUFGEGANGEN/EVENING SONG: Matthias Claudius wrote the text in 1778; the melody was based on the spiritual evening song "Nun ruhen alle Wälder" ("Evensong"), which was written by the Lüneberg composer Johann Abraham Peter Schulz in 1790, and published in volume three of the collection *Lieder im Volkston (Popular Folk Songs)*. Schulz, who was a court conductor in Copenhagen, was a member of the Berlin school of song writing, which consciously tried to evoke the "appearance of the familiar." The text of this song was eventually set to music by more than twenty composers.

DER REVOLUZZER/THE AMATEUR REVOLUTIONARY: Erich Mühsam dedicated this text to German social democracy, whose leaders at the highest level he accused of cooperation with politically reactionary forces. Mühsam was imprisoned for six years. He was sent to Oranienburg concentration camp in 1933, where he was murdered in June 1934.

DER ROTE WEDDING/THE REDS FROM WEDDING: The social democratic police chief of Berlin, Zörgiebel, had forbidden demonstrations for May 1, 1929, and ordered the demonstrations, which took place nevertheless, broken up by force of arms. The second verse expresses the workers' outrage over the SPD's "betrayal" of the working class. In a few hours, Weinert and Eisler wrote this song, which quickly became one of the favorite battle songs not only of the German workers' movement, but of the international one as well. Weinert later altered the text several times according to the changing political situation.

DEUTSCHER SONNTAG/A GERMAN SUNDAY: The lawyer Franz Josef Degenhardt, who was born in northern Germany in 1931, became well known as an active member of the Extra-Parliamentary Opposition (APO), particularly during the German student movement in the Federal Republic in the 1960s. In the 1960s, he took part in the jamboree at Castle Waldeck that was so important for the development of music. In addition to songs, Degenhardt also published novels. In "Deutscher Sonntag" (1965), the songmaker's severe criticism of everyday life in the Federal Republic—a life that, according to him, thwarts all critical reflection by an overemphasis on appearances and an unconditional maintenance of given norms—becomes clear in an exemplary fashion.

DIE ARBEITSMÄNNER/THE HYMN OF THE PROLETARIAT: After the founding of the German Social Democratic Workers' Party in 1869, this became an important song and, until 1918, was one of the songs most frequently sung within the German workers' movement. Johannes Most wrote the song in 1869 while imprisoned in Vienna; in spite of being banned, the song very quickly became popular. The melody is based on the song "Zu Mantua in Baden" ("To Mantua in Baden").

DIE BEIDEN GRENADIERE/THE TWO GRENADIERS: Heinrich Heine wrote the text around 1850; Robert Schumann wrote the melody (op. 49, no. 1).

DIE GEDANKEN SIND FREI/THOUGHTS ARE FREE: This was originally a Middle High German text from around 1230. The song appeared in numerous broadsides between 1780 and 1800 and quickly became known throughout all of Germany primarily due to wandering apprentice craftsmen. It is also contained in the anthology *Des Knaben Wunderhorn*. It was banned during the time of the Revolution of 1848 and for years stood on the list of writings forbidden by state censorship. This song acquired great importance in the concentration camps during the period of German fascism. During the student movement in the Federal Republic of Germany, it again enjoyed great popularity. Pete Seeger sang the song against Senator Joseph McCarthy at the Newport Folk Festival in Rhode Island in 1964.

DIE HAB ICH SATT!/I'M SICK OF IT!: (See "Das Barlach-Lied")

DIE INTERNATIONALE/THE INTERNATIONALE: This is the song of the 1871 Parisian Commune, the first "workers' republic" in history, through which many reforms were achieved. The song was written by Eugene Pottier after the bloody suppression of the commune and set to music seventeen years later in 1888. The "Internationale" became the manifesto, the hymn of freedom of all revolutionary and protest movements around the world and was to be translated into many languages. The song first appeared in 1907 in German workers' song books—and was immediately confiscated by the police.

DIE JUNGE GARDE/THE YOUNG GUARDS (also called "Lied der Jugend" or "Dem Morgenrot entgegen"): This was the first song of the organized German working class youth. The Bonn teacher Heinrich Eildermann wrote the text in 1907; it appeared in the social democratic newspaper *Arbeiterjugend* (*Working Class Youth*) in 1910. Because of his position, Eildermann published the song in imperial Germany under the pseudonym Heinrich Arnulf. Andreas Hofer's song "Zu Mantua in Baden" ("To Mantua in Baden") served as the musical model, to which Johannes Most had already written a progressive text back in 1879.

DIE LORELEY/THE LORELEI: The Lorelei legend was freely adapted by Clemens Brentano. In 1799, he wrote an accompanying ballad, which he used in his novel *Godwi*. In 1823, Heinrich Heine condensed the material to just three double-verses that have been set to music by countless composers. The melody by Friedrich Silcher, published in Silcher's collection *Volkslieder* (*Folk Songs*) in 1837–38, became the best known.

DIE MOORSOLDATEN/THE PEAT-BOG SOLDIERS: This song was first sung in Börgermoor concentration camp in 1934 at an event improvised by prisoners in protest against a pogrom that had occurred during the night. The song was forbidden after two days, yet it is still famous throughout the world today. Hans Eisler did a version of it in 1935. The singer Ernst Busch took the song with him to the International Brigades in Spain in 1937. This song is a testimony to the resistance of antifascists who were imprisoned under Hitler and whose will could not be broken even after years of imprisonment and torture in concentration camps.

DIE MORITAT VON MACKIE MESSER/THE CRIMES OF MACKIE THE KNIFE : Bertolt Brecht wrote the text, Kurt Weill the melody; the song is part of Brecht's *Dreigroschenoper (Three Penny Opera)* (1928).

DIE THÄLMANN-KOLONNE/THE THAELMANN COLUMN: The Thaelmann Battalion was part of the International Brigades that defended the elected popular front government against Franco's fascist putschists in the Spanish Civil War from 1936 to 1939. Thousands of German antifascists were members of the various international brigades. Paul Dessau composed the song in exile in Paris in 1936; it was also sung by the American Lincoln Brigade.

DU, DU, LIEGST MIR IM HERZEN/YOU, YOU ARE MY TRUE LOVE: This is a folk song from northern Germany, circa 1820.

EIN FESTE BURG IST UNSER GOTT/A MIGHTY FORTRESS IS OUR GOD: Martin Luther wrote this song in 1528, basing it on Psalm 46. It was circulated as a broadside and became one of the most popular songs of the sixteenth century. Although Luther distanced himself from the revolutionary goals of segments of the peasantry in his work *Against the Thievish and Murderous Hordes of Peasants*, it was exactly the lower classes who were riled up by the song. Friedrich Engels thus described it as the "'Marseillaise' of the seventeenth century."

EIN HELLER UND EIN BATZEN/A PENNY AND A FORTUNE: Count Albert Schlippenbach wrote the text to the melody, which is from the period of the German youth movement.

EIN JÄGER AUS KURPFALZ/A HUNTER FROM KURPFALZ: The text already existed as a broadside in 1763; the melody was sketched in Swabia in 1807 and published in 1839 by Erk-Irmer. It quickly became popular, especially in the Palatinate.

EIN MÄNNLEIN STEHT IM WALDE/A LITTLE MAN STANDS IN THE WOODS : The song is based on a folk melody from the Lower Rhine; Hoffmann von Fallersleben, who, between 1830 and 1837, had already written many children's songs based on traditional folk proverbs, also wrote this riddle song in 1843.

EIN NEUES LIED/A WINTER'S TALE: The text was published by Heinrich Heine as a part of his *Deutschland Ein Wintermärchen* (1844, Caput 1), which was immediately outlawed in Prussia because of its massive criticism of political conditions. Dieter Süverkrüp (see "Der Baggerführer Willibald"), who uses historical texts in several of his melodies, wrote the melody to this text.

EIN VOGEL WOLLTE HOCHZEIT MACHEN/THE BIRD WEDDING: The oldest broadside version is probably from the beginning of the sixteenth century. In Hainhofer's lute tabulature of 1604, the song has forty verses. This song was sung in many variants at weddings throughout all of Germany; the number and the text of the verses varies. Yet the song is always based on the melody that was sketched by Bunzlau and Haynau and that was published by Hoffmann von Fallersleben and Ernst Richter in *Schlesische Volkslieder mit Melodien (Silesian Folk Songs with Melodies)* in 1842.

EINHEITSFRONTLIED/UNITED FRONT SONG: The idea of a united front of all political forces in the struggle against fascism was thematized in this song by Brecht and Eisler in 1934 and was portrayed in part as a precondition for avoiding a predictable world war. It was commissioned by the International Music Office (Erwin Piscator) in Moscow, to which workers' music organizations from various countries belonged, and written in exile in London. The song originally had verses in different languages. It first appeared in the small song book *Lied der Zeit* (*Song of the Time*), which was edited by Ernst Busch.

ERMUTIGUNG/ENCOURAGEMENT: The songwriter Wolf Biermann wrote this song in the middle of the 1960s at a time when he was living in the German Democratic Republic (GDR). (See "Das Barlach-Lied")

ERSCHRÖCKLICHE MORITAT VOM KRYPTOKOMMUNISTEN/DREADFUL BALLAD OF THE CRYPTO-COMMUNIST: Dieter Süverkrüp (see "Der Baggerführer Willibald") published this song in 1966 at a time when the Cold War in Europe dominated public opinion among large segments of the population and the fear of a communist subversion of institutions was an important topic. The satirical form of the text was acclaimed as a successful example of the combination of social criticism and humor and quickly made the song popular, particularly in oppositional circles.

ES, ES, ES UND ES/IT, IT, IT, AND IT (Also: "Seine Arbeit, die gefällt mir nicht"): There are many versions of the song, most of which were handed down by word of mouth but also appear in early folk song books (such as in 1826). This is one of the best known apprentice craftsmen songs. Apparently, it was not wanderlust that moved the apprentice craftsmen to look for a different workplace. Guild rules required at least three years of wandering prior to the master craftsman's examination.

ES DUNKELT SCHON IN DER HEIDE/DARK IN THE HEATH: The textual motive was already addressed in the *Rostocker Liederhandschrift* (*Rostock Song Manuscript*) of 1471. Numerous variations of text and melody subsequently arose, the best known of which is the present one, which is originally an eastern Prussian spinning room song.

ES IST EIN ROS ENTSPRUNGEN/LO, HOW A ROSE IS GROWING: In the oldest versions of this song, such as in the 1599 *Kölner Gesangbuch* and the 1605 *Mainzer Cantual*, this is a Catholic devotional hymn to Mary, based on the legend of a rose that blooms at Christmas time. In reality, the word "Ros" (i.e., "Reis" or "rice") is a reference to the geneology of Jesus, which is said to go back to Jesse of Bethelehem, the father of King David. The evangelical cantor Michael Praetorius wrote today's oft-sung version of the melody in 1609. The original title of the song "Ein alt catholisch Triersch Christ liedlein" ("A Little Old Christian Catholic Song from Trier") indicates that the song was composed much earlier (fifteenth century). The third verse was written during the nineteenth century (Friedrich Layritz, 1844).

Es ist ein Schnitter, heißt der Tod/Behold the Reaper: This song was circulated as a broadside during the Thirty Years' War. The song's political character is unmistakable: it threatens the nobility with death and annihilation. This reaper's song was considered to be (in Goethe's words) a "Catholic church song and dirge. [It] deserved to be Protestant."

Es klappert die Mühle am rauschenden Bach/The Rattling Water Mill: Leipzig teacher Ernst Anschütz wrote the first version of the text and melody; the song was published in 1830. The text became known in conjunction with the older melody of the folk song "Es ritten drei Reiter zum Tore hinaus" ("There Were Three Horsemen Riding out of the Gate") which was first published in Rome in 1774. A German beggar is said to have sung this song in the streets of Rome in 1770.

Es tönen die Lieder/Now Spring Is A-Springing: This is a traditional song from the nineteenth century that was frequently sung as a canon and became very popular in all of Germany.

Es waren zwei Königskinder/Two Royal Children: This ballad is based on the ancient Greek myth of Hero and Leander. The words were in German texts as early as in the twelfth century; by the fifteenth century, the ballad was widely common. The melody comes from Brandenburg; it was published by the folk song collectors Büschling and Von der Hagen in the *Sammlung deutscher Volkslieder* (*Collection of German Folk Songs*) in 1807. Hoffmann von Fallersleben sketched the well-known High German version as a student in 1819.

Freifrau von Droste-Vischering/Milady Droste-Vischering : Rudolf Löwenstein wrote the text in 1844. In this "biting satire of the belief in miracles" (Steinitz), the public presentation of the "holy kilt of Jesus" by the Catholic bishop of Trier in 1844 is criticized. This article of clothing allegedly had miraculous power. Among the public, there was a strong reaction even in the bourgeois press against this idolatry. The last such exhibition of the relic took place in 1959. Dieter Süverkrüp updated the song.

Freiheit, die ich meine/Come, My Gentle Freedom: The East Prussian poet Max von Schenkendorf wrote the text in 1813 to rally support for the liberation struggle against Napoleon. There were many musical versions. The melody by the theologian Karl August Groos (1818), which first appeared in 1822 in the *Auswahl deutscher Lieder für Hallesche Burschen* (*Selection of German Songs for Halle Students*), was the most popular.

Frieden im Land/Peace in the Land: See "Ach, du mein schauriges Vaterland"

Fuchs, du hast die Ganz gestohlen/Fox, You've Stolen the Goose (also: "Gänsedieb"): Ernst Anschütz wrote the words and melody in 1824 on the basis of the old children's song "Wer die Ganz gestohlen hat" ("He Who Stole the Goose"). With slight changes in the melody, the song later became well known from Brandenburg with the words "Ei, ei, ei ihr Hühnerchen".

FÜR M. THEODORAKIS/FOR M. THEODORAKIS: This song expresses international solidarity with the struggle for democracy in Greece, of which Theodorakis is the representative. Franz Josef Degenhardt (see "Deutscher Sonntag") wrote this song in 1968.

GEH AUS, MEIN HERZ, UND SUCHE FREUD/GO OUT, MY DEAR, AND FIND JOY: The melody is taken from the song "Heut singt die liebe Christenheit" ("Today Sings Dear Christianity"), which Nikolaus Hermann composed in 1560 and for which he wrote the words. Paul Gerhardt (1607–76) combined this melody with new words in 1656. In 1813, A. Harder wrote the version that is most common today.

GLÜCK AUF, GLÜCK AUF/GOOD LUCK! GOOD LUCK!: The words of this, the most famous of miners' songs, first appeared in the collection *Neuvermehrtes vollständiges Berglieder-Büchlein* (*Newly Enlarged Complete Booklet of Miners' Songs*), which was published in Saxony around 1730. There are countless versions of this song from various German-speaking regions.

GROßES GEBET DER ALTEN KOMMUNISTIN OMA MEUME IN HAMBURG/THE COMMUNIST GRANDMA MEUME'S GREAT PRAYER IN HAMBURG: In his texts, Wolf Biermann (see "Das Barlach-Lied") frequently complemented aspects of far-reaching social criticism and of specific criticism of the society of the GDR with aspects from his personal biography and thereby made them concrete (see "Moritat auf Biermann seine Oma Meume in Hamburg").

GUTEN ABEND, GUT' NACHT/CRADLE SONG: In 1868, Johannes Brahms wrote this piano song (op. 49, no. 4) for the Viennese woman Bertha Faber, whom he had gotten to know during his time in Hamburg when he was the director of the women's choir; it has now become a popular folk song. The first verse is from the eighteenth century; Georg Scherer is thought to have authored the second verse in 1849.

HEIDENRÖSLEIN/THE WILD ROSEBUD (also: "Sah ein Knab ein Röslein stehen"): Johann Wolfganng von Goethe wrote the text in 1771, which is based on a folk song from 1602, "Sie gleicht wohl einem Rosenstock" ("She Is Like a Rosebush"). Many composers have set the words to music, including Reichardt (1794), Schubert (1815), and Schumann (1849). In 1827, Heinrich Werner composed the melody which is still popular throughout the world even today.

HOCH AUF DEM GELBEN WAGEN/ATOP THE YELLOW CARRIAGE: Rudolf Baumbach wrote the words in 1879; the melody is by Heinz Höhne (1922).

HÖRT, IHR HERRN, UND LAß EUCH SAGEN/LISTEN TO ME, GENTLEMEN: The first part of the text is from traditional sources from the sixteenth century; the second part was first published in 1821. The melody of the first part is from the seventeenth century. Originally a hymn, it was provided with the most various texts, especially in southern Germany, and thus served night watchmen and others in their hourly proclamations. The song appeared in various anthologies as a "watchman's song" at the beginning of the nineteenth century; it was most popular during the twentieth century in the German youth movement.

HORCH, WAS KOMMT VON DRAUßEN 'REIN?/HARK, WHO'S COMING INSIDE HERE?: This folk song from the Baden Palatinate was very popular, especially in student circles after 1870; its protest against traditional burial customs was an innovation. The first variants of the song go back to the eighteenth century.

ICH BIN DER DOKTOR EISENBART/I AM DOCTOR IRONBEARD: This song, a jocular folk song from the eighteenth century (1745), was handed down by word of mouth. Dr. Johann Andreas Eisenbart (1661–1727) was a historical personality; his students probably wrote the song for fun.

ICH BIN EIN FREIER BAUERNKNECHT/I AM A FREE PEASANT: This song by a peasant is from the second half of the seventeenth century and expresses the peasants' self-consciousness and pride about their class and work, a pride that could not be broken even by feudalistic rule.

ICH BIN EIN GUTER UNTERTAN/A LOYAL SUBJECT AM I THEN: This song was written in the revolutionary year 1848 by the famous Berlin couplet writer Adolf Glasbrenner, who would be known today as a songmaker. He was especially well-known in Prussia as the author of local Berlin farces.

ICH BIN SOLDAT, DOCH BIN ICH ES NICHT GERNE/A SOLDIER AM I, BUT DON'T LIKE TO BE: An expression of the ideas of proletarian internationalism and of antimilitarism at the time of the Franco-Prussian War of 1870–71. Because of the song's clear goal, singing as well as even possessing the song were subject to the severest punishment, as officials saw in this oppositional solider's song a danger to the German army's readiness to engage in battle against the "arch-enemy," France.

ICH STEH AN DEINER KRIPPE HIER/I STAND BESIDE THY CRADLE HERE: Johann Sebastian Bach composed his own version of this Christmas song in 1736; the words were written by Paul Gerhardt (1607–76) in 1650.

IHR KINDERLEIN, KOMMET/O COME, LITTLE CHILDREN: Johann Arbaham Peter Schulz originally wrote this melody for a different song in 1794. Christoph Schmidt, a priest and writer of young people's books, was already known for his six-volume *Biblische Geschichte für Kinder* (*Biblical History for Children*) when he combined the new words with the melody.

IM FRÜHTAU ZU BERGE/HIKING IN THE MOUNTAIN DEW: This was originally a Swedish student song from 1905. G. Schulten translated it in 1917. The German version was published in 1923 by Walther Hensel. It has since become one of the most frequently sung songs about this topic.

IM KRUG ZUM GRÜNEN KRANZE/THE EMERALD GARLAND: The words of this folk song from the nineteenth century were written by Wilhelm Müller in 1821. The melody was joined to this text in 1843; before that, the melody had been sung to older songs, such as to the ballad "Ich stand auf hohem

Berge" ("I Stood upon a Mountain High"). In view of the failed Revolution of 1848, the new words were a reminder to achieve democracy. A parody of this song appeared in a social democratic song book in 1898.

IM MÄRZEN DER BAUER/FARMWORK SONG: This folk song from northern Moravia was written down by Joseph Pommer in the *Liederbuch für die Deutschen in Österreich (Songbook for Germans in Austria)*, which was published in Vienna in 1884; there are numerous textual variants of the song. The most frequently sung version is W. Hensel's from 1923.

IN EINEM KÜHLEN GRUNDE/THE BROKEN RING (also: "Das zerbrochene Ringlein" ["The Little Broken Ring"]): Joseph von Eichendorff wrote the text in 1809 and published it in Tübingen in 1813 under the pseudonym Florens. Tübingen theology student Friedrich Glück set it to music one year later. Yet it became known and widely common in Friedrich Silcher's version, which was published in the collection *Volkslieder für vier Männerstimmen (Folk Songs for Four Men's Voices)* in 1826.

INNSBRUCK, ICH MUß DICH LASSEN/INNSBRUCK, NOW I MUST DEPART: There are various sixteenth-century versions of this song. The words were probably written around 1500 in southern German apprentice craftsmen's circles. After the Reformation, the song was sung at funerals and public executions, and the secular wanderer's song thereby became, in Kröher's words, a "pilgrim's song of blessed eternity." The melody is based on a version by Heinrich Isaac (ca. 1450–1517), who was a musician at the courts of various princes. Isaac's text and melody are in the collection by the Nuremberg physician Georg Forster, *Auszug guter alter und neuer teutscher Liedlein (Selection of Good, Old, and New German Songs)*, which was published in Nuremberg in 1539.

JA, DIESES DEUTSCHLAND MEINE ICH/THIS IS THE GERMANY I MEAN: (See "Deutscher Sonntag")

JEDEN MORGEN GEHT DIE SONNE AUF/EVERY MORNING: The words were written by Hermann Claudius; the melody is by Karl Marx.

JETZT FÄNGT DAS SCHÖNE FRÜHJAHR AN/LOVELY SPRING: The first version of this folk song, which is still the most common one today, came from the Lower Rhine from around 1880. Later, there were many other versions in various German-speaking regions.

KEIN FEUER, KEINE KOHLE/ SECRET LOVE (also: "Heimliche Liebe"): The text of this folk song appeared as a broadside from 1786 as the text of a Silesian shepherd's song with eight verses. One well-known version is from the *Sammlung deutscher Volkslieder (Collection of German Folk Songs)*, which was published by von Büschling and Von der Hagen in Berlin in 1807. Silcher's version for men's choir is from 1825.

KEIN SCHÖNER LAND/THERE ARE NO OTHER LANDS: August Wilhelm Florentin von Zuccalmaglio wrote the first two verses in 1838 and took part of the melody from two old folk songs, "Ade, mein Schatz, ich muß jetzt fort,"

("Ade, My Dear, I Must Now Go") and "Ich kann und mag nicht fröhlich sein" ("I Can Not Be and Do Not Like to Be Merry"). The song was published in 1840; it appeared in the *Preußisches Soldatenliederbuch* (*Prussian Soldier's Songbook*) in 1884. It became very well known after 1918 due to the German youth movement.

KINDER/CHILDREN: Born in Berlin in 1946, Bettina Wegner studied accounting in the GDR; her citizenship was revoked because she demonstrated against the intervention of Soviet troops in Prague in 1968. Since 1973, she has been active as a songmaker in the Federal Republic and has become known most of all for her sensitive yet critical texts.

KIRSCHEN AUF SAHNE/CHERRIES AND CREAM: (See "Der Baggerführer Willibald")

KOMINTERN-LIED/COMINTERN: In 1929, Hanns Eisler composed the melody for the text that was written by Franz Jahnke and Maxim Vallentin.

KOMM, LIEBER MAI, UND MACHE/YEARNING FOR SPRING: Lübeck poet Christian Adolf Overbeck wrote the poem entitled "Fritzchen an den Mai" ("Little Fritz Speaks to May") in 1775; it was published in the *Vossischer Musenalmanach* (*Vossisch Muses' Almanac*) one year later. Wolfgang Amadeus Mozart composed the musical version in the form of piano song in the year of his death, 1791. Ludwig Erk published a simplified melody with an abridged text in 1824, which was responsible for the song's becoming very popular as a children's song and school song as well as a song for adults.

KOMMET, IHR HIRTEN/COME, YE MEN AND WOMEN: A similar melody was already known as a Christmas song in Bohemia in 1605. In translating the text from Old Bohemian, Leipzig choir director Carl Riedel also changed the melody and, in 1880, published a version that, in the collection *Altböhmische Gesänge* (*Old Bohemian Songs*), is still common today.

KOMMT EIN VOGEL GEFLOGEN/LITTLE BIRD: This song is a part of a Viennese magic opera and was written in Austrian dialect by Adolf Bäuerle in 1822; Wenzel Müller wrote the melody.

KUCKUCK, KUCKUCK/CUCKOO, CUCKOO: Hoffmann von Fallersleben freely adapted the text and melody from the Lower Austrian folk song "Stieglitz, 's Zeiserl is krank" (1817).

LATERNE, LATERNE/LANTERN, LANTERN: This folk song from northern Germany has been known in various texual and melodic variants since 1740. It is sung in the form of a refrain by children in lantern parades on St. Martin's Day.

LIED DER DEUTSCHEN ARBEITER/SONG OF THE GERMAN WORKERS: The fiery melody of the "Marseillaise" inspired several writers to make German versions. After Georg Herwegh's version of 1849, Jacob Audorf wrote his verses for the General German Workers' Union in 1864.

LIED DER INTERNATIONALEN BRIGADEN/SONG OF THE INTERNATIONAL BRIGADES: International Brigades defended the Spanish Republic from 1936 to 1939. Soliders' songs having political import were written there.

LIED FREYER LANDLEUTE/SONG OF THE FREE COUNTRY FOLK: The text is from 1792–93 and was sung to the melody of the "Marseillaise." The symbol of the tree of freedom is noteworthy.

LIED VOM BÜRGERMEISTER TSCHECH/THE MAYOR TSCHECH SONG: There are very many versions of this song; the authors are unknown; it first appeared in Dittfurth's *Historische Volkslieder: 1815–1866* (*Historical Folk Songs: 1815–1866*). The text is based on a real occurrence: Mayor Ludwig Tschech of the small Brandenburg town of Storkow injured the Prussian royal couple with two shots that he fired in Berlin in 1844. The song's motif is his disappointment over the fact that his petitions to the king were rejected. Tschech was executed in December 1844. The song's form, which is in part satirical, expresses the people's sympathy for the assassin. Lied von der

GEDANKENFREIHEIT/FREEDOM OF THOUGHT SONG: Walter Mossmann wrote the text and melody of this song at a time when applicants for public service were examined for their loyalty to the constitution.

LOBE DEN HERREN/ PRAISE TO THE LORD: The reformed Pietist Joachim Neander (1650–80) published his *Bundeslieder* (*Confederacy Songs*) in 1679. They were based in part on old reformed versions of psalms and in part on new melodies that he had written, and made him the revitalizer of the song in reformed churches. This very popular church song is from that collection.

MANCHMAL SAGEN DIE KUMPANEN/THESE DAYS THE GUYS MIGHT SAY: See "Deutscher Sonntag."

MARIA DURCH EIN'N DORNWALD GING/MARY WALKS AMID THE THORN: A text with a similar beginning was first mentioned in 1608. The text and the melody have been very common since 1850. The song was again made popular at the beginning of this century by the German youth movement.

MARSCH DER MINDERHEIT/MARCH OF THE MINORITY: Born in 1925 in Moers on the Lower Rhine, Hanns Dieter Hüsch became known in the 1950s as a cabaret artist; for the following generation of song makers, he was the trailblazer.

MEIN VATER WIRD GESUCHT/THEY'RE LOOKING FOR MY FATHER: Many people in the opposition emigrated after the fascists assumed power. Hans Drach, living in exile in the Soviet Union, wrote the text in 1936 and asked Gerda Kohlmey, who was in exile in Prague, to set it to music. The text was a manifest indictment of the Nazis' methods of hauling people off; it quickly became famous throughout the world.

MORITAT AUF BIERMANN SEINE OMA MEUME IN HAMBURG/MORITAT FOR BIERMANN'S GRANDMA MEUME IN HAMBURG: See "Das Barlach-Lied."

MUSS I DENN/SINCE I MUST . . .: Only the first verse of this Swabian folksong is traditional. Heinrich Wagner, a student of Ludwig Uhland and a friend of Silcher, wrote the second and third verses in 1824. Silcher wrote a version for men's choir in 1825–26. Today, the song still sounds over the Elbe at Blankenese when a ship coming from the harbor of Hamburg goes by.

NATIONALHYMNE DER BUNDESREPUBLIK DEUTSCHLAND/NATIONAL ANTHEM OF WEST GERMANY: Joseph Haydn composed the melody in 1797; Hoffmann von Fallersleben added his three-verse text to the melody in 1848. The first verse ("Deutschland, Deutschland über alles, über alles in der Welt"), in particular, was subsequently used by conservative circles, and especially by representatives of fascist ideology, to realize their objectives. Because of their undemocratic content, the first two verses have now been banned since the birth of the Federal Republic of Germany. The third verse is the national anthem of the Federal Republic of Germany.

NATIONALHYMNE DER DDR/NATIONAL ANTHEM OF THE GDR: Johannes R. Becher wrote the text; the melody was written by Hanns Fischer in 1949.

NATIONALHYMNE ÖSTERREICHS/NATIONAL ANTHEM OF AUSTRIA: The Austrian cabinet proclaimed this song to be the country's national anthem on February 25, 1949. The text was written by Paula von Preradovic; the melody is attributed to Johann Holzer, although some music scholars believe that Mozart was the composer.

NATIONALHYMNE DER SCHWEIZ/NATIONAL ANTHEM OF SWITZERLAND: The original version of the song is from 1841. Leonard Widmer is said to be the author, Alberich Zwyssig (Otto Kreis) the composer. This song was officially named as the national anthem of Switzerland in 1961.

NUN ADE, DU MEIN LIEB HEIMATLAND/SWEET HOMELAND, FAREWELL!: August Disselhoff wrote the text in 1851; the melody is based in part on a Westphalian soldier's song and in part on the Swabian folk song "Muß i denn."

NUN DANKET ALLE GOTT/NOW THANK WE ALL OUR GOD: Martin Rinckart (1586–1649) originally wrote the text as a table prayer in 1630; not until the years of the plague—during which he had to conduct more than four thousand funerals as a pastor—did he make a song of thanks out of it around 1638. The melody is by J. Crüger.

NUN RUHEN ALLE WÄLDER/EVENSONG: The melody has been known since the fifteenth century. Paul Gerhardt wrote the text in 1647, which eventually became a model for the song "Der Mond ist aufgegangen."

NUN WILL DER LENZ UNS GRÜSSEN/SPRING SENDS US HEARTY GREETINGS: The text was written by the German minnesinger Neidhart von Reuenthal; the melody is based on the seventeenth-century song "Wilhelmus von Nassauen." The song can be seen as an example of the many variations of historical texts and melodies that were very popular in the German youth movement at the beginning of this century.

O DU FRÖHLICHE/OH, YOU JOYFUL: Johannes Falk wrote the first verse in 1816; Johann G. Holzschuher wrote the second and third verses in 1829. The melody is based on the popular Sicilian air "O sanctissima."

O HAUPT VOLL BLUT UND WUNDEN/OH, SACRED HEAD NOW WOUNDED: Paul Gerhardt (1607–76) wrote the song on the basis of the Latin text "Salve caput cruentatum" by Arnulf von Löwen (ca. 1200–1250). The melody follows the 1601 air "Herzlich tut mich verlangen" by Hans Leo Hassler. The very popular melody was combined with various spiritual texts.

O KÖNIG VON PREUßEN/OH, KING OF PRUSSIA: A very popular oppositional soldier's song from the early nineteenth century; existing versions are almost exclusively manuscripts, as it seemed too dangerous to most printing shops to print the text because the Prussian kings did not shy away from persecuting and taking reprisals on people who made such personal criticisms.

O TANNENBAUM/OH CHRISTMAS TREE: The song's existence is documented already from the end of the sixteenth century, and various textual variations were widely known, including in England. This well-known mazurka melody was originally set to student songs such as *Lauriger Horatius* or *Grüß Gott dich, Bruder Straubinger*. In 1820, the Potsdam educator August Zahneck combined this melody with the text of a cheerful love song that began with the words *O Tannenbaum*. The Christmas tree was first made the topic of the song by the Leipzig teacher Ernst Anschütz in 1824; this is the version common today.

O WAG ES DOCH NUR EINEN TAG/OH, JUST DARE, IF FOR JUST ONE DAY: This song convincingly documents the fact that many German-language writers (such as Heinrich Heine, Hoffmann von Fallersleben, and Ferdinand Freiligrath) tried to have an influence on the political events of 1848 through their writings and assumed clear positions in order to bring about a change in political conditions. Georg Herwegh formulated the text for a traditional melody in 1845.

O, WIE WOHL IST MIR AM ABEND/OH, HOW LOVELY IS THE EVENING: This canon for three voices was passed on by word of mouth and is very common.

OSTERMARSCHLIED 68/EASTER MARCH SONG 1968 (also: "Argument der Straße" [Street Argument], "Da habt ihr es" [There You Have It], and "Zweiter Juni" [Second June]): The student Benno Ohnesorg was shot to death by a policeman—who was later acquitted of the deed—during a West Berlin demonstration against a visit by the shah of Iran on June 2, 1968. In this song, Franz Josef Degenhardt expressed the demonstrators' outrage and horror over official and public reaction.

REVEILLE: Claude-Joseph Rouget de Lisle wrote the melody in 1792; the text is by Ferdinand Freiligrath. The song was first performed at an event celebrating freedom in Cologne in 1844.

SCHÖN IST DIE WELT/THE WORLD IS BEAUTIFUL: This Hessian folk song was published by Franz Magnus Böhme in 1895 in the collection *Volkstümliche Lieder der Deutschen* (*Folksongs of the Germans*). The editor is thought to be the author.

SIEBEN FRAGEN EINES SCHÜLERS UND SIEBEN FREIHEITLICH-DEMOKRATISCH-GRUNDORDENTLICHE ANTWORTEN/SEVEN QUESTIONS FROM A SCHOOLBOY AND SEVEN, FREE, DEMOCRATIC, CONSTITUTIONALLY APPROPRIATE ANSWERS: Born in 1941 in Karlsruhe, Walter Mossmann gave his first public performance at the 1965 song festival at Castle Waldeck. He has since supported numerous activities of the students' and citizens' movements with his songs. This song should be seen in conjunction with the witch hunts of public officials (such as teachers) and employees in public service conducted by state institutions in the face of the student movement and the actions of the Red Army Faction (RAF). These "examinations" took place in an attempt to determine whether the person under consideration recognized and helped "protect the constitutional order" of the Federal Republic.

SO TREIBEN WIR DEN WINTER AUS/LET'S DRIVE OUT OLD MAN WINTER: The melody of this song became well known through Martin Luther's parody "Nun treiben wir den Babst heraus" ("Let's Drive Out the Pope"), which appeared in Wittemberg in 1545; the text first appeared in a discussion about the Gregorian Calendar in 1584. The old custom of driving out the winter was very common in Germany: on the third Sunday before Easter, a straw puppet symbolizing the winter was burned in order to welcome the spring.

SOZIALISTENMARSCH/THE SOCIALIST MARCH: This march was written after the proclamation of the law against the socialists and was first played in October 1891 at the SPD's second party convention in Erfurt, at which a new party platform was debated and passed. Max Kegel wrote the text, Carl Gramm the music.

SPIEL NICHT MIT DEN SCHMUDDELKINDERN/DON'T PLAY WITH THOSE FILTHY CHILDREN: Franz Josef Degenhardt quickly became known in the Federal Republic of Germany with this song. He first sang it publicly in the autumn of 1964 at a jamboree sponsored by Sender Freies Berlin (Radio Free Berlin).

STILLE NACHT/SILENT NIGHT: The text of this song was written on December 23, 1818. The author was the cleric Joseph Mohr, who lived near Salzburg. The teacher Franz Gruber set the text to music a short time later. Tyrolian troubadours brought the song to Leipzig, where it was published as a "Tyrolian folk song" and began to gain fame that would eventually extend throughout the entire world.

TOCHTER ZION, FREUE DICH/DAUGHTER OF ZION, COME REJOICE: In 1820, Heinrich Ranke wrote the text to a 1747 melody by Georg Friedrich Händel.

TROTZ ALLEDEM/DESPITE IT ALL: The text is based in part on verses by the Scotsman Robert Burns; the first German-language version was written in

December 1843; Freiligrath wrote his version in 1848. The text is a criticism by the working class of the contradictions and cowardice of the German bourgeoisie, which entered into an agreement with the nobility after the bougeois-democratic Revolution of 1848 in Germany and allowed the partial reinstitution of the feudalistic system of power. Freiligrath wrote his poem shortly after the suppression of the uprising and published it in *Neue Rheinische Zeitung* (*New Rhenish Times*), which was edited by Karl Marx and others. The melody is taken from the song Lady Mackintosh's Reel. The German songmaker Hannes Wader made the song very popular during the German student movement.

ÜB IMMER TREU UND REDLICHKEIT/BE ALWAYS TRUE AND RIGHTEOUS: The socially critical text by Christian H. Hölty from 1775 was seldom printed in its entirety. Mozart's melody from *Die Zauberflöte* (*The Magic Flute*, 1791) was first circulated in Freemasons' song books and later in school song books.

UND ALS WIR ANS UFER KAMEN/AND WHEN WE REACHED THE LAKE SHORE: See "Das Barlach-Lied."

VOM HIMMEL HOCH/FROM HEAVEN ABOVE TO EARTH I COME: The melody is based on the old fifth-century church hymn "A solis ortu cardine." A version was published as a dance song in Nuremberg in 1530. In Schumann's song book (Leipzig, 1539), the version known today was published before Martin Luther, who shaped the text and melody. The melody has also been known since 1616 in conjunction with the text "Ein Kind geborn zu Bethlehem" ("A Child Born in Bethlehem"). There are also versions of the song in the 1623 *Kölner Gesangbuch* and in the 1628 *Mainzer Gesangbuch*.

WANN WIR SCHREITEN SEIT AN SEIT/WHEN WE'RE MARCHING SIDE BY SIDE: This song, which came from the antimilitaristic workers' movement of World War I, was first performed at the founders' convention of the Free Youth of Hamburg-Altona in 1916. It became one of the most beloved working class youth songs of the next decades. Hermann Claudius wrote the text in 1915; Michael Englert, the melody in 1916.

WAS NOCH FRISCH UND JUNG AN JAHREN/ANYONE WHO'S SPRY AND YOUTH-FUL: The text and melody have been known since the eighteenth century.

WAS SOLL DAS BEDEUTEN/I KNOW IT'S MIDNIGHT: Part of the text of this Silesian Christmas song was published by J. G. Meinert in 1817 in the collection *Volkslieder aus dem Kuhländchen* (*Folk Songs from the Cow Pastures*). Hoffmann von Fallersleben and Ernst Richter published the complete version most common today in 1842 in the collection *Schlesische Volkslieder mit Melodien* (*Silesian Folk Songs with Melodies*). Because of its content, the song might be derived from a folk pastoral song.

WEM GOTT WILL RECHTE GUNST ERWEISEN/WHOMEVER GOD DECIDES TO FAVOR: Joseph von Eichendorff wrote this poem in 1822 and published it four years later in his novel *Aus dem Leben eines Taugenichts* (*From the Life of a Do-Nothing*). The Swiss conductor Friedrich Theodor Fröhlich set it to music for men's choir and published it in the collection *Lieder im Volkston* (*Popular Folk Songs*). Today, this version by Fröhlich is better known than Felix Mendelssohn Bartholdy's musical version.

WENN ALLE BRÜNNLEIN FLIEẞEN/THE FLOWING BROOKS: This Swabian folk song was first published around 1520 in a manuscript under the title *Die Brünnlein, die da fließen, die soll man trinken* (*One Ought Drink from the Brooks That Flow There*). There were many variations of the melody; the text remained largely unchanged. It is based on Mozart's Papageno song "Ein Mädchen oder Weibchen" from *Die Zauberflöte* (*The Magic Flute*, 1791). Versions of this folk song from southern Hessia and Swabia are known; the 1855 melody by the composer and folk song scholar F. Silcher allowed the song to achieve popularity in the twentieth century.

WENN DER SENATOR ERZÄHLT/WHEN THE SENATOR TELLS HIS TALES: See "Deutscher Sonntag."

WENN ICH EIN VÖGLEIN WÄR/IF I WERE BUT A BIRD (also: "Der Flug der Liebe" ["The Flight of Love"]): The melody of this song, which was originally a Freemason song, was published in Halle in 1784 and performed by J. F. Reichardt in an operetta in 1800. Reichardt is also thought to have been the composer. Six years before that, Herder had published the text, which was derived from older versions, in the 1878 collection *Stimmen der Völker in Liedern* (*Voices of the Nations in Song*).

WER JETZIG ZEITEN LEBEN WILL/WE NEED A HEART OF COURAGE NOW: This song from the seventeenth century shows in the crude style of German baroque language one of the fundamental problems of German feudalism: the push by many small princes for economic and territorial power.

WINTER, ADE!/WINTER, GOOD-BYE!: The melody is based on the 1816 Franconian folk song "Schätzchen, ade!"; Hoffmann von Fallersleben wrote the text in 1835.

WIR SIND DES GEYERS SCHWARZER HAUFEN/GEYER'S PITCH-DARK GANG ARE WE: This song is based on two peasant proverbs from the fifteenth century; a new version was written around 1820. The quote, "As Adam dug and Eve was spinning, who was there the nobleman?" existed in English as early as 1381 in a chronicle by Wat Tyler. The text criticizes the relation between the oppressed peasants and their feudal lords who were allegedly installed by God.

WOHLAUF IN GOTTES SCHÖNE WELT/GOD'S GORGEOUS WORLD: The text, which was published in 1908, is by the Hessian writer Julius Levy (alias Rodenberg). He combined the text with an old Franconian melody from around 1820 that had appeared in the collection *Deutscher Liederhort* (*Treasure of German Songs*) published by Erk and Boehme.

Translated by Lance W. Garmer

ACKNOWLEDGMENTS

Every reasonable effort has been made to locate the owners of rights to previously published works and translations printed here. We gratefully acknowledge permission to reprint the following material:

The songs by Deiter Süverkrüp are reprinted with the kind permission of the songwriter.

The songs by Franz Josef Degenhardt are reprinted with the kind permission of Aufbau-Verlag, Berlin and Weimar.

"Wir sind die Moorsoldaten": music by R. Goguel/ H. Eisler reprinted with the permission of C. F. Peters, Frankfurt/ M.

English translations of the hymns by Martin Luther, "From Heaven Above to Earth I Come" and "A Mighty Fortress Is Our God" copyright © 1978 *Lutheran Book of Worship*. Reprinted by permission of Augsburg Fortress Publishers.

The English translations of the following songs: "Frieden im Land" by Konstantin Wecker, "Kinder" by Bettina Wegner, "Kirschen auf Sahne" by Dieter Suverkrüp, and "Marsch der Minderheit" by Hanns Dieter Hüsch are reprinted from *Dimension* volume 19/1 (© 1991) with the permission of the editor, A. Leslie Willson.

"Ach, du mein schauriges Vaterland" and "Frieden im Land" by Konstantin Wecker are reprinted by permission of Ehrenwirth Verlag, Munich.

"I'm Sick of It," "Encouragement," "The Old Communist Grandma Meume's Great Prayer in Hamburg," and "Moritat für Biermann's Grandma Meume in Hamburg" from *Song and Ballads* by Wolf Biermann, translated by Steve Gooch, published by Pluto Press, London, 1977.

The music to "Trotz alledem," "Die Thälmann-Kolonne," and "Wann wir schreiten Seit' an Seit'" is reprinted with the permission of Friedrich Hofmeister Musikalien-Verlag.

The songs by Walter Mossman are reprinted with the permission of Rotbuch Verlag, Hamburg.

"Ballade von der 'Judenhure' Marie Sanders," "Einheitsfrontlied," and "Die Moritat von Mackie Messer" by Bertolt Brecht are reprinted with the permission of Suhrkamp Verlag.

The music to "Einheitsfrontlied" is reprinted with the permission of Deutscher Verlag für Musik.

The English translation of "Lantern, My Lantern" is reprinted by permission of Plough Publishing House.

The English translation of "Oh Christmas Tree" appeared in *Folksinger's Wordbook*, edited by Irwin and Fred Silber. Copyright © 1973 by Oak Publications, a division of Music Sales Corporation. International Copyright secured. All Rights Reserved. Reprinted by permission.

The English translation of "Said Wealth to Toil" is reprinted by permission of the Fabian Society, London.

The English translations of the national anthems of the German-speaking countries appeared in *National Anthems of the World*, edited by W. L. Reed and M. J. Bristow, and are reprinted by permission of Cassell PLC, London.

The English translation of "Hymn of the Proletariat" Copyright 1975 by the Board of Trustees of the University of Illinois. Used by permission of the University of Illinois Press.

"Hoch auf dem gelben Wagen" © 1923 by Richard Birnbach Musikverlag, D-82166 Lochham.

The German text of the songs by Wolf Biermann are reprinted by arrangement with Verlag Kiepenheuer & Witsch, c/o Joan Daves Agency as agent for the proprietor.

Index of Composers

Bach, Johann Sebastian, 1, 175
Biermann, Wolf, 104, 114, 116, 125, 127, 142, 152
Brahms, Johannes, 206
Bülow, Hans von, 59

Cruger, J., 184

Daniel, Peter, 100
Degenhardt, Franz Josef, 108, 123, 129, 138, 144, 150, 153
Degeyter, Pierre, 66
Dessau, Paul, 100

Ebel, Eduard, 179
Eisler, Hanns, 62, 78, 85, 89, 96, 160
Englert, Michael, 83
Espinosa, Rafael, 92

Fröhlich, Fr. Theodor, 216

Glück, Friedrich, 265
Goguel, Rudi, 96
Gramm, Carl, 81
Groos, Karl August, 14
Gruber, Franz Xavier, 190

Händel, Georg Friedrich, 192
Harder, Augustin, 204
Haßler, Hans Leo, 186
Haydn, Franz Joseph, 158
Heinz, Peter, 59
Herman, Nikolaus, 204
Hofer, Andreas, 69
Höhne, Heinz, 237
Holzer, Johann, 166
Hüsch, Hans Dieter, 140

Isaac, Heinrich, 244

Kohlmey, Gerda 95
Kreis, Otto, 163

Leopoldi, Hermann, 86
Luther, Martin, 169, 193
Lyra, Justus Wilhelm, 230

Marx, Karl, 208
Mossmann, Walter, 136, 146
Mozart, Wolfgang Amadeus, 222, 248
Müller, Wenzel, 268

Palacio, Carlos, 92
Pfitzner, Hans, 53
Praetorius, Michael, 172

Reichardt, Johann Friedrich, 199
Reinitz, Bela, 74
Rinck, C. H., 171
Rinck, Johann Christian, 198
Rohland, Jürgen, 28
Rouget de Lisle, Claude-Joseph, 20, 44,

Scherchen, Hermann, 58
Scheu, Josef, 51
Schlippenbach, Albert, 232
Schubert, Franz, 225, 228, 262
Schultz, Johann Abraham Peter, 176, 201
Schumann, Robert, 48
Silcher, Friedrich, 171, 253, 267, 269, 271, 273
Strauss, Richard, 53
Süverkrup, Dieter, 30, 105, 117, 133

Wecker, Konstantin, 102, 121

Wegner, Bettina, 131
Weill, Kurt, 98
Werner, H., 262

Zelter, Karl Friedrich, 279
Zöllner, C., 228
Zwyssig, Alberich, 163

Index of Poets

Anschütz, Ernst, 189, 287, 289
Audorf, Jacob, 71

Bäuerle, Adolf, 268
Baumbach, Rudolf, 237
Becher, Johannes R., 160
Biermann, Wolf, 104, 114, 116, 125, 127, 142, 152
Böda-Löhner, Fritz, 86
Brecht, Bertolt, 62, 85, 98

Claudius, Hermann, 83, 208
Claudius, Matthias, 201

Dach, Simon, 253
Degenhardt, Franz Josef, 108, 123, 129, 138, 144, 150, 153
Dehmel, Richard, 53
Disselhoff, August, 246
Drach, Hans, 95

Ebel, Eduard, 179
Eichendorff, Joseph von, 216, 265
Eildermann, Heinrich, 69
Ernst, Karl, 100

Falk, Johannes, 185
Fischer, A., 212
Freiligrath, Ferdinand, 28, 44, 46

Geibel, Emanuel, 230
Gerhardt, Paul, 175, 186, 204, 220
Glasbrenner, Adolf, 36
Goethe, Johann Wolfgang von, 262

Heine, Heinrich, 30, 48, 269
Hensel, Walther, 227, 242
Herder, Johann Gottfried von, 253
Herman, Nikolaus, 204
Herwegh, Georg, 40, 51, 59

Hey, Wilhelm, 169
Hoffman von Fallersleben, A. H., 15, 158, 198, 215, 260, 276, 279, 281, 292
Hölty, Ludwig Christoph Heinrich, 248
Holzschuher, J. G., 185
Hüsch, Hans Dieter, 140

Jahnke, Franz, 89

Kegel, Max, 81
Kleber, Leonard, 273

Langhoff, Wolfgang, 96
Lehne, Friedrich, 20
Levy, Julius, 218
Löwen, Arnulf von, 186
Löwenstein, Rudolf, 31
Lüchow, J. Chr., 43
Luckhardt, Emil, 66
Luther, Martin, 1, 170, 193

Mohr, Joseph, 190
Mossmann, Walter, 136, 146
Most, Johannes, 54
Mühsam, Erich, 74
Müller, Wilhelm, 225, 228, 241

Neander, Joachim, 180

Overbeck, Christian Adolf, 222

Pfau, Ludwig, 23
Pottier, Eugène, 66
Preradović, Paula von, 166

Radin, Leonid P., 58
Ranke, Heinrich, 192
Reuenthal, Neidhard von, 212

Richter, Ernst, 15
Riedel, Carl, 178
Rinckart, M., 184

Salis-Seewis, Johann Guadenz
    Freiherr von, 199
Schanz, Ludwig, 34
Schenkendorf, Max von, 14
Schlippenbach, Albert, 232
Schmid, Christoph von, 176
Schulten, G., 239
Süverkrüp, Dieter, 105, 117,
    133

Thunman, Olaf, 239

Vallentin, Maxim, 89

Wagner, Heinrich, 271
Wecker, Konstantin, 102, 121
Wegner, Bettina, 131
Weinert, Erich, 78, 92
Widmer, Leonard, 163

Zahneck, August, 189
Zuccalmaglio, August Wilhelm Flo-
    rentin von, 211

Index of Titles and First Lines

Abend wird es wieder, 198
Ach, das waren finstre Zeiten, 136
Ach, du mein schauriges Vaterland,
    102
Ach Mutter mach die Fenster zu,
    104
Achtzehnhundertvierzig und acht,
    52
Achtzehnter März, 51
Alle Jahre wieder, 171
Alle Vögel sind schon da, 276
Als meine Oma ein Baby war, 142
Am Brunnen vor dem Tore, 225
Annchen von Tharau, 253
Auf, auf, zum Kampf, 57
Auf Bruder! Auf! Die Freiheit lacht,
    11
Auf, du junger Wandersmann, 227
Auf einem Baum ein Kuckuck, 277
Auf, Sozialisten, schließt die Rei-
    hen!, 82
Auferstanden aus Ruinen, 162
Aus tiefer Not schrei ich zu dir, 169

Badisches Wiegenlied, 23
Ballade von der "Judenhure" Marie
    Sanders, 85
"Bet' und arbeit!" ruft die Welt, 60
Brüder, zur Sonne, zur Freiheit, 58

Buchenwaldlied, 86
Bundeslied, 59
Bunt sind schon die Wälder, 199
Bürgerlied der Mainzer, 11
Bürgerlied, 26

Da habt ihr es, das Argument der
    Straße, 144
Da sind sie, die Konzern- und
    Landbesitzer, 123
Da, wo die Arbeit und, 129
Das Barlach-Lied, 104
Das Blutgericht, 25
Das Heckerlied, 34
Das Hölderlin-Lied, 127
Das Land steht stolz im Feiertagsge-
    wand, 121
Das Proletariat, 43
Das Wandern ist des Müllers Lust,
    228
Das war' ne heiße Märzenzeit, 47
Dem Morgenrot entgegen, 70
Der Arbeitsmann, 53
Der Baggerfuhrer Willibald, 105
Der gute Bürger, 28
Der Kuckuck und der Esel, 279
Der Mai ist gekommen, 230
Der Mond ist aufgegangen, 201
Der Revoluzzer, 74

Der rote Wedding, 78
Deutscher Sonntag, 108
Die Arbeitsmänner, 54
Die beiden Grenadiere, 48
Die Gedanken sind frei, 15
Die hab ich satt!, 114
Die Internationale, 66
Die junge Garde, 69
Die kalten Frauen, die mich
   streicheln, 114
Die Loreley, 269
Die Moorsoldaten, 96
Die Moritat von Mackie Messer, 98
Die Thälmann-Kolonne, 100
Die beiden Grenadiere, 48
Du, du, liegst mir im Herzen, 257
Du, laß dich nicht verhärten, 116

Ein feste Burg ist unser Gott, 1
Ein Heller und ein Batzen, 232
Ein Jäger aus Kurpfalz, 280
Ein Männlein steht im Walde, 281
Ein neues Lied, 30
Ein Vogel wollte Hochzeit machen,
   283
Einheitsfrontlied, 62
Einigkeit und Recht und Freiheit,
   160
Ermutigung, 116
Erschröckliche Moritat vom Kryp-
   tokommunisten, 117
Es dunkelt schon in der Heide, 258
Es ist am Morgen kalt, 106
Es ist ein Ros entsprungen, 172
Es ist ein Schnitter, heißt der Tod, 3
Es klappert die Mühle am rauschen-
   den Bach, 287
Es klingt ein Name stolz und
   prächtig, 34
Es quillt und keimt von unten auf,
   43
Es tönen die Lieder, 203
Es waren zwei Königskinder, 260
Es, es, es und es, 233

Freifrau von Droste-Vischering, 31
Freiheit, die ich meine, 14

Freunde, noch sind wir wenige, 140
Frieden im Land, 121
Frisch auf, mein Volk, mit Trom-
   melschlag, 41
Frisch auf zur Weise von Marseille,
   44
Fuchs, du hast die Gans gestohlen,
   290
Für M. Theodorakis, 123

Geh aus, mein Herz, und suche
   Freud, 204
Glück auf, Glück auf, 236
Großes Gebet der alten Kommu-
   nistin Oma Meume in Ham-
   burg, 125
Guten Abend, gut' Nacht, 206

Heidenröslein, 262
Hier im Ort ist das Gericht, 25
Hoch auf dem gelben Wagen, 237
Horch, was kommt von draußen
   'rein?, 263
Hört, ihr Herrn, und laßt euch
   sagen, 173

Ich bin der Doktor Eisenbart, 290
Ich bin ein freier Bauernknecht, 5
Ich bin ein guter Untertan, 36
Ich bin Soldat, doch bin ich es nicht
   gerne, 64
Ich steh an deiner Krippe hier, 175
Ich weiß nicht, was soll es bedeuten,
   270
Ihr Kinderlein, kommet, 176
Im Frühtau zu Berge, 239
Im Krug zum grünen Kranze, 241
Im Märzen der Bauer, 242
In dem kleinen Café, 134
In diesem Lande leben wir, 127
In einem kühlen Grunde, 265
In Nürnberg machten sie ein Gesetz,
   85
Innsbruck, ich muß dich lassen, 244

Ja, dieses Deutschland meine ich,
   129

Ja, wenn der Senator erzählt, 153
Jeden Morgen geht die Sonne auf, 208
Jetzt fängt das schöne Frühjahr an , 209

Kein Feuer, keine Kohle, 267
Kein schöner Land, 211
Kinder, 131
Kirschen auf Sahne, 133
Komintern- Lied, 89
Komm, lieber Mai, und mache, 222
Kommet, ihr Hirten, 178
Kommt ein Vogel geflogen, 268
Kuckuck, Kuckuck, 292

Land der Berge, Land am Strome, 167
Laterne, Laterne, 293
Leise rieselt der Schnee, 179
Lied der deutschen Arbeiter, 71
Lied der Internationalen Brigaden, 92
Lied freyer Landleute, 20
Lied vom Bürgermeister Tschech, 39
Lied von der Gedankenfreiheit, 136
Links, links, links, links!, 79
Lobe den Herren, 180

Manchmal sagen die Kumpanen, 138
Maria durch ein'n Dornwald ging, 182
Marsch der Minderheit, 140
Mein Vater wird gesucht, 95
Moritat auf Biermann seine Oma Meume in Hamburg, 142
Muß i denn, 271

Nach Frankreich zogen zwei Grenadier, 48
Nationalhymne der Bundesrepublik Deutschland, 158
Nationalhymne der Deutschen Demokratischen Republik, 160
Nationalhymne der Schweiz, 163

Nationalhymne von Österreich, 166
Nun ade, du mein lieb Heimatland, 246
Nun danket all Gott, 184
Nun ruhen alle Wälder, 220
Nun will der Lenz uns grüßen, 212

O du fröliche, 185
O Gott, lieber Gott im Himml, hör mich betn, 125
O Haupt voll Blut und Wunden, 186
O König von Preußen, 17
O Tannenbaum, 189
O wag es doch nur einen Tag, 40
O, wie wohl ist mir am Abend, 213
Ob wir rote, gelbe Kragen, 27
Ostermarschlied 68, 144

Reveille, 44

Sag mal, sag mal, sag mal Herr Lehrer, 146
Schlaf, mein Kind, schlaf leis', 23
Schon ist die Welt, 247
Sieben Fragen eines Schülers und Sieben freiheitlich-demokratisch-grundor-dentliche Antworten, 146
Sind so kleine Hände, 131
So hab ich's doch nach all den Jahren, 28
So sprach die Mutter, sprach der Vater, lehrte der Pastor, 150
So treiben wir den Winter aus, 214
Sozialistenmarsch, 81
Spaniens Himmel breitet seine Sterne, 100
Spiel nicht mit den Schmud-delkindern, 150
Stille Nacht, heilige Nacht, 190

Tochter Zion, freue dich, 192
Trittst im Morgen rot daher, 164
Trotz alledem, 46

Üb immer Treu und Redlichkeit, 248

Und als wir and Ufer kamen, 152
Und der Haifisch, der hat Zähne, 98
Und weil der Mensch ein Mensche ist, 62

Verlaßt die Maschinen, heraus, ihr Proleten!, 90
Vom Himmel hoch, 193

Wacht auf, Verdammte dieser Erde, 67
Wann wir schreiten Seit an Seit, 83
War einmal ein Revoluzzer, 77
Was noch frisch und jung an Jahren, 251
Was soll das bedeuten, 195
Wem Gott will rechte Gunst erweisen, 216
Wenn alle Brünnlein fließen, 273
Wenn der Senator erzählt, 153
Wenn der Tag erwacht, eh' die Sonne lacht, 88

Wenn die Sonne bezeichnenderweise im Osten und rot, 119
Wenn die Spinne Langeweile, 110
Wenn ich ein Vöglein wär, 274
Wer jetzig Zeiten leben will, 7
Wer schafft das Gold zutage?, 55
Wer war wohl je so frech, 39
Winter, ade!, 215
Wir haben ein Bett, wir haben ein Kind, 53
Wir, im fernen Vaterland geboren, 93
Wir sind des Geyers schwarzer Haufen, 9
Wohin auch das Auge blicket, 97
Wohlan! es geht! es ist gegangen!, 20
Wohlan, wer Recht und Wahrheit achtet, 72
Wohlauf in Gottes schöne Welt, 218

The German Library
in 100 Volumes

Wolfram von Eschenbach
Parzival
Edited by André Lefevere

Gottfried von Strassburg
Tristan and Isolde
Edited and Revised by Francis G.
  Gentry
Foreword by C. Stephen Jaeger

German Medieval Tales
Edited by Francis G. Gentry
Foreword by Thomas Berger

German Mystical Writings
Edited by Karen J. Campbell
Foreword by Carol Zaleski

German Humanism and Reformation
Edited by Reinhard P. Becker
Foreword by Roland Bainton

Immanuel Kant
Philosophical Writings
Edited by Ernst Behler
Foreword by René Wellek

Friedrich Schiller
*Plays: Intrigue and Love and Don
  Carlos*
Edited by Walter Hinderer
Foreword by Gordon Craig

Friedrich Schiller
Wallenstein and Mary Stewart
Edited by Walter Hinderer

Johann Wolfgang von Goethe
*The Sufferings of Young Werther and
  Elective Affinities*
Edited by Victor Lange
Foreword by Thomas Mann

German Romantic Criticism
Edited by A. Leslie Willson
Foreword by Ernst Behler

Friedrich Hölderlin
Hyperion and Selected Poems
Edited by Eric L. Santner

Philosophy of German Idealism
Edited by Ernst Behler

G. W. F. Hegel
*Encyclopedia of the Philosophical
  Sciences in Outline and Critical
  Writings*
Edited by Ernst Behler

Heinrich von Kleist
Plays
Edited by Walter Hinderer
Foreword by E. L. Doctorow

E. T. A. Hoffman
Tales
Edited by Victor Lange

Georg Büchner
Complete Works and Letters
Edited by Walter Hinderer and Henry
  J. Schmidt

German Fairy Tales
Edited by Helmut Brackert and
  Volkmar Sander
Foreword by Bruno Bettelheim

German Literary Fairy Tales
Edited by Frank G. Ryder and Robert
  M. Browning
Introduction by Gordon Birrell
Foreword by John Gardner

F. Grillparzer, J. H. Nestroy,
  F. Hebbel
Nineteenth Century German Plays
Edited by Egon Schwarz in
  collaboration with
  Hannelore M. Spence

Heinrich Heine
Poetry and Prose
Edited by Jost Hermand and Robert
C. Holub
Foreword by Alfred Kazin

Heinrich von Kleist and Jean Paul
German Romantic Novellas
Edited by Frank G. Ryder and Robert
M. Browing
Foreword by John Simon

German Romantic Stories
Edited by Frank Ryder
Introduction by Gordon Birrell

German Poetry from 1750 to 1900
Edited by Robert M. Browning
Foreword by Michael Hamburger

Karl Marx, Friedrich Engels, August
Bebel, and Others
*German Essays on Socialism in the
Nineteenth Century*
Edited by Frank Mecklenburg and
Manfred Stassen

Wilhelm Raabe
Novels
Edited by Volkmar Sander
Foreword by Joel Agee

Theodor Fontane
Short Novels and Other Writings
Edited by Peter Demetz
Foreword by Peter Gay

Gerhart Hauptmann
Plays
Edited by Reinhold Grimm and
Caroline Molina y Vedia

Rainer Maria Rilke
Prose and Poetry
Edited by Egon Schwarz
Foreword by Howard Nemerov

Robert Musil
Selected Writings
Edited by Burton Pike
Foreword by Joel Agee

Essays on German Theater
Edited by Margaret Herzfeld-Sander
Foreword by Martin Esslin

Hermann Hesse
*Siddhartha, Demian, and Other
Writings*
Edited by Egon Schwarz
in collaboration with
Ingrid Fry

Friedrich Dürrenmatt
Plays and Essays
Edited by Volkmar Sander
Foreword by Martin Esslin

Max Frisch
Novels, Plays, Essays
Edited by Rolf Kieser
Foreword by Peter Demetz

Gottfried Benn
Prose, Essays, Poems
Edited by Volkmar Sander
Foreword by E. B. Ashton
Introduction by Reinhard Paul Becker

German Essays on Art History
Edited by Gert Schiff

Contemporary German Fiction
Edited by A. Leslie Willson

Hans Magnus Enzensberger
Critical Essays
Edited by Reinhold Grimm and Bruce
Armstrong
Foreword by John Simon

All volumes available in hardcover and paperback editions at your bookstore or from the publisher. For more information on The German Library write to: The Continuum Publishing Company, 370 Lexington Avenue, New York, NY, 10017.